SOMETHING MORE

CATHERINE MARSHALL

SOMETHING MORE

Guideposts Associates, Inc.
Carmel, New York 10512

Book Designed by Marcy J. Katz

Guideposts edition published by arrangement with
McGraw-Hill Book Co., Inc.

to
Peter Christopher
and
Amy Catherine
children of the King, now with Him
and to
Mary Elizabeth
and
Peter Jonathan
whom He has loaned to us

Acknowledgments

I want to express my gratitude to my long-time editor and friend, Edward Kuhn, Jr., who believes in excellence, hard work, and humility for authors; to Elizabeth Sherrill for sensitive and penetrating critique; to Dr. William R. Felts of Washington, D.C., for much helpful information on medical details; to Marguerite Shuster, who contributed her insights as well as her knowledge of Biblical Hebrew; to my talented and versatile secretary, Jeanne Sevigny, who has patiently typed and retyped manuscript with unflagging enthusiasm; to Emma Mulrean and Frances Orgain, who also helped with last-minute typing; to my husband, Leonard LeSourd, for many constructive suggestions and for being always an honest and discerning sounding-board.

Finally, to all the friends who through the pages of this book have been willing to share so generously of their innermost joys, sorrows, and victories, I offer my deepest appreciation.

Contents

	Foreword	xi
1	Yes, God Is in Everything	1
2	The Golden Bridge of Praise	19
3	Forgiveness: The Aughts and the Anys	35
4	The Law of the Generations	58
5	The Joy of Obedience	78
6	"To Sleep! Perchance to Dream…"	96
7	The Fallen Angel	117
8	The Unholy Spirit	137
9	The Enigma of Healing	159
10	The Roof on the House	174
11	The King's Treasury	197
12	The Dilemma of Our Rebellion	219
13	Run for the Strong Tower	243
14	The Helper	264
	Notes	293
	Index	305

Foreword

The other day I pulled a copy of my book *Beyond Our Selves* from the bookshelf and was startled to note again its date—1961. Thirteen years! It scarcely seemed possible!

Writing it seems like only yesterday. Yet there have been so many changes that the thirteen years might have been fifty. For the world of the seventies is very different from the world of the late fifties and early sixties.

My personal world has seen changes too. In the Foreword of *Beyond Our Selves*, I wrote,

> Just at the point when I thought child-rearing was over, Len's three children have joined Peter John in calling me "Mother."...A man swimming a horse across a turbulent stream does not stop to take a picture of the experience. I'll get my colts across the stream, see them thoroughly dried off, well fed, and on their way—then perhaps the picture.

Well, it has happened. The colts are on the far bank. Jeffrey, a tot of five when I wrote *Beyond Our Selves*, is now a senior at the McCallie School. Chester is a junior at Taylor University. Linda has graduated from college and has a job with Cornerstone, a Christian organization, in Washington. Peter John and his wife, Edith, minister to a lively, bursting-at-the-seams congregation on Cape Cod.

At times during the crossing, the stream was rough, the current swift, the wind shifty. Yet these thirteen years have been exhilarating, a learning process all the way. The pages that follow are not a photograph album of the crossing, but here and there snapshots are tucked in.

The setting of our lives has changed from Chappaqua, New York, to the east coast of Florida with frequent stops at Evergreen Farm in Loudoun County, Virginia, where my mother, after whom I modeled the heroine of my novel *Christy*, still lives, delighting in organic farming and conservation and enjoying her family and friends who come to her from all over the world.

The involvement of first, Peter John Marshall and then Linda LeSourd with facets of the rebellion of the young, together with the death of two grandchildren have forced me to reexamine my faith, groping for ever-surer foundations.

At further range, the rapidly changing worldscene, creating its own uncertainties, has challenged the tensile strength of our faith. Even in the early sixties most nations were full of hope. Surely, we thought, progressive education and our expanding social consciences would gradually eliminate the problems of society. As the dark side of human nature was educated out and away, together with the marvellous advances made possible by scientific knowledge, a golden age, Utopia, would eventually emerge.

Now we are in a position to see clearly that the progress we hoped for has not been achieved: we are not golden men living in a Utopia. Violence and crime have risen to new heights. The home and family units, the chief crucible from which our stability and creativity should have come, are a shattering vessel.

The present generation looks with skeptical eyes on both education and science and refuses any longer to regard either as a god. Standards of ordinary truthfulness, honesty, unselfishness, reverence for life, cherishing children, sexual morality previously accepted by past generations (even when individuals did not themselves measure up to those standards), are now under serious attack as not being necessarily desirable. Situation ethics have gotten us into increasing difficulty. Moral and sexual perversions are being flaunted in books and motion pictures, with crusades mounted to make the perversions "legal." Superstitious practices involving witchcraft and the occult have reappeared from the subterranean depths in which they had lain since the Middle Ages and are quite literally courting the Devil. Confusion reigns.

Principles, laws, institutions, positions of trust on which we have depended for structure, are crumbling all around us. Over most of the world a leadership vacuum has left men feeling rudderless with a sense of betrayal. Fear seeps like dank fog across the earth creating suspicion and mistrust, damaging relationships, and raising the specter of economic disaster.

Where do we turn for help in times like these? Is there nothing on which we can depend?

A long time ago when Roman civilization had also reached an impasse because of its corruption and state of decay, one small group of people who were certain they had the answer called themselves followers of "The Way." They were disciples of a Jew named Jesus who had been executed about the year A.D. 29 in an obscure province of the Empire under the Roman governor Pontius Pilate.

"Seek a new way."...The Way, they called it.

But is it really? If the way advocated by Jesus is the way for us today—then why hasn't it worked? Why hasn't Christianity eliminated poverty and war and brought us the good life? Because we have still never tried Jesus' way. Not enough of us. Not on a large enough scale.

Could it be that His way contains an answer that we have almost completely overlooked? Perhaps the reason we haven't found the answer all these centuries is that all the while it has lain in that portion of man we have mostly ignored—the spirit. Is it possible that the sole agent who can knit each human being back together, heal the wounds, and bridge the gaps between the heterogeneous elements of society is the one agent neither secular society nor the organized Church really takes seriously—the Spirit? By which I mean a specific: the divine Spirit tabernacling within each man's spirit—the Creative agent in life, writ small enough to live within each of us, to work through mind, body, emotions, will, and conscience, not only synthesizing them, but demonstrating a new and creative way—The Way—in every one of life's arenas.

The itinerant rabbi Jesus told us that we—you and I—would be living in the era of the Spirit of Truth.

We have never needed truth so desperately.

The pages that follow offer you experiences from my life and the lives of people well known to me as case histories of what happens in the twentieth century when we say "Yes" to the Spirit of Truth, allowing Him to invade us and lead us out into the light. These are men and women from all walks of life with backgrounds and temperaments as varied as humankind itself is varied. Their experiences come from every aspect of life—where evil strikes into the lives of "good" people, in matters of health, family relationships, rebellion, business and money, safety, remorse, resentments, and estrangements.

There are some surprises in this raw material from life. For the Christian the emphasis is usually on the original commitment to the religious life as symbolized by joining a church. Most sermons and religious books do not lead us to expect much to happen spiritually between our "entering in" and the end of life. The "rewards" are to come in afterlife.

Yet the true stories related here tell us that commitment

is only our birth into the new life. Then begins learning and growth. The process of being molded into a mature person in Christ Jesus becomes more challenging with each year that passes. I am finding that the knowledge of God grows often by means of the very experiences that would sweep us downstream, the turbulence I would prefer to escape.

As we grow older the pace and dimension of physical life must wind down. But it is meant to be just the opposite with the spiritual life—growth at an ever-accelerating pace. The heights and depths of the spirit, and enthusiasm for God isn't for children. In the latter half of life the normal Christian almost breaks into a jog or a run. Excitement and aliveness build. An altogether new quality of joy is given to us. It has little to do with the circumstances of our lives—good or bad—but everything to do with knowing Him who is managing the circumstances. It is joy that has the feel of permanence, even of eternity about it. Deep within we know that nothing that befalls us today or tomorrow can ever defeat that joy.

There are other reasons for the joy too. How great it is to realize, for instance, that the Holy Spirit did not limit His revelations to the truths contained within the canons of the Old and New Testaments. "I have much more to tell you," this Jesus told His companions around the table during His Last Supper talk with them, "but you cannot bear to hear it now. When He the Spirit of Truth is come, He will reveal all."

All—more and more. Always something more.

No matter how late the hour, no matter how desperate the moment, we cannot despair; the joy and the riches He has promised us stretch like a shining road into the future!

Catherine Marshall
Boynton Beach, Florida
March 4, 1974

SOMETHING MORE

1

Yes, God Is in Everything

At last we were safely airborne. December winds buffeted the little Cessna 205 four-seater as if it were a helpless leaf tossing in the vastness of the sky. There was room only for the pilot and my son Peter, his wife Edith, and me. Directly behind Edith and me was the baby's casket—so tiny with a spray of pink rosebuds atop it. It was the casket of my first grandchild, Peter Christopher Marshall, who lived for only two weeks. The special flight was the only way we could make it that day from the funeral service in West Hartford, Connecticut, to the graveside service at Fort Lincoln Cemetery outside Washington.

Inside the plane the noise shut out conversation. Pictures kept intruding on my thoughts. So much had happened in only fifteen days.... Peter's first telephone call on December 3rd, "It's a boy, Mom." But his voice was not as excited as a man's should be over his first child. Then it came. "Something's wrong, Mom. 'Poor muscle tone,' the doctors say."

Lung congestion had followed, the threat of pneumonia.

That Sunday Peter had crawled in under the oxygen tent to christen the baby Peter Christopher—"Christ-bearer" or "light-bearer."

I remembered that morning in Florida thirteen days later when the inner release to go to Connecticut had finally been given me. The message had been so clear, "Go—and crown My prince with thanksgiving."

Then that seemingly interminable three-and-a-half-hour delay at New York's Kennedy airport. Something was happening to the baby. I could feel it. Later I found out: Peter Christopher had stopped breathing; he had turned blue, then stony white. Loving hands had been laid on the baby in prayer and miraculously, he had begun to breathe again.

But not for long enough.

Sitting there in the bumpy little plane with the roar of the engines and the shriek of the wind in my ears, I could shut my eyes and remember my first glimpse of my grandson— pink and normal looking, that perfect round head with its suggestion of blond hair.

I had wanted to cuddle him—but first, I must do what He had told me to do. So there in the hospital room we offered up our sacrifice of thanksgiving, crowning His little prince with His own blessing.

Thirty-five minutes later, the young doctor had spoken. Simply, "He is gone."

Lord, I don't understand. When Peter Marshall died Your sure word to me was that "goodness and mercy would follow me all the days of my life." Lord, is this goodness and mercy?

Scarcely a person but knows similar earthly partings or heartache or loss. The mail I read day by day dramatizes our shared human plight: the young wife who had received one of those dreaded telegrams from Vietnam: "Killed in action"; a grandmother struggling to save her grandson from drug abuse; a husband with an alcoholic wife; a doctor's verdict of terminal cancer; a brush fire that destroyed one's home and possessions; a businessman cheated by a dishonest partner; a marriage breaking up in disillusionment and bitterness.

"How can God permit such things to happen?" is the cry that rises from our hearts. If He exists at all and is a loving God, He would not want such evils to befall us. Yet how could He be God and not have the power to prevent these disasters? These are the most difficult of all questions for those embarked on the Christian walk. Certainly for me this problem of evil has been a real stumbling block.

In my groping to understand, back in the forties during a long illness I "discovered" a body of Christian literature unknown to me. It was experiential, the true personal experiences of other people. Compared to most church literature which I knew so well—largely theory—this was exciting reading. I gobbled up everything that A. E. Simpson, Glenn Clark, Starr Daily, Rufus Mosley, Frank Laubach, Rebecca Beard, Dorothy Kerin, Roland Brown, and later on, C. S. Lewis and Agnes Sanford wrote. In addition, I began to search out the journals and letters of some who had lived in other eras—Brother Lawrence's *Conversations,* John Foxe, John Wesley, Hannah Whitall Smith, George Müller, Evelyn Underhill. These journals and letters proved a rich mine of personal experience.

I recognized that the experiential approach had firm New Testament precedent. For example, when John the Baptist sent messengers to Jesus to ask if He was really the long-awaited Messiah, Jesus' response was not a theological discourse. Instead, He pointed John to His miracles—the healing of all manner of disease, of the blind, the deaf. These facts were the evidence.

And I remembered the ringing words of Jesus' apostles to

those who would silence them, "We cannot but speak the things we have seen and heard." [1]

But thrilling and helpful as those books were, there was one chapter in Hannah Smith's *The Christian's Secret of a Happy Life* over which I had stumbled. Able to accept and profit from all the rest of Hannah's book, my rebellion was violent against chapter twelve entitled "Is God in Everything?" I asked myself how God could be "in" the death of a three-year-old who wandered into the street in the path of a truck? Was God in war? In cancer? The answer that welled up inside me was a resounding "Certainly not!" Further, I even considered such submissiveness wrong when Christians confronted with such tragedies, intoned, "Then it must have been God's will"... and piously quoted old harassed Job, "The Lord gave, and the Lord taketh away; blessed be the name of the Lord." [2] To me this seemed an especially cruel and offensive form of piosity.

But despite myself there were two bits of Hannah's chapter twelve that stuck to my mind like glue. The first was an illustration. The author related how at an informal prayer and sharing meeting one night, a woman had risen and told this story....

She had been much troubled by the seeming contradiction of a God supposed to have all power in heaven and on earth versus human instrumentality or "second causes." It seemed to the woman that stubborn, evil mankind was always messing up God's perfect plans. So she had pleaded with God to set her straight on this question.

The result had been an interior vision:

> She thought she was in a perfectly dark place, and that there advanced toward her, from a distance, a body of light which gradually surrounded and enveloped her and everything around her. As it approached, a voice seemed to say, "This is the presence of God! This is the presence of God!" While surrounded with this presence, all the great and awful things in life seemed to pass before

her—fighting armies, wicked men, raging beasts, storms and pestilences, sin and suffering of every kind.

She shrank back at first in terror; but soon she saw that the presence of God so surrounded and enveloped herself and each one of these things that not a lion could reach out its paw, nor a bullet fly through the air, except as the presence of God moved out of the way to permit it.

And she saw that if there were ever so thin a film, as it were, of this glorious Presence between herself and the most terrible violence, not a hair of her head could be ruffled, nor anything touch her, except as the Presence decided to let the evil through. Then all the small and annoying things of life passed before her; and equally she saw that there also she was so enveloped in this presence of God that not a cross look, nor a harsh word, nor petty trial of any kind could affect her, unless God's encircling presence moved out of the way to let it.[3]

So for this woman (and subsequently for Hannah Smith too), one of life's most thorny questions was forever settled: God is in everything. The events of our lives do come to us, moment by moment as from His hands, no matter how evil the instrumentality or second cause may appear to us to be.

The acceptance of this principle, Hannah Smith asserted, was the only possible basis for the Scriptural admonition (repeated over and over—Old Testament and New): "In everything give thanks: for this is the will of God in Christ Jesus concerning you." [4] And "everything," she insisted, did mean everything—bad things as well as good.

It was Hannah's warning that unless we do accept God in an all-inclusive "everything" we can know no contentment. In that case a life of faith and victory becomes a romantic mirage. For how can we accept or give thanks for what is less than good, or even evil, if we do not believe that God's shielding Presence has deliberately stepped aside to allow those forces to get to us? Even more, that His purpose in stepping aside is for good—not evil?

Well, the matter may have been settled for Hannah Smith. But not for me. I could not understand her explanation fully. I convinced myself I was hanging the matter on a hook for further consideration. Practically speaking, this was simply rejection.

But surely few are as stubborn as I! I held out on Hannah Smith's thesis from 1945 until 1972. Twenty-seven years!

In those twenty-seven years a great deal happened, including the worst I could imagine: on the morning of January 25, 1949, with only a few hours' warning, my husband Peter Marshall slipped over into the next life.

For the first week, I was supernaturally carried over and above grief. Then inevitably, I fell to the bottom of the pit asking, "Why? Why?" Even—"Have I been mistaken to put my faith in God? Has everything I've ever believed been wrong?"

In essence, my husband's death at only forty-six had thrown me squarely back once more against Hannah Smith's assertion that God *is* in everything—either to accept or refuse it....

> What is needed is to see God in everything, and to receive everything directly from His hands, with no intervention of second causes....
>
> An earthly parent's care for his helpless child is a feeble illustration of this. If the child is in its father's arms, nothing can touch it without that father's consent, unless he is too weak to prevent it. And even if this should be the case, he suffers the harm first in his own person before he allows it to reach the child. If an earthly parent could thus care for his little helpless one, how much more will our Heavenly Father!...[5]

But I was still not quite ready for that "completely restful" life of the spirit. Perhaps my mind, always questioning, always seeking the answer to "Why?" got in the way of the deeper life, the longer view.

I did understand and could accept the difference between God's ideal will and His permissive will. For the
Creator refused to make His creatures puppets whose
strings He could manipulate to force us to obey. He took
the risk of giving us free will. Therefore, men are sometimes going to go their own stubborn way, bringing unhappiness, grief, and horror into human life. Upon those
occasions, God "permits" the disobedience. Thus the permissive will of God is a fact of our life on earth.

In Peter's case, I am certain that it was not God's ideal
will that he die of coronary occlusion at forty-six. Why
then, did God "permit" it? I had some clues, but not the
final answer.

In the meantime, I forced myself to stop asking "Why?"
and face stark reality: I was a widow with a young son to
rear without his father. So what was I to do next? What was
God's ideal will for me right then?

Lovingly and surely, I was taught one of the greatest
lessons any of us can ever learn. In essence, it could be
summarized like this... Sin is in the world. And sin is
"missing the mark," missing God's perfect plan. There is so
much of this missing the mark that it is going to impinge on
every person's life at some points.

If God left us with only this, real happiness or victory in
this life would be an impossible mirage. But the Gospel
truly is good news. The news is that there is no situation—
no breakage, no loss, no grief, no sin, no mess—so dreadful
that out of it God cannot bring good, total good, not just
"spiritual" good, if we will allow Him to.

Our God is the Divine Alchemist. He can take junk from
the rubbish heap of life, and melting this base refuse in the
pure fire of His love, hand us back—gold.

Out of that understanding I was led to claim for my
personal crisis and for my young son the promise that, for
me, is gold:

And we know that all things work together for good to

them that love God, to them who are the called according to his purpose.[6]

The results of this claiming were amazing. Gently and
tenderly, God brought to my mind the teen-age dream of
wanting to write. "Now is the time," I seemed to hear God
saying. "Go forward and I'll open the doors before you."

The words soon became fact. The first venture was my
editing some of Peter Marshall's sermons. This became *Mr.
Jones, Meet the Master.* I was hard at work on it within six
weeks of Peter's death. A year or so later, thousands of
people were reading Peter Marshall's words. Clearly the
Lord was telling me, "Catherine, your job is to spread his
message."

From that time the path has gone on and on through my
delight in the editing and writing of eleven books. Of
course, the "good" that God, the Alchemist, worked for me
has gone far beyond merely a satisfying career as an author.
Blessings have been heaped upon me, including eventually, eleven years after Peter's death, marriage to Leonard
LeSourd and the challenge of taking on a new family—
Linda, Chester, Jeffrey. The new family responsibilities in
addition to my writing have taken all my resources of
physical and spiritual strength and have given back a full
life.

There have been many joyous experiences. Like that
when my granddaughter Mary Elizabeth Marshall was
born. On the second day of the baby's life, the head nurse
on Maternity had bounced into Edith's room. "Of all the
babies I've seen born in this hospital," she announced
jubilantly, "yours has the greatest muscle tone!"

"It was like a direct message," Edith told us later. "That
nurse didn't know about Peter Christopher. It was like the
Lord saying, 'See, I've handed you a special joy. I've
heaped it up.'"

My cup overflowed.... The total rapture of a one-year-old as she received her first doll.... The fun of painting Christopher Robin and Pooh Bear figures on a little girl's bedroom furniture, of reading to her and watching understanding grow and unfold.

In the midst of such joy it seemed to me that I could forget Hannah's challenge—that God *is* in everything, good and bad. I left it on the hook where I had hung it years before. I still wasn't convinced.

Then in 1971 a family crisis brought it to the forefront again. On July 22nd of that year a third child was born to my son Peter John Marshall and his wife Edith. It was apparent from her birth that Amy Catherine had suffered severe damage to internal organs because of some unknown genetic difficulty. Medically speaking, there was no hope.

The family decided that we could but pray in total faith, asking for a miraculous healing. We were joined by Peter's congregation on Cape Cod, by a group of sixteen who flew in for days of intensive prayer in a retreat situation, and by many, many others. If ever a family went out on the end of a limb of faith, we did. As for me, not since Peter Marshall's first heart attack had I thrown everything I am and have, every resource of spirit and mind and will into the battle for a human life.

Meanwhile, the sixteen people gathered there were experiencing in the space of a few days extraordinary answers to prayer: one of the group prayed for a little girl on the same floor with Amy Catherine at Boston Children's Hospital and later found that the child's miraculous recovery had begun that day; our daughter Linda experienced a cataclysmic reordering of her life, lifting her out of darkness and confusion into a new beginning; our friend Virginia Lively was given the key to her daughter's health; a woman's life, blighted twenty years before, which no amount of prayer, counseling, and psychotherapy had alleviated, was lovingly restored; a man's resentment against his father, festering since childhood, was healed; a floundering marriage was made right again.

It was as if the tiny baby Amy became a divine catalyst, calling forth a concentration of God's power and love for others.

After the retreat, I stayed at the Inn near Children's Hospital in Boston while Peter and Edith took turns keeping the vigil over Amy and driving back and forth to Cape Cod to be with Mary Elizabeth. Day after day we sat beside the baby who was stretched out on a slanting "Heat Bed" under a big light. Amy was hungry and would open her mouth expectantly like a baby bird, yet she was too weak to suck; she had to be fed intravenously, the seemingly endless tubes sticking out in all directions.

"She needs to feel loving arms," my heart kept telling me. Finally, the nurses assented and one morning carefully placed her in my arms, tubes and all. She cuddled up, nuzzling me. After that it became a ritual, and I was holding our baby only minutes before her heart stopped beating. Amy Catherine's time on earth had been but six weeks.

Had I long before received the truth of "Is God in Everything?," then I could have endured Amy's death in the spirit in which I had accepted Peter Marshall's. But the years of nonacceptance had taken a larger toll than I had realized. I fell on my face. There followed months of rebellion against God, sharper questioning than ever: what can we believe about healing through prayer?"

I experienced the most intense misery I've ever known. Life went gray. Nor was it all psychological or spiritual. Events in the exterior world began going against me. Things like: a major Hollywood studio purchased my novel *Christy*, then decided not to produce it. The fiction manuscript on which I was working was presenting problems so great that I began to see that after pouring myself into it for three years, I was going to have to suspend work on it. An almost wild succession of small, vexing personal inconveniences came on in waves: the dishwasher went out; the bathroom plumbing went awry; a truck driver backed into our mailbox and demolished it; the lawn developed chinch bugs; the car kept stopping cold on us.

> When sorrows come, they come not single spies,
> But in battalions! [7]

wrote Shakespeare. It is true. Trials do have a way of piling up. The question is—why?

Once again I was brought back to Hannah's thesis. If we don't accept the circumstances God's permissive will has allowed and ask, "Lord, what is Your will for me in the midst of these circumstances?," then He permits the difficulties to heap up. For most of us that's the only way He can get our attention.

In my misery He had my attention all right. Obviously, I was meant to turn off my grumbling and wait upon Him. I was to listen and to learn.

Finally the words of truth began to break through.... "His loving allowance for us"..."Must see all of life as coming directly from His hands." Hannah Smith again! After twenty-seven years of rejecting her!

To explain the evolution of my belief to that moment when I knew that I'd made connection with the transcendent power of God, I must backtrack briefly. When still in my twenties a lung condition had put me to bed. After a year and a half of the four walls of my bedroom, desperation had set in. Every other way medically and spiritually had failed me. I had been forced to the Prayer of Relinquishment, "I stop demanding anything. I want only what You want for me, whatever it is." There I had touched the hem of His garment and found health. And is not relinquishment very close to the "acceptance" Hannah wrote about?

Yet I had been puzzled, as had others, about a seeming contradiction between relinquishment and praying with faith. For how can we pray "Thy will be done, whatever it is, even unto death," and mean it, and at the same time have faith for healing?

Suddenly, it was as if a searchlight played upon my own experience of relinquishment [8] to illumine it for me further. Having ascertained through reading of the four Gospels that God's will is for health (as Satan's is on the side of disease, death, and destruction), I had felt myself to be in accord with God's will in asking for healing. I loathed the idea of disease and of being sick and had self-righteously set myself not to submit to illness. Thus in my mind there was the sharpest kind of dichotomy between, on the one hand, disease and sickness—the Destroyer's territory, and on the other, wholeness of spirit, mind, body—God's kingdom.

Yet back in 1943 a year and a half of asking on the basis of that dichotomy and of "believing" to the limit of my ability (what I thought was faith) had resulted in—nothing. The reason was, I perceived now, that God would not allow me to get well *until I saw Him even in my illness.* Disease is of Satan's kingdom, but God had allowed it for me. Blame it on Satan, I might, but see God *in* it, I must. He would hold me at that point until I did.

He held me firmly right there, until out of desperation, I bowed to Him. That was all He required. I had dropped my human "reasoning"—the basis of my authority in asking—and had laid everything at the feet of the Creator: He had taught me through hard experience that as His creature, I had no authority of my own. When I finally acknowledged that, He raised me up speedily.

I realized then what I'd really been saying to Him. "I'll keep a certain amount of rebellion and pin it to a good cause (against disease)." Then I had added with due piety, "Of course, God, I only insist on this because I know it's Your will."

But God's reply had never varied. "You can't insist on anything. I will not let you harbor rebellion for any cause. Lay your arms down."

I had also been guilty of a Pharisaical stance in relation to my understanding of prayer, healing, and the like—a fearsome trap laid for those who have done their homework by reading a lot of books, attending many meetings, complemented by a minimum of experience. I cringed as I saw myself alongside that Pharisee in the temple,[9] standing and praying with myself, "God, I thank thee that I am not as other men are. I've done so much reading and thinking and praying. I have more understanding than most of them."

My situation was perfectly set forth in this incisive statement in Romans 1 : 21:

> Because that, when they [rebellious men] knew God, they glorified him not as God, neither were thankful, but became vain in their imaginations, and their foolish heart was darkened.

No wonder God had been unable "to justify" me! No wonder I couldn't hear His voice at all until I had deposited my "understanding" along with my "proper rebellion" at His feet. Then I heard (I don't know about other people, but He doesn't always speak to me in King James English), "You did read the Gospels correctly about healing. But the important thing is not whether your ideas are right. Learn this: you can't trust in your own understanding any more than you can trust in your own righteousness. I am offended by even one odious whiff of intellectual or spiritual self-exaltation."

Thus it was that the searchlight playing on my healing through relinquishment lighted up some ugly facts about myself. I saw that previous to being willing to bow before God and worship Him, lifting only empty hands, I had been steadily refusing to recognize the totality of God's authority in my situation. God *is* in everything—even illness.

I recognized better what Hannah had meant by God being "in" everything. Further, new light was shed on one of Jesus' best known teachings:

> Are not two sparrows sold for a farthing? and one of them shall not fall on the ground without your Father.
>
> But the very hairs of your head are all numbered.
>
> Fear ye not therefore, ye are of more value than many sparrows.[10]

The Greek word for "without" (verse 29) is a strong word implying more than sympathy or even empathy. I was told by those knowledgeable in New Testament Greek that this word "without" can be used not only as "without the knowledge or consent of" but also as "without the Father's *participating presence.*"

Then I was given an insight on a facet of Jesus' teaching that had escaped me—His identification with every human being in need. The Gospel accounts show Him with a passion for helping those in trouble. He has not changed! The minute we need saving from anything, He stands ready in His role as Saviour.

He illustrated this identification in a variety of ways to show us that it is a real fact of our world. When we minister to someone hungry or poverty-stricken or ill or in prison, we are ministering to Him.[11] When we persecute others, we persecute Jesus.[12] When we receive and welcome one little child, we receive and welcome Him.[13] Frank Laubach has put this in a memorable way: "At the center of every need He stands pleading with us to help Him as He moves to help others."[14] He is not only "in" trouble and sorrow, but is there in a particular way—to have dialogue with us, to teach us, and then to rescue us.

Putting this together with the hairs-are-numbered passage, Jesus was telling us that since not even one insignificant sparrow can perish without the knowledge and consent of a loving Father and, more, His participating presence (since He stands waiting at the center of every need), then we should have no fear. Each of us is infinitely precious in the Father's sight, so much so that He knows every detail about us, even to the number of the hairs on our head.

Therefore, nothing can happen to us without His knowledge, His consent, and *His participating Presence* as Saviour. All of that Hannah had meant by God being "in everything."

Now, so many years later, God had given me this new insight to illuminate the heartbreak of Amy Catherine's death. Once again, I had been making the same errors: once again, I had been leading with my "understanding" that it was surely God's will to heal an innocent baby. As before, I saw Satan's work all over the physical problem, the tiny, genetically damaged body. And just as steadily, I was refusing to see God "in" the situation at all. So I had been attributing Amy's death to the combined factors of our failure in prayer plus the power of evil. Seeing it that way, I had not been able to receive the baby's death as from God's hands in a greater scheme of things not yet given to me to understand.

It was a shock to realize that as a result of this defective thinking I had actually ascribed more power to evil than to God. To the mind of Jesus, as consistently portrayed to us in the Gospels, this would be unthinkable. For any one of us to believe that His Father could be frustrated or vanquished by any rival power would surely call forth His sad, "O ye of little faith! How long must I bear with you?"

Nor is this the viewpoint of the Gospels alone. Like a great bell tolling and tolling over all the land, deep-

throated, its echoes ringing in our ears, the consistent voice
of the sovereign power of God reverberates throughout Old
Testament and New. He is the God of the supernatural—
omnipotent, omnipresent, omniscient in this life and the
next. We cannot believe this and also think that our God is
no match for the evil of the world.

Yet even believing in God's power doesn't help in our
crisis situations if we cannot also believe that He wants to
help *us*. Frequently, we hear people say, "I know God has
power—'if it be His will' to use it . . " Like that leper who
pleaded with Jesus, "Lord, if You only choose, You can
cleanse me."

Jesus ringing response leaves no doubt: "I do choose. Be
cleansed." [15] And Jesus is the portrait of God. Here is the
One who leaves the ninety-nine sheep safely in the fold and
goes out after the one lost lamb—because He cares.[16] By
every word and deed, Jesus made it clear that His Father
not only cares, but that no detail of any life is too
insignificant for His loving providence.

The accounts of Jesus' miracles portray Him working out
His Father's love for each man, each woman, each child.
He went about demonstrating the Father's delight in
restoring deranged minds to sanity, sight to blind eyes,
hearing to deaf ears, the joy of unfettered motion to the
lame and the paralyzed; in satisfying hunger, dispelling
pain, curing diseases of all sorts—no matter how far gone
or how hideous.

So often the styluses of the Gospel narrators etched the
word "compassion." No wonder! In Jesus they had encountered a caring of such depth and magnitude, yet often
stooping to attend to such minute detail, that language
failed them in describing it. He who was the embodied
revelation of God had the profoundest sense of the sacred-
ness of human personality of any man in history. The
Galilean's tender love for any human being in misery or
pain or need is the Gospels' eternally true message about
God. In the eyes of Jesus today, our Contemporary Lord,

no set of facts in any century should ever shake this central core of truth about the character of His Father.

Yet as the twentieth century has progressed men have found the truth that God cares about each one of us increasingly difficult to believe. We need to be searchingly honest here. As children of a scientific age we have grown up indoctrinated with the concept of a mechanistic universe. Machines have all but taken over our everyday lives. The individual has come to feel lonely. Is anyone at home in the cosmos? Perhaps God *is* dead. And machines are not much company.

To loneliness is added helplessness. The individual feels like an all-but-worthless cog in the machinery of huge industrial bureaucratic nations. No wonder we find it a long leap from our century's framework of thinking to Jesus' sure teaching about the Fatherhood of God.

Yet whenever we are emboldened to accept and act on Jesus' revelation of the Fatherhood of God, always and always we find solid ground beneath our feet.

With a love and patience beyond imagining, God brought me slowly back step by step to take a fresh look at Hannah Smith's thesis, at what's wrong with grumbling about our lot in life—even baby Amy's death and at the relinquishment that brings such miraculous results. He seemed to be saying, "Now that you're fully persuaded of the value of relinquishment, you're ready for the next lesson. *But relinquishment is only a stopping place on the way to praise. It's as nothing compared with the power of praise.* Now begin to praise."

My thoughts went back to the Apostle Paul's "In everything give thanks: for this is the will of God in Christ concerning you."

"You mean, Lord," I asked, "that in the midst of tragic circumstances, by an act of will I'm to praise You? How can I make it real? Wouldn't it be just words, almost hypocritical?"

"Obedience means turning your back on the problem or the grief and directing your eyes and attention toward Me. Then I will supply the emotion to make the praise real."

One early morning not long after Amy Catherine's death I went out on the patio to begin. Hadn't nature always brought me closer to God? Birds sang in the branches of the fiscus tree in the back yard. The sky was still gray-white with the faintest suggestion of blue. I began to praise that first time hesitatingly, woodenly:

"Lord, I think I'll begin with the small irritations first— that truck driver demolishing the mailbox. Surely, I'm not supposed to thank You for *that*! I can see, Lord, as I talk to You that the mailbox is of no consequence. Looking at You puts petty problems into perspective in a hurry. I can feel Your humor that I took it so seriously. So thank You, Lord, for perspective. Thank You for humor. Thank You for You."

As I persisted on down the list, another instruction was given. "Now write down every situation in your life that seems less than good, that you would like to see changed."

That wasn't hard. I went inside to get my red notebook and a pen and proceeded to fill five pages. But what came next *was* hard: "I want you to go down the list and praise Me for every item."

"Lord, I can see praising You for bringing good out of all these things, but I still don't understand how I can praise You for the bad things. Doesn't that make You the Author of evil?"

"I am Lord over all—good and evil. You start praising. I'll supply the understanding."

Step by hesitant step, I was being led on an exciting spiritual adventure.

2

The Golden Bridge of Praise

My first discovery was that I knew almost nothing about praise, neither what it was nor how to praise. Beyond some joyous hymns and a few "Praise Gods" and "We adore and worship Thee" with the lips, what then? We Protestants sitting so properly in straight rows of pews staring straight ahead, how can we know how to praise? The subject is mentioned occasionally as a nice worship exercise, a sort of icing on the cake as a gesture to God, but praise as the key to answered prayer, no. That was a new concept altogether.

A short time after I began my amateurish praise efforts with the five-page list, a new book came in the mail one day: *Prison to Praise* [1] by a former Army chaplain, Merlin Carothers. The author's thesis is that God steps in to change unhappy or even disastrous situations in our lives when we thank Him *for the situation itself.* This makes sense only when we see that life as it comes to each of us day by day is our schoolroom. That, in turn, can be true only when we at last understand that God is "in" every

circumstance—good or bad—that He allows to come to us.
Growth comes at the point of our hang-ups and problems
when we take an active step toward God who stands waiting
for us at the center of the problem. The quickest way to go
to meet Him is through praise. No wonder we meet Him
there, for Scripture goes on to teach us that God actually
"inhabits" (lives in) the praises of His people.[2]

Carothers concedes that when most people are first
presented with the concept of praising God for unhappy
situations, they are resistant and even incensed, as I was
when I was told to offer praise after baby Amy's death. But
Chaplain Carothers records incident after incident of
miraculous answers to prayer following praise.

There is such a thing as the "fullness of time" for an idea.
Following Carothers' writings on praise, books by other
writers on the same subject began appearing on booksellers'
lists, such as *Let Us Praise* by Judson Cornwall and *Praise
the Lord Anyway* by Frances Gardner Hunter.

The Scriptural basis for this is not only solid but overwhelming, such as:

> Rejoice evermore.
> Pray without ceasing.
> In every thing give thanks: for this is the will of God....[3]
>
> Continue in prayer, and watch in the same with thanks-
> giving.[4]

But out of many such passages,[5] it was the concept of
praise as a sacrifice which began to show me the way:

> By him [Jesus] therefore let us offer the sacrifice of praise
> to God continually, that is, the fruit of our lips giving
> thanks to his name.[6]

The fact that the word "sacrifice" is used tells us that the
writers of Scripture understood well that when we praise

God for trouble, we're giving up something. For sacrifice means "the surrender or destruction of something prized or desirable for the sake of something considered as having a higher or more pressing claim." [7] What we're sacrificing is the right to the blessings we think are due us!

We are also sacrificing our human desire to understand everything. Obviously, praising God for trouble makes no sense from the earthly side. Human reason asks, "Why should I thank God for dark and negative circumstances when He is the Author of light and goodness alone? So when we bypass our "right" to understand and offer up suffering to God in praise, the Bible is right in calling this a "sacrifice of praise."

When we offer thanksgiving in the face of circumstances such as Habakkuk set forth, that's a sacrifice.

> Although the fig tree shall not blossom, neither shall fruit be in the vines; the labour of the olive shall fail, and the fields shall yield no meat; the flock shall be cut off from the fold, and there shall be no herd in the stalls:
>
> Yet will I rejoice in the Lord, I will joy in the God of my salvation. [8]

The Bible gives us many illustrations of praise being the hinge upon which great events turned. Just one example among many is the story of how King Jehoshaphat of Judah pleaded with God for help when the Moabites joined with the Ammonites to come against his little country. The answer came: Jehoshaphat and his people were to turn their back on their enemies and spend their time worshiping God...

> And when he [Jehoshaphat] had consulted with the people, he appointed singers unto the Lord, and that [they] should praise the beauty of holiness, as they went

out before the army, and to say, Praise the Lord; for his
mercy endureth forever.

And when they began to sing and to praise, the Lord set
ambushments against the children of Ammon and
Moab...which were come against Judah: and they were
smitten.[9]

When we turn to the New Testament there are many
examples. There was the time Paul and Silas were cruelly
beaten at Philippi and put in jail under maximum security
with their feet chained in stocks.[10]

In this crisis the prisoners gave themselves to prayer,
which is understandable. But to praise? So exuberant did
their rejoicing become that it flowed over from words of
thanksgiving into songs of praise.

Praise for what? we might ask cynically. That their backs
were raw and bleeding from the "stripes" so cruelly laid
upon them! That they were in prison with all the city
authorities against them? That with their feet in stocks,
they couldn't even move around their cell? Thanking God
for that? From any human point of view, it makes no sense.
It's foolishness, maybe even hypocrisy. Foolishness, that is,
so long as we are looking at the human circumstances and
not at God.

Paul admits to us that anything about Christ's cross or
about the crosses you and I bear in life is "foolishness" to
the world. But he had learned that God allows us to have
disappointments, frustrations, or even worse because He
wants us to see that our joy is not in such worldly pleasures
as success or money or popularity or health or sex or even
in a miracle-working faith; our joy is in the fact that we
have a relationship with God.[11] Few of us ever understand
that message until circumstances have divested us of any
possibility of help except by God Himself.

It is a stripping process that we experience as we go on in
the Christian life. The process has gone by many names in

Christian literature: "the dark night of the soul"... "inward desolation"..."the winter of the Soul"..."the way of the cross"..."the Valley of the Shadow"..."the Dispensation of Darkness."

Once we have only God to depend on—as Paul and Silas had at Philippi—then we can *with joy* "draw water out of the wells of salvation."[12] We draw out the precious water by rejoicing in Christ, our Deliverer, not in our circumstances or in anything about ourselves. Not even pride at our wonderful experiences or our faithfulness, or what we've learned, or even our joy.

About midnight, as Paul and Silas, still bruised and bleeding, turned their minds from self and sang their thanksgiving to the Lord, rejoicing in Him, an earthquake rocked the city of Philippi, shook the foundation of the prison, burst the gates and wrenched the chains from the walls. Two other miracles followed quickly. The jailer and his entire household became followers of the Way. And when morning dawned the city authorities in a complete about-face withdrew all charges and bade Paul and Silas "depart, and go in peace."

As the former prisoners strode on their way, Paul could exult, "I have learned, in whatsoever state I am, to be content." [13]

Out of such a framework, we would do well to listen to this giant among apostles when he admonishes us to

> Rejoice in the Lord *alway*: and again I say, Rejoice...
> in every thing by prayer and supplication with thanksgiving let your requests be made known unto God.[14]

Just to be certain that we fully understand, Paul carefully details for us some of the difficulties he had undergone in the midst of which he had practiced "rejoicing": official scourgings of thirty-nine stripes—five separate times; three times beaten with rods; stoned once; three shipwrecks;

innumerable journeyings in peril of robbers and other enemies; weariness; pain; hunger and thirst.[15] Few of us can match Paul's list.

Even as God asked praise of Jehoshaphat and of Paul and Silas, so He asks it of each one of us. And the longer one ponders this matter of praise and experiments with it, the more evidence comes to light that here is the most powerful prayer of all, a golden bridge to the heart of God. No human situation is too burdensome, no circumstances too calamitous for praise to bring as marvelous results today as it did then.

Gladys, a missionary in Ecuador, has written me several times. One of her letters related her brother Clem's story. His marriage had broken up after the couple's only child, a three-and-a-half-year-old boy, had died in a drowning accident. Clem was an efficiency expert for an industrial consultant firm, traveling a great deal, usually staying in one place about three months until he could get a particular company's problems straightened out. Yet he was handling the problems of his own life with anything but efficiency; Clem was miserably estranged from God.

Clem's and Gladys's father had died suddenly when Clem was fifteen. Ever since, the boy had been angry at God. Whatever church services she and her brother would attend, he viewed every preacher and every congregation with a critical eye. Gladys had been praying for her brother's change of heart for twenty years. So far as she or anyone else could see, nothing had happened as the result of these prayers. Indeed, a deterioration process was apparent in her brother's life.

Then the Prayer of Praise came to Gladys's attention. She decided to praise God for Clem's life just as it was, believing that God was working in spite of outer circumstances.

Almost immediately a chain of unexpected events began. Clem's employer, based in Chicago, sent him to Seattle on a six weeks' consulting job. There he met some distant relatives who were retired missionaries. He had long talks with the missionaries, finding them easy to confide in. They took Clem to their church where for the first time he found the atmosphere to his liking—warm and friendly and loving.

Then Clem's work in Seattle was over and unwillingly he went back to Chicago. The rest of the story was in Gladys's letter:

Clem decided that he would get right with God someday, but he could do this best in Seattle where the atmosphere was more to his liking.

In the ensuing months Clem consistently put the cart before the horse by trying to solve his problems and *then* he would give his heart to God. Dejection set in.

At last there came an opportunity for him to be in Seattle over a weekend, staying at the home of the same relatives.

On that Sunday morning Clem awoke overwhelmed with the knowledge that Jesus loved him. At a Sunday evening service Clem was also aware that many of the people there were praying for him. That night the pastor asked anyone who wanted to hand his life over to God and to become a follower of Jesus to stand.

Secretly (so Clem told me later) he had told the Lord that he would go forward if the pastor asked. But he would not rise.

After the service, outside in the church parking lot, Clem felt that God was talking to him, "You have to have your own way even in this? You are saying, 'I will accept God on my terms.' The terms will have to be Mine, none of yours; or there will be no acceptance."

Clem drove as rapidly as he dared back to the relatives' home. "I can't hold out any longer," he announced as he rushed into their living room.

It ended up with their shoving the piano bench to the middle of the room to double as an altar. There my brother knelt and handed his life over to the Hound of Heaven who had pursued him for so long.

Gladys's letter ended with these words:

Five months of praising God for Clem *just as he was* was more effective than twenty years of begging God in prayer to rescue my brother.

Or here is another incident.... Redeemer Temple in Denver, Colorado, is an unusual church. Its worship services are attended by a cross-section of Christians from the main-line Protestant denominations—Lutherans, Presbyterians, Methodists, Disciples of Christ—as well as by Roman Catholics. Many of these worshipers are still members of their own denominations and of a Sunday morning attend an early service in their own church before going on to Redeemer Temple. "It's because in this church the Book of the Acts is being lived out before our eyes," one of them told me, "that we can't stay away."

As in the Acts a large group in the church has been led to communal living. A group of hippies who had stumbled into Redeemer Temple one Sunday and subsequently had their lives turned right side up, were led to buy a run-down house in the heart of the ghetto and renovate it as the headquarters of a Christian commune. There at the "House of Grace" they minister to other hippies. The Redeemer Temple congregation enthusiastically agreed to sponsor and help finance it.

On Sunday, May 17, 1970, the sanctuary at Redeemer Temple was crowded to the doors. Suddenly a young man sitting in the center block of pews got to his feet and stumbled down the aisle toward the platform. His appearance suggested that he had come from the hippie commune. Since the services at Redeemer are more informal than most and often filled with surprises, no one reached out to stop the man.

But it was apparent to everyone that he was drunk. "My name's Clarence," he announced, his voice thick. "I'm a man of color and proud not to be a white, proud to be a Black Panther." He was waving a black beret aloft.

At first Pastor Lou Montecalvo had courteously stepped back allowing the young man the floor. As it became obvious that this was a canned speech filled with clichés and memorized hate talk, the pastor walked over to the intruder and put one arm around his shoulders. "Clarence, you're delivering your speech to the wrong people. We care about you here."

Gently, the pastor began leading Clarence back toward his seat, talking to him as they walked. "See all those people out there? They love you, Clarence, not for the usual human reasons, but because they know how much Jesus loves you."

The congregation was hushed. At the foot of the chancel steps, two ushers took over from the pastor and quietly escorted Clarence back to his seat.

Pastor Lou returned to the pulpit and began the morning prayer. But as he began to pray, the voice of the drunk man in the pew was heard again, muttering and complaining. It was rapidly becoming a duet between the complaining from the pew and the praying from the pulpit.

Then a strange thing happened. All over the church people began quietly praising God aloud. "Thank You, Lord"... "We praise You for what is happening..." First a quiet steady hum of voices, then an harmonious chorus of thanksgiving and praise. After a few moments of this, the chorus diminished again. Finally the voices ceased.

Then everyone saw—Clarence was no longer there. Somehow in the midst of the praise he had slipped out of the church. As the people were realizing this, a member of the congregation rose. "I believe that I have a word of prophecy for all of us. It's this: 'My children, this day I have

been showing you, teaching you this lesson. Satan, the
enemy, is routed by praise, and only through praise.'"

Then he sat back down and Pastor Lou quietly picked up
again, incorporating into his prayer gratitude for the
tremendous object lesson that pastor and people alike had
just been taught. Not long afterwards, in the same church,
Clarence rose and made a public apology for his behavior
on May 17th. Then he asked for prayer for the Black
Panther organization.

"We know," one of those who heard him told me, "that it
is only a matter of time until Clarence will have his own
personal confrontation with Christ and become one of us."

It was a sign of the spiritual maturity of the Temple
people that they responded to this situation by:

> Giving thanks *always for all things* unto God and the
> Father in the name of our Lord Jesus Christ.[16]

"Always...for all things" is inclusive. It offers us no
loopholes, however awkward or irritating the situation,
wherein we are not to praise. Even in the relatively minor
emergency of an interuption to a worship service, praise
wrought its own miracle.

Grim circumstances of quite a different nature faced our
Dutch friend Corrie ten Boom and her sister Betsie during
World War II in Ravensbruck, the Nazi concentration
camp. The sisters had been hauled off to prison for aiding
Jews in the Dutch underground in their native village of
Haarlem.

Corrie is now a vigorous eighty-two, traveling and speaking all over the world. She remains one of the most
enjoyable guests who has ever graced our home and has
often regaled us with anecdotes of her prison life. One of
my favorites is her flea story....[17]

At one period of their imprisonment Corrie and Betsie
were transferred from crowded cells (where they had been

separated for months) to Barracks 28. Within the hour they discovered that their reeking straw bed pads were crawling with fleas.

"How can we live in such a place!" Corrie wailed softly.

Without answering, Betsie immediately began praying, "Show us, Lord. Show us how." Then a moment later excitedly, "Corrie, He's given us the answer! I read it in the Bible this morning. Here—read that part again."

It was in I Thessalonians. "Rejoice always, pray constantly, give thanks in all circumstances, for this is the will of God in Christ Jesus—"

"That's it, Corrie! We're to thank Him for every single thing about the new barracks."

"Such as?" Corrie was trying to look with fresh eyes at the half-dark, foul-smelling room.

"Such as being together here."

"Oh, *yes*."

"And having managed so far to hang onto that Bible."

"Yes—oh, yes. Thank You, Lord, for *that*."

"And for the fleas—"

"Betsie, I see no way I can thank God for fleas."

"But fleas are part of this place where God has put us. 'Give thanks in all circumstances,' it says. Not just pleasant circumstances."

So the two women thanked God for the fleas.

As the days wore on the prisoners in Barracks 28 discovered that there was an astonishing lack of supervision or interference. Corrie and Betsie used the unprecedented freedom to talk to the other prisoners, read the Bible to them, minister in myriad ways.

Then one day a supervisor tipped her hand as to why they were given so much latitude. Some of the women had called through the grilled door to ask the supervisor to come and settle a dispute. She refused, as did the guards. "That place is crawling with fleas," the supervisor said. "I wouldn't step through the door."

Corrie's mind rushed back to their first hour in the

barracks and to their rueful prayer thanking God for fleas. When she looked up, Betsie was chuckling, her eyes sparkling, "So now we know why we were supposed to praise Him even for fleas. Even the fleas had to be His instrument for our good."

As time has gone on, I have begun to see why praise is such a miraculous key. As we begin our praising in each circumstance, ever-fresh insights follow. This much I already see.... Just as a genius in mathematics can skip over many interim plodding steps to get the answer to the algebra or calculus problem, even so praise is the genius-shortcut route to our answer—God. This is because praise is faith in action, faith in its most vigorous form. When we praise...

> We are letting self go by turning our backs (through an act of will) on the problem or grief where self has been most involved.
>
> We stop fighting the evil or less-than-good circumstances.
>   With that, resentment goes;
>   Self pity goes.
>   Perspective comes.
> We have turned our back on the problem and are looking steadily at God.
>
> We are acting out our belief in the character of God—His goodness, His love.
>
> We are acting out our belief in the present power of God—in His participating Presence.[18]

We have to experience the delights of it to know what glory His participating Presence adds even to life's unpretentious moments. Soon I made a discovery that thankfulness, as nothing else does, enables us to live in the present moment. Not often do any of us grasp one shining moment, live fully in its "presentness," and consciously enjoy it. I shall not soon forget one such moment....

After dinner one evening my mother and I were comfortably settled in our living room. Through the room and around us flowed the music of a fine recording, the London Philharmonic Orchestra playing Mendelssohn's *Violin Concerto in E Minor*. As we listened, our hands were busy working on some table mats that were to be a gift. The singing, soaring melody was a delight not just to the eardrums but to the emotions.

All at once it happened. My heart overflowed with praise. Silently, I lifted all of it to Him, aware now of His presence.... *This quiet room, the comforts and the peace of it. No bombs are falling outside. No Gestapo is going to pound on the door.... By Your mercy and grace, Mother is still with us, the inimitable Christy, so gentle, yet so full of her own kind of ginger. You love her too. Isn't it great that she and I have such rapport that often conversation isn't even necessary!... This music, so glorious. It must be pleasing You too. Work for my hands to do, work that I enjoy. You know all about work with the hands. This moment—what delight—what an oasis—in the midst of busy life.*

The thankfulness bubbled up and up, and still I had not spoken.

Three evenings later at the dinner table I shared the experience with Leonard and Mother and in the telling, found tears in my eyes.

Then I marveled that such a quiet, unassuming moment had meant so much. Why, I wondered?

The word "consciousness' is probably the key to the answer. The thankful heart raised in praise and adoration, verbal or silent, becomes the vessel to hold the sense impressions and the distilled essence of the presentness of life.

In my sorrow after Amy's death, I had been promised

that when I obeyed God by beginning to praise, He would
show me how and why. Some of the understanding He has
supplied has been given directly, some through others. At
my request a friend who knows Hebrew and Greek made a
study of Old and New Testament verbs and nouns denoting
praise. Here are some of the insights which resulted:

> An arresting Biblical concept is that true praise and
> thanksgiving actually blesses and magnifies God; that
> what we do and our attitudes are important to Him for
> His sake, not just for ours.[19]

> The Hebrew root for "thank" also means "to acknowl-
> edge," "to confess." It is also related to the word for
> "hand," probably meaning the gestures used in
> worship.[20]

> Confession of wrongdoing goes hand in hand with praise
> because it is the other side of God's sovereignty.[21]

> Anything but praise attributes more power to someone or
> something than to God.

Now I began to see how God's Presence can be the
catalyst to turn evil events and situations into good ones.
We could compare it to the process that a photographer
goes through to develop a negative into a beautiful print.
(The word "negative" is intriguing here.) When we hold a
photo negative up to a light, all objects are reversed: black is
white, white is black. Further, the character lineaments of
any face in the picture are not clear.

Once plunged into the developing solution, what pho-
tographers call "the latent image" is revealed in the print—
darkness turns to light and lo, we have a beautiful picture.

Even so, we must begin by obeying Jesus' injunction
"Resist not evil." So we stop fighting whatever form evil is
at the moment taking in our life, even as the worshipers in
Redeemer Temple did not resist the interruption of a
drunken man.

"Resist not evil" however, does not mean mere passivity or submission. That would make us "slaves of sin," which is hardly what Jesus meant. When we praise by an act of the will, by our own free choice, first we accept present circumstances, then we take up a positive position. By beginning to praise God for the evil, we take our less-than-good situation and plunge it into the photographer's fluid—the Presence of God.

Even as the photographer has to wait while the chemicals in the solution do the developing work, we too have to wait—meanwhile continuing to praise—while the Spirit does the work. And as we wait and praise, often unable to see any change in exterior circumstances, we understand what Paul meant when he wrote, "I am become a fool in glorying."

Paul was right. There are times when praise makes any one of us feel foolish. I remember the pain, the agony, of my loss as I resolutely but awkwardly began the Prayer of Praise for my granddaughter Amy Catherine. "Lord, thank You for being with all of us during those weeks of Amy Catherine's battle to live. You certainly were a participating Presence, else that other little girl wouldn't have been healed, all those other great answers to prayer would never have happened

"Lord, I see it: There's still a lot of selfishness and introversion in me, or I would be as overflowing with praise for those others getting blessed as I would have been if Amy had been gloriously healed. Thank You for showing me this." Now the pain was subsiding, the praise flowing more naturally.

"Lord, I see now what You mean about everything that happens being part of the lesson material in Your schoolroom. I really can praise You that You refuse to let us stay children, that you keep insisting on our growing up. Thank You for caring that much about us.

"And thank You most of all that Your love for each one

of us goes right on despite our stubborn refusal to understand until You have shown us the light again and again."

The matter of praise is obviously still one of my growing edges. I am convinced that living at the point of praise and seeking it will lead us to the richest discoveries we have ever made.

3

Forgiveness: The Aughts and the Anys

Joan is forty-six years old, a successful merchandiser of women's clothing, yet extremely unhappy. She resents her father to the point of hatred because she blames him that she never married. Her father so missed having a son that he pressed Joan into a too-masculine role from childhood on.

Roger, another acquaintance, is sixty, ill with a series of physical problems. He has drifted in and out of undemanding jobs beneath his ability. Roger's heart knows seething bitterness for a business partner who cheated him. Roger was the one who had to pay with a six-months' jail sentence. Constantly he harks back to this so that people do not like to be with him. His face looks so angry that children are always thinking he is mad at them.

In both Joan's and Roger's situation the inability to forgive has built to a point where all the people involved are frustrated and miserable.

Most of us are aware that Christ requires us to forgive. Yet forgiving is not easy when the other person is clearly in

the wrong. This is especially true in actions that violate
God's and man's laws and the good that God wants for His
world.... The rape-murder of a little girl. Ruthless exploitation of a small country by a large and powerful one. The
Dachau extermination camps. Did Jesus mean that we
must also forgive evil of that kind? And if He did, how can
we?

For years I attached a condition to my forgiveness: if the
other person saw the error of his ways, was properly sorry,
and admitted his guilt, then—yes, as a Christian, I was
obligated to forgive him. Finally I had to face the fact that
this was *my* pat set of conditions, not Christ's. For He said,
"Forgive, if ye have aught against any...." [1] "Any" can
have only one meaning: anybody—everybody—all-
inclusive. As for the particular wrongs we are to forgive,
Jesus is just as demanding on us there too. His instructions
are to forgive "aught." The dictionary definition of "aught"
is "anything whatsoever." Again, all-inclusive.

The scope and inflexibility of Jesus' teaching on forgiveness staggered me. Obviously I was missing something.
Basically two questions clamored for answers. First, how
can a righteous God ask us to forgive a rapist, an exploiter,
or a murderer with blood on his hands? Would not forgiving the unrepentant murderer be the same as saying that all
value-judgments are wrong?

Secondly, approaching it from the psychological side,
Jesus, we are told in Scripture, "knows what is in man." He
understands human nature all through; furthermore, the
Carpenter of Galilee is intensely practical. Therefore, He
would not command human beings to forgive in a way that
is impractical, cuts across all morality, and is frankly
impossible for us.

Now I knew I was missing something.

When a pastor listens to an individual pour out his
problems, often he sees clearly that at this point or that

one, the person on the other side of his desk has been in the wrong. If the pastor has been trained in nondirective counseling, he will carefully withhold these opinions.

Even so, he is caught in a dilemma. The minister knows that a spirit of condemnation in him, even though unexpressed, will set up an immediate barrier to further confidences. Yet liberation for the needy one can only come from seeing himself as he really is and wanting to change. Without that there is no hope, as experience in a group like Alcoholics Anonymous has long demonstrated.

I remember Peter Marshall coming home from many such confrontations in his church office, marveling, "Nothing—but nothing—is as difficult as for one human being ever to bring another person to the conviction of sin. Why, oh why do we ever try it?"

And that's exactly what the Bible tells us. "When He (the Comforter, the Holy Spirit) is come, He will reprove the world of sin.".... [2] Here we have Jesus telling us that convicting one another is not, and never was, our work: it's the Holy Spirit's business. The pastor can point to the ideal, even be specific about what the Bible teaches. Beyond that, each of us must receive illumination about his guilt from the inside.

But can we? Is there any way we can facilitate the work of the Spirit? I was given help on that by David du Plessis, a minister formerly of South Africa.

Back in 1961 when I was writing about David du Plessis' insight that there is no such thing as inherited Christianity because "God has no grandsons," [3] I wrote of him as "a new friend." Now that the du Plessises live in the United States, we see them more often. In 1971, at a time when certain family prayers were still unanswered, David gave us an insight as powerful as the "no grandsons" one.

Over coffee in our living room he pointed out to us a verse of Scripture that had long puzzled me:

Verily I say unto you, whatsoever ye shall bind on earth
shall be bound in heaven: and whatsoever ye shall loose
on earth shall be loosed in heaven.[4]

"For a long time I was puzzled," David told us,
"about what 'loosing' and 'binding' meant. Then I found
out: it means that by hanging onto my judgment of another, I can bind him to the very conditions I'd like to see
changed.

"By our unforgiveness, we stand between the other
person and the Holy Spirit's work in convicting him and
then helping him. By stepping out of the way through
releasing somebody from our judgment, we're not necessarily saying, 'He's right and I'm wrong.' Forgiveness
means, 'He can be as wrong as wrong can be, but I'll not be
the judge.' Forgiveness means that I'm no longer binding a
certain person on earth. It means withholding judgment.

"How I wish," David continued, "that I'd been taught
that from the beginning. My whole Christian life would
have been different. Judge, judge—there are no more
judgmental people in the world than Christians. It was
certainly so in my life! When the Lord made me face up to
that, He told me, 'You're not forgiving. You're a public
prosecutor, judging everybody in sight. And I want you to
be a public defender—not public prosecutor.'"

David put down his cup of coffee. "Weren't you and Len
telling me that you're troubled by some unanswered
prayers? Well, in my life I've found this forgiveness business a key to getting prayers answered. A couple of years
ago I was going through one of those prayers-not-getting-
beyond-the-ceiling periods and I prayed, 'Lord, I don't
have enough faith. Give me the gift of faith.'

"'It isn't your faith,' the reply came. 'I can see faith even
if it's as small as a mustard seed. No, it's something
else.... When you stand praying—forgive if ye have aught
against any. That's your trouble. That's why your prayers

aren't answered. *You go about with a lot of aughts against a lot of anys.'*"

As David concluded his story, I thought to myself, "Our aughts against all the anys.... What a shaft of light!" So now we saw why certain of our prayers had not been answered and we set ourselves to the work of forgiveness.

My husband Len and I started on a systematic releasing of our "aughts against all the anys" in our respective lives. We agreed to spend about thirty minutes each morning, each with a cup of coffee in a separate room, getting our Aughts on paper. After that we would meet together for verbal prayer release of each person on our lists. Then we would tear the lists into small bits, put them in a large manila envelope. Eventually we would burn them.

Long ago we had learned the principle that it is necessary to get the past confessed and straightened out (as far as is possible) before we can live abundantly in the present. So we began as far back as we could remember, working on a different period of our life each morning, searching out people and situations buried deep in our unconscious.

For instance, since I've always been fascinated with history, many long-dead characters are as large as life to me, like the English Tudor king, Henry VIII. For reasons not altogether clear, I have always had a personal loathing for that man. On each trip to the British Isles, I could never seem to escape him. In the Tower of London, his coarse, obese presence hovered in the shadows as I would peer through the slit of a window to the green below where such a procession of his subjects had their heads chopped off at his instigation—Sir Thomas More, Bishop John Fisher, the aged Margaret Pole, and two of Henry's wives—Anne Boleyn and Catherine Howard.

Even in Scotland at the ruins of Dryburgh and Melrose abbeys, who should appear but Henry VIII! As I stood in the grassy aisle, the guide intoned, "In May, 1544 Henry VIII commenced what he called his 'rough wooing' of

Scotland. The Earl of Hertford marched on the Border, looting, murdering, burning. Behind them in England, 3,219 abbeys already lay in ruins, which had added treasure to His Majesty, the King, of 161,000 pounds. Scottish abbeys, including Melrose and Dryburgh, were also soon put to the torch."

So that's why Dryburgh was a ruin! Even as my eyes reveled in the beauty of the stone fretwork looking like delicate lace against the sky, I seethed at the thought of all those cathedrals and abbeys destroyed by order of Henry.

Now back home in Florida, during one of those quiet thirty-minute periods of a morning, my "aughts" against Henry VIII kept hammering at me. How, I wondered impatiently, could someone I'd never known in the flesh be such a personal affront to me? And this historical Aught seemed too trivial to bother with. After all, this particular character had already been dead 425 years and more pressing forgiveness work awaited me nearer home.

But the answer came, "No, this is valid for you. Get on with the cleaning out. That's real emotional energy you've been spending on history. The point is not whether the target for your emotions is past or present, the dead or the living, valid or invalid. The point is to get into the proper relationship with Me: assume your creaturely role, and give back to Me the sole right to judge."

So...marveling at my own foolishness, I released His Majesty King Henry from my unforgiveness. After that, I could rejoice in no longer having to arraign Henry for his black deeds and let God handle that one.

On another morning, I tackled all my Aughts in connection with my hatred of war, like the armament makers of World War I, the Senate leaders who had defied Woodrow Wilson and blocked America's entrance into the League of Nations; more latterly, certain gentlemen of the Pentagon.

Some Aughts surfaced from my childhood. Childish resentments, to be sure, but needing to be unloaded. My baby brother Robert had crawled in amongst my doll furniture, wrecking everything. Not only that, fascinated with dolls' eyes that open and shut, with an exploratory forefinger he had punched the dolls' eyes back into their heads. When I discovered sightless sockets looking up at me as Mrs. Eagen's and Mrs. Ogen's "eyes" rattled around in their heads, I was so angry that Mother had to restrain me from pummeling brother Bobby with my fists.

Mornings later an especially difficult Aught surfaced from Peter Marshall's first heart attack. Sometime before that attack he had stopped smoking. Nine days into his convalescence, the doctor had put a cigarette in Peter's mouth because he was so fearful of "nervousness." The passing of the years with all we know now about smoking and heart disease only made this Aught harder to release.

Then I came to that Aught from my first years in the writing-publishing world. On editing Peter's sermons from his manuscripts (meant only for oral delivery, hence not carefully annotated), a particular clergyman had not been given proper credit because I had not caught this in preparing the book manuscript. The publisher had received an angry letter. As one Christian to another, I had written the man a letter of detailed explanation (my fault—not Peter's) and apology, promising the proper credit line in the next printing and all subsequent ones. The only reply had been a terse, "From henceforward you will address me only through my lawyer." In the end, the retribution exacted had been a small sum of money. Curdled by the episode, this Aught had clung. Now it had to go.

As Leonard and I dealt with our respective Aughts out of the past and proceeded to present areas needing forgiveness, we had continually to guard against merely flashing around our negative opinions and analyses rather than relying on God to remedy the situation. But gradually we found that by dropping personal judgments we could clear out tons of emotional debris that had obscured the real issues involved.

It did not take many mornings to see that the contemporary parallel of my Henry experience involved that category of persons who had never injured me, but whom I would rather avoid. There are many ways of expressing the feeling. "He rubs me the wrong way"... "Oh, I don't know, some chemical reaction between us—not good"... "Just allergic to her, I suppose." That would not do in Jesus' eyes, I discovered. So those people, too, had to be released to be themselves whether or not I happened to like their looks, their habits, or their life styles.

Jesus' direction about love is clear: "You shall love the Lord your God with all your heart, soul, and mind... and love your neighbor as much as you love yourself." [5] In all honesty, we know how little genuine love we bring to God even in moments of what is supposed to be worship, how feebly and selectively we love our neighbor. The love God demands can only be the gift of God. Yet He cannot give us that gift so long as bitterness and resentment have slammed shut the door of the heart and unforgiveness stands sentinel at the door lest love open and enter. Forgiveness is the precondition of love.

The "how" of forgiveness is through knowing how to use our will—the rudder of our life. We are responsible for the set of this rudder; once we have willed a course of action, God will be responsible for our feelings if we will hand them over to Him. Otherwise, nothing we can do would change these feelings.

When I put that conclusion alongside David du Plessis' statement, "Forgiveness means, 'The other person may be as wrong as wrong can be, but I'll not be the judge,'" I saw that forgiveness is simply the decision of our wills to release a particular person, followed by verbalizing that to God. It can be a simple prayer like, "Lord, I release _____ from my judgment. Forgive me that I may have bound him and hampered Your work by judging. Now I step out of the way so that Heaven can go into action for _____." Obviously, there is nothing impossible about praying like that.

As for faith that such a nonemotional release would result in changes in the other person's life, I confess that we began with deficient faith. The process of releasing the Aughts seemed too simple, too pat.

We were about to be shown that when we follow Jesus' directions, the simplest ways are the most powerful.

Every human being has problems of relationship with other people. The other (positive) side is that in interaction between people we learn most of life's needed lessons. Yet grown-ups as well as children are inclined to avoid correction. Any of us can plan a life style which skirts around our foibles, hang-ups, and selfishness.

By 1959 after ten years of widowhood, with Peter John in college, I realized that I was developing exactly such a life style. Though I had decided to build a house and settle down in Washington, there were inner warnings. I saw that too much protected solitude was a danger to me. It jeopardized aliveness and those fresh discoveries that are part of spiritual growth. By then I also understood that even the most earnest prayer and disciplined Bible reading leaves out another whole area through which God reaches us—people. What to do about it?

Today many people who seek an answer to all this are entering into communal living so that interaction with others can deal with character flaws. In the fifties and sixties however, there were only faint rumblings of movements toward community living.

For my solution I had turned my eyes toward the Church of the Saviour. This was a small interdenominational church shepherded by Gordon Cosby. One of its requirements of church membership was a high degree of commitment not only to the Lordship of Christ but to the group itself. I had all but decided to take this important step when Leonard LeSourd and his three children walked into my life.

Soon it became apparent that for me God had planned a different sort of involvement and commitment. The house I was building was almost finished. Inside its insulated, climate-controlled walls I could have slipped into the rut of a padded middle age much too early. There I would have been secure from the jostles and jabs of normal family living. In that perfect step-down office adjoining my bedroom, I might even have completed my novel *Christy* in three or four years rather than the nine years it took.

But what growing pains of the human spirit (my own included) I would have missed! How little I would have understood of what life is all about compared to what I've learned during the hurly-burly years since. Though I have still had little experience with living in community (only an occasional retreat and a three-generation household) I now see the family as another one of life's important training grounds for learning how to deal with the Aughts.

So I sold the house and undertook the rearing of a second family. The years since have dramatized what I already knew, that I am no expert in child rearing, only a constant learner. I know that I share with other parents those situations in a family where varying interests and personalities whittle away at selfishness and impatience, force us to run the risk of sharing our innermost selves, so that we are bent and then rebent into flexibility. The bumps and bruises and turbulence are part of the price you pay for life's richness.

During the early years of my marriage to Leonard, some of the turbulence came from infighting between Chester and his young brother Jeffrey, two bear cubs frolicking about the house, rolling over rugs, colliding with furniture.

There was the morning I heard loud noises from the direction of the boys' room. Then came the sound of a slap and a door banging. Chester and Jeffrey were at it again!

Chester's angry voice met me as I crossed the living room. "Jeff, open that door. Open it!"

From the bedroom side of the door came an impudent reply that further infuriated fourteen-year-old Chester. He hauled back his right foot and kicked the door. There was a crunch. With dismay I saw that the toe of Chester's shoe had punched through the wood paneling.

I rapped sharply on the door. "Jeff, unlock this door this instant—or I promise you such a scorched bottom you won't sit down for the next week!"

He slid back the bolt and stood there looking sheepishly at us.

"He hid my English paper and I have to turn it in today." Chester's voice was still shaking with rage. "He refused to give it to me."

"Did you do that, Jeffrey?"

"Yes-s."

"I'm disgusted with you. That's baby stuff." Then I turned on Chester. "When are you going to control that temper of yours? The door," I moaned. "Just look at that door! It's ruined."

Such a bear-cub scene was not made easier for me by Len's genial disinclination to punish for infighting. His attitude tended to be a relaxed, "Well, that's the way boys are."

Soon after Len and I were married and were living in Westchester County, New York, my new daughter Linda was entering the sixth grade. It became apparent that my stepmother role was not going to be easy. There was the usual playing of one parent against the other and the tussles over clothes and curfews most mothers have with their daughters.

In the sixth grade, Linda was bright and freckle-faced with the instincts of a tragic actress. This was the period when the fad was to wear dirty sneakers to school—preferably with no socks. One day Linda and I had just returned from purchasing a new pair of sneakers. Several minutes later, I looked out the front window and saw our daughter in the rock garden on her hands and knees, the shoe box open on the ground beside her, carefully dragging one white sneaker, then the other through the black soil.

Loudly I voiced my objections, "Do you really want to look as if you've come out of a pigsty?"

The gaze she turned on me was withering. "Mom, everyone wears dirty sneakers. I'll look ridiculous if mine are all new and white."

The emotional temperature was soaring, so I dropped the subject. That afternoon when I happened to be near the junior high school, I dropped in to see for myself. Classes were just changing. Sure enough, all the way down the corridor moved hundreds of pairs of dirty sneakers. Standing there, I remembered how humiliated I had been when Mother made me wear galoshes to school on a rainy day when my classmates didn't.

But sneakers and the like were minor points compared to something that neither Len nor I understood. When fun times were planned especially for Linda, such as a party or a shopping trip, immediately afterward she would turn into her worst self. This odd sequence happened so often that we knew a warped force was at work. If was as if she was saying, "Please, I can't stand any special demonstration of love."

On the other side, when punishment was necessary (usually the withdrawing of some freedom or privilege) no sooner was the discipline given than Linda would become a veritable angel with a winsome disposition.

Such behavior was especially discomfiting to a step-mother. The relationship to which I had looked forward was not what I had hoped. I felt like a rejected parent. Then I caught myself resenting this child and her attitudes. Since this was not my image of the "good mother," I tried to ignore or bury such emotions.

I still remember some moments of realization one Sunday morning in the First Congregational Church in Chappaqua. The winter sunlight was streaming in the tall arched windows laying long patterns of light across the white Colonial sanctuary. I was sitting there thinking about Linda. Suddenly in my mind and heart His voice was speaking to me with particular clarity and intensity. *Unless you love her, you don't love Me.*

"Lord, I know that's true." The thought stabbed me. "But *how* do we love a person when we hate some of the things they do? Please tell me how. And Lord, I have another problem. I can't manufacture love. Nobody can. I need help."

With the issues thus clearly drawn I struggled on. Over and over I would take a fresh grip on my willingness to love Linda, no matter what she did—all the way from minor infractions to slipping out of her bedroom window after midnight for a date with a senior football star five years older than she. As I willed to love, I asked God to take care of my emotions and make my love real. For a time it would work and our home would know contentment and harmony. Then another crisis would develop and I would fall on my face.

The difficulties that had surfaced in early adolescence grew until Linda was finding life all but unmanageable. For years, schoolwork had been difficult. Here was a bright girl whose grades seesawed wildly between A and Flunking. Almost every term report carried teachers' comments about "Poor attitude and motivation" and "Work not up to level of ability." Tutors and extra sessions and a prep school brought no demonstrable results.

During these years her father and I had tried everything we knew—guidance counselors, a child psychologist, counseling with Christian friends, group prayer, prayer at Linda's bedside while she was asleep—every type of prayer we could think of. There had been some minor breakthroughs, but Len and I knew that the root problem remained. It seemed to be centered in her will. She appeared to be unable to want to be any different.

In college the trouble grew. To academic difficulties was

added the Youth Revolution of the late sixties. Linda plunged wholeheartedly into it: life pattern; clothing styles —levis, long hair, wire-rimmed spectacles; protest meetings, campus sit-ins, hitchhiking to peace marches and rallies.

Most of us parents with children caught up in all this know the feeling... wondering whether our sons and daughters might be ensnared in experiences dark enough so that we would prefer not to know specifics. Especially when they were away from home, we told ourselves that "what we don't know won't hurt us," meanwhile knowing full well that the ostrich never solved anything with his head in the sand.

Graduation day came for our daughter. Linda's father, grandparents, and I got to the graduation scene to find a very tense girl on our hands. There was a thin veneer of happiness but flashes of irritation and anger kept breaking through to us. The strain in the relationship between Linda and me was obvious, her dissatisfactions deep. Watching the academic procession walk by on sneakers, dirty white shoes, T-thong sandals, with mortarboard caps tilted on the heads at every possible angle, I wondered what the other graduates were feeling. Were most of them unhappy too, with life somehow out of kilter, values all a jumble?

The scene left me with such heaviness of spirit that after our return home to Florida I spent one morning working on the release of all Aughts against Linda stretching back over the years to age ten. To my astonishment, I filled three pages. Neither Len nor I told Linda anything about our prayer of release.

We did not have long to wait to see results.

Several weeks later on Cape Cod during that tumultuous summer of 1971 came the climax to our long years of struggle with this particular situation. When my grandchild Amy Catherine Marshall was born on July 22nd with severe liver, kidney, and brain damage, a group of us gathered on the Cape for concentrated prayer. On an impulse I telephoned Linda, who was working in her grandmother's gift shop in Maine. Would she care to join us?

There was a moment's silence. Then, "Yes," she said, "I'd like to be there."

Afterward Linda told me that she wanted to come because I was the one who had telephoned and invited her. What happened when she got there literally reversed the direction of Linda's life. The details of the story are hers alone to tell. As is usually the case, people other than Len and me—her parents—were used by God as the catalyst for our daughter. The turning point that followed is best told in her words...

> On the afternoon after my arrival at the retreat I was about to take a shower. A particular moment is crystallized forever for me. I had one foot on the bathroom rug, the other in the shower stall. At that instant like a bolt the realization hit me that one foot in, one foot out was an accurate representation of my life. Several times I'd gone through the motions of committing my life to God. Yet I did not have an obedient heart. I was living in outright rebellion against Him.
>
> I sensed that this was the moment to decide—for Him, or against Him. There could no longer be any middle ground.
>
> Standing there, I carefully weighed what choosing the Lord's side would cost me. Obviously, some things in my life would have to go. But I was tired of living in two worlds and not enjoying either. Desperately, I longed for His peace in my heart.
>
> I took a deep breath and said aloud, "I choose You, Lord." Then I got in the shower. That shower was my true baptism.

The following day came many hours of agonizingly honest dialogue with us. We heard things we didn't want to hear. Tears flowed. After that I understood why the direction given me in the Chappaqua church—*Unless you love her, you don't love Me*—had been so difficult for me.

"I thought I wanted a loving relationship with you when you married Dad," Linda told me. "But resentment crowded in. The reason was that at a gut level I thought you were taking Dad away from me. I would no longer be Number One in his life."

During this long evening of honesty and confession among the three of us, many barriers came crashing down. For Linda it was the release of years of hostility and guilt. For us, it was a facing up to mistakes and fears and lack of understanding. To cap all of this emotional upheaval, Linda had a "believer's baptism" in the ocean followed by a communion service on the beach.

That was not the finish of this particular Aught-Any episode. I was to get my come-uppance the morning after the communion service.

During the intervening hours, my mind must have flicked at some secret thoughts along the line, "*All that...* all those years of agony she put her father and me through, then she's forgiven by God *instantly*. Isn't that too easy a forgiveness?" Ugly secret thoughts—except God knew.

The next morning I was awakened to the clear incisive internal message, "Remember My story of the prodigal son? You're in grave danger of taking the place of that elder brother.[6] That morning in Florida, you didn't quite mean business about finally releasing all those Aughts against Linda, did you? I heard and answered anyway. *Now let them go.* For now, take the lowest seat at My banquet table, below Len, below Linda. And I want you to confess all this to Linda this morning."

Thus I was properly zapped, as our boys would say. Humbly and a trifle haltingly, at breakfast I made my confession to Linda. She wept again, this time from joy, and then ecstatically hugged me.

Now that Len and I had released Linda of our Aughts against her, she was free to become the very person we had longed for. A new life began for her. For several months she stayed with Edith and Peter Marshall under their direction and guidance. Gradually she began to get answers to those crucial questions, "Who am I? Why am I on the earth? Where am I going?" Linda now lives in Washington where she is part of a unique Christian fellowship at Trinity House, living cooperatively and ministering to students and young career people.

All of this give and take with my new family enabled me to identify with many friends who were having trouble with rebellious teen-agers. One close friend, Sybil Jones, who lives in Virginia a few miles from our Evergreen Farm, was having a problem with her niece Fay. Because of the personal nature of the events, I have changed names and some unimportant details.

One night in Florida I received a call from Sybil. "Catherine, I just have to talk to you. It's about Fay."

As Sybil talked on, I was remembering Fay's family. I have known her parents, Loretta and Tim Randle, for many years and have watched with apprehension the way they have catered to their only daughter. Each Christmas would come a family picture of the three of them with the golden-haired Fay always the center of their adoring smiles. As the years passed the Christmas cards showed the child was growing up into a beautiful girl—a pert face, slender body, lovely. Except that when she was fifteen a look was developing on Fay's face that bothered me—a touch of arrogance in the eyes? Selfishness around the mouth? Or was I imagining?

We would see the three Randles in the summertime when they came to Virginia to visit my friend Sybil, who was Loretta's sister. Aunt Sybil had always been a sort of spiritual godmother to Fay. She read Bible stories to her as a little girl, taught her special prayers. Fay stayed with her Aunt Sybil while her parents took long cruises or trips abroad. During those periods she would try to provide the disciplined home life that Fay was obviously not getting.

While the Randles were churchgoers, although only in a hit-or-miss way, they saw no connection between Christian faith and the way they structured their home. And whatever Fay wanted she usually got.

When Fay reached her seventeenth birthday that May she wanted a Corvette hardtop automobile. Her parents gave it to her. Then Fay began to want things not even they would give her—like drugs and weekend trips with boys.

Soon an ominous personality change developed in their daughter. Fay became withdrawn, moody, secretive. She had been a good student; suddenly she didn't seem to care. That was when they discovered the marijuana.

"I've no idea how long Fay has been smoking marijuana," Sybil told me. "As if that isn't bad enough, her father found a big supply of 'downers' in her room. When he discovered the marijuana and the downers—she had been using six or seven of them a day—he hit the roof. He took her car keys for a month. One night about a week ago Fay packed a bag and drove off in her Corvette. Apparently she had a spare set of keys.

"Her father almost went out of his mind," Sybil continued. "Days passed with no word from Fay. He alerted the police, then hired a private detective to find her." There was a long silence as I prepared for—I did not know what. "Last Friday they found her and some boy named Bart living together in a dirty apartment in the French Quarter of New Orleans."

I commiserated with Sybil the best I could, promised to pray for Fay, and hung up the phone thinking, "How many, many parents are going through this same kind of experience!" I knew of ten or more friends who had watched in anguish as rebellious children left home. Some had returned; one had died of a drug overdose; two had been killed in car accidents, others injured with one paralyzed for life; some were still missing.

When Fay's father confronted her and her boy friend in

the New Orleans apartment, there was a stormy scene. "I'm tired of your respectable middle-class life," Fay shrieked at him. "It's phony. You and your friends kill yourselves with cigarettes and booze. Let me alone to do what I want to. Bart is the only real thing I've ever found in life. Except maybe Aunt Sybil."

Her father stared at her, at the long-haired boy beside her, then turned around and left. "I don't have a daughter any more," Tim told his wife when he got home. During the next few months his wife and friends watched him age ten years.

That Christmas no card came from the Randles.

But while Tim Randle had given up on his daughter, his wife and Sybil had not. They persisted in keeping in communication with the young couple.

The next summer while at Evergreen Farm, I had an unexpected visit from Sybil, visibly upset.

"I'm afraid I've done the wrong thing," she began. "Yesterday morning Fay and the boyfriend, Bart, arrived suddenly at my house. I had sent them some money to visit me, but they didn't tell me they were coming. They had hitchhiked all the way from New Orleans. I guess they've had to sell Fay's car.

"I greeted them lovingly, fed them a big meal. Then suddenly they asked where they were to sleep. 'Are you married?' I asked. They shook their heads. 'Then I'll give you separate rooms,' I said.

"'Separate rooms!' The look on their faces was something. 'You're a phony like everyone else,' Fay shouted at me. Before I could stop them they'd picked up their things and walked out the front door."

Sybil looked at me, her eyes full of tears. "Did I do the wrong thing?"

We talked and prayed together. The answer to our prayers was clear guidance: Sybil had done the right thing. She had showed them love, but since Fay and Bart sleeping together as an unmarried couple violated the moral code of Sybil's faith and her home, she had to ask them to take separate bedrooms.

During our time together I told Sybil about the Aughts against the Anys principle. For a long moment she considered the question: was there judgment and condemnation in her heart for Fay and Bart?

"Yes, I do think there is judgment on my part," she admitted. "But how can I honestly pray to get rid of it?"

We did it together. Then Sybil raised a new point. "My releasing judgment against Fay and Bart may help my relationship with them. But the real problem is between Fay's parents and these kids. And the Randles are coming to visit me next week."

Sybil had before her the formidable task of trying to bring the Randles to the point where they not only forgave and released their daughter from judgment, but did the same for Bart.

"You know, Bart isn't hard to like," Sybil confided to me as she was leaving. "Behind all that hair there's a gentleness and yes, even a sweet spirit. Fay calls him 'a hip beautiful person.'" Bart, too, had left a middle-class family situation in Arkansas in rebellion against his parents.

When the Randles came to visit there was complete stubbornness on Tim's part toward any reconciliation. Finally, Sybil bluntly told them that their hardness of heart would keep God from doing His forgiving work in all the lives involved. It had not been a pleasant time.

Months later she was on the telephone again, her voice jubilant. "Fay and Bart have moved into a small apartment just two miles from here. They hitchhiked from New Orleans weeks ago, both now have jobs. I had them for dinner last night. Do you know what they asked me? Did I know a minister they could talk to? I sure did."

The next letter had good and bad news. Bart's and Fay's talks with the minister had resulted in their deciding to get married. Living together unmarried had seemed racy and amusing. But they had few close friends and could find no real place in the community. There also came an inner dissatisfaction they couldn't define. They then had decided that marriage made more sense than they had thought.

So Bart and Fay were married one afternoon in a quiet church ceremony. The bad news was that Fay's parents had refused to come to the ceremony.

I had trouble sleeping that night, grieving over the Randles' unforgiving stubbornness. What was the Lord trying to tell parents through experiences like this? That what we have called love for our children is largely sentimentality, not strong enough to be redemptive? That the permissive giving of so many material possessions to children is really a form of self-gratification without the quality of love Paul talks about in the thirteenth chapter of Corinthians?

Fay's mother, it turned out, had desperately wanted to go to the wedding, but felt she should not come without her husband. Heartbroken by the situation, she thought of Sybil's words about their hardness of heart and the necessity of releasing their Aughts against Bart and their daughter Fay.

The morning of the wedding, Loretta Randle alone in her quiet bedroom took two important steps. She gave her life to the living Lord she had never known. Then she spent two hours getting on paper her Aughts against Fay stretching back to about age ten. She had not realized how many resentments against Fay she had acquired.

Loretta felt lighthearted, happier than she had been in years. So she persuaded Tim to work on his Aughts too. He found it especially hard to release Bart, who in his eyes had "seduced his little girl." All of this was done with no communication with Fay and her new husband Bart. Slowly, painfully, hundreds of miles away they were being released from judgment.

There came the memorable day in Sybil's living room when Fay and Bart were reconciled with her parents. Fay asked her father's forgiveness for the harsh statements she had made that day in New Orleans. She hugged her mother—and wept. Then to Sybil's astonishment her niece knelt at her feet. "Aunt Sybil," she said revealingly, "you were right that day—when you wanted to put me and Bart in different rooms. One reason I got so mad was because I knew you were right. That's the reason Bart and I came here to live because we felt you were the one person we could trust. You stood for something and deep down we wanted what you had."

Later Sybil wound up her report to me with a little vignette. "The Randles," she wrote, "arrived two days ago for a week's visit. From my window I can see Bart with Tim Randle out by the front fence. Bart is handy with tools, so Tim has enlisted his help in making a new gate for me. Already there's an easy camaraderie between the two men. Isn't it great the way this has turned out! How can I ever thank you for the Aughts and the Anys?"

After we had seen such miracles of restored relationships, I began to understand why Jesus gave us the Aught-Any command immediately following His clarion call to "have faith in God" and His challenge to get on with a mountain-removing faith.[7] The sequence can mean only one thing—that our Aughts, big or just pesky, are always the chief block to prayer power.

Once we see this truth, many examples spring to mind, such as that of Stephen, that personable, eloquent young man who became the first Christian martyr. As the murderous stones flung by a frenzied mob bruised flesh and broke bones and the bloody stones piled up at Stephen's feet, Saul of Tarsus stood watching, holding the witnesses' outer garments so that they could better hurl stones at the condemned man. Saul heard Stephen's last words before death, "Lord, lay not this sin to their charge." So it was Stephen's release of his Aughts against his executioners that made it possible for heaven to go into action for Saul of Tarsus.

Shortly thereafter, as Saul traveled toward Damascus, heaven opened to bring Saul to his knees in one of the most dramatic turnabouts in recorded history. He would become Paul, missionary-traveler over all the known world, great apostle to the Gentiles, and spiritual father to all of us in the Western world.

As each of us bemoans the severing of so many relationships, we may recognize that we can't really expect anything else when we leave God out of our lives. As always, Jesus challenges His followers to be out in front showing the way: "Forgive, if ye have aught against any...."

There's no way to get our world back together again except as each of us begins with himself and with his own family.

4

The Law of the Generations

For years I felt the same despair as everyone else under the continual barrage of articles and true-life situations telling of estrangement between parents and children and issuing dire predictions of the imminent demise of the family.

The cover of a national news magazine dramatized it, a picture of a father, mother, son, and daughter—square, robotlike people, with the caption, "The U.S. Family: 'Help!'"

Statistics followed: one in every four marriages now ends in divorce; a high 70 percent rate of divorce exists in some California communities; 40 percent of all married women with children hold out-of-home jobs; half a million teenagers run away from home each year; the rate of school drop-outs is steadily rising; the "new morality" with utter rejection of premarital chastity has been accepted by a large percentage of young people.

During the 1960s the world's youth had center stage. The young had become our obsession: either they were glorified, with even their hair and clothing styles copied by their elders, or they were feared, resented, and blamed for everything. After a while it became apparent that neither extreme could be right since we had found so few solutions.

It was about then that I was startled to find in the Old Testament a brief but applicable description of society's plight in our time:

> Thou shalt beget sons and daughters, but thou shalt not enjoy them; for they shall go into captivity.[1]

All of us know the ways in which we do not enjoy our children. We are afraid of what is happening to them. Or we feel cut out of their lives. Then there's the basic fear that our children will "go into captivity." In the seventies we are discovering that the captivity of drugs, of the occult, of sexual promiscuity, is every bit as real a captivity as it was for the Israelites who were physically carried into Babylon centuries ago.

How different is this from those other descriptions in Scripture of parents who do enjoy their children, described joyfully as "a fruitful vine by the sides of their house"... "a quiver full of arrows"... "the crown" of old age... "olive plants round thy table."

Startled by how pointedly and powerfully the Deuteronomy verse speaks to our hearts today, I sought out the original setting of the words. The author and compiler of Deuteronomy[2] has Moses speaking them as part of a prophetic warning as given him by God. The forty years of Israel's wilderness wanderings were over. The second generation then stood poised, ready to enter the Promised Land. Moses would soon die; he would not enter Canaan with them. Before formally commissioning Joshua as his successor, the venerable leader gave a farewell charge to Israel. This charge is the book of Deuteronomy.

Reading this book is like looking through a window into the amplitude of Moses' spirit. In his speech there is no note of an old man's sentimental nostalgia, rather the entire thrust is into the future. Warm with feeling and persuasively eloquent, Moses focused on this one significant point:

> See, I have set before you life and death, the blessing and the curse...
>
> Therefore choose life...[3]

The rest of the Old Testament narrative tells us what happened: all too often the descendants of those to whom Moses had given his charge did not "choose life." History records that these descendants did go into captivity literally as well as spiritually.

Each generation then, as now, has a choice: life or death... the blessing or the curse.

"Why shouldn't I do as I please—as long as it doesn't hurt anyone else?" we are hearing frequently today.

The truth is that whether we are young or old, we cannot do as we please and not hurt other people in the process. As Dr. Francis Schaeffer, philosopher and theologian, states it, "Man is drowning in cosmic alienation." Scripture continually insists on the principle of our connectedness as a fact of human life: "We are... every one members one of another."[4] In this Law of the Generations, as I call it, we are linked to previous generations behind us. Our ancestors are in our genes, in our bones, in our marrow, in our physiological and emotional makeup. We, in turn, will be written into the children who come after us.

I was at home alone one night recently when I heard a noise in the kitchen. Dropping my mending in my lap, I tensed, listening for any other sounds however faint. Those cat burglars I'd been hearing about... was someone there?

Hearing nothing more, I went to investigate. The kitchen was so dark! Suddenly, I felt that familiar prickling at the base of my neck.

Then came a surge of annoyance at myself. "You're not going to let that fear of the dark return," I told myself sternly. Resolutely, I walked into the kitchen and flipped on the light. A tray had toppled from its place beside the refrigerator.

Most of my life I've struggled with an assortment of fears, many of them foolish ones. As I sought through prayer for a reason for so many fears, I was pointed back to my father's mother, Grandmother Sarah.

My girlhood recollections of this grandmother are rather negative ones. I remember that she spent most of her days sitting in a comfortable chair in the bay window of the living room, often with a huge Bible open on her lap. She used it as a sort of scrapbook; it bulged with clippings, cards, letters, and snapshots tucked between its pages. The expression on her face was usually dour. I cannot recall any of her grandchildren sitting in her lap to be cuddled.

Yet Grandmother Sarah had an immense capacity for friendship and hospitality. I can remember no meal in that home without guests and boarders, not even breakfast. She and the two daughters who ran the house were superb cooks in the best of Southern tradition.

But I began to see that the overall effect of my grandmother's fear-ridden personality on me was not good. My mother remembers a significant event that occurred when I was six weeks old. Grandmother and Grandfather had agreed to baby-sit for me one night while my father and mother went to a lecture.

"About midway in the evening, an usher handed a note to the lecturer," Mother recalled. "He asked if a Mrs. Wood was in the audience? If so, there was a message for her at the door of the auditorium. There stood your grandfather. 'It's the baby,' he panted. 'She's cried herself blue in the face.'

"He and I started for home almost on a run. Halfway

home I could hear you screaming. Yet the instant I dashed into the room and picked you up, the crying stopped as though a faucet had been turned off. You were frightened and my presence reassured you. Grandmother had searched so fearfully for an open safety pin, a Florida mosquito chewing on you, or a rash, she had made you more afraid. She was so tense."

Can it be that a baby's sensitive antenna can pick up the tone of people surrounding him? If his family is happy and their relationship harmonious, the baby's reaction is contentment; if there is strong negativism like fear, the baby senses this and protests. Child psychologists and those who work with babies in institutions affirm that this is exactly so.

As I grew up, I discovered the nature of Grandmother's fears. Since she thought the night air dangerous, she would not allow Grandfather to raise any windows in their bedroom winter or summer. Many a morning we would see Grandfather stagger pasty-faced and dripping with perspiration from the sweatbath of their stifling sleeping quarters.

To this was added an abnormal fear of thunderstorms. As the skies would begin their fireworks, Grandmother Sarah would dash for her feather bed, cover herself with a comforter and stay there until the last bit of lightning had faded and the last drop of rain had fallen.

Later, when I was about eleven, Grandmother Sarah kept me and my younger brother and sister while my father, dangerously ill, spent three months at Johns Hopkins Hospital with Mother there beside him. It was a time of real fear and tension for all of us. At this impressionable time of my life, I somehow focused on Grandmother's fears of night air, drafts, thunderstorms, the dark, washing hair too often, staying out in the sun—things which seemed to me ludicrous and absurd. Such phobias were the last things I wanted to imitate.

Yet so strong is the Law of the Generations that even what we scorn can still come down to us. In my case it was not Grandmother Sarah's particular fears—rather simply an overinclination to fear. In my life it centered on a dread of germs and illness; a horror of mice or small dead animals, and during my childhood, fear of the dark, ghosts, and the like.

The time came when I realized that in Jesus' eyes, fear is a sin since it is acting out a lack of trust in God. Then my attention was drawn to that part of the second commandment which follows the injunction not to "make for yourself a graven image": "For I the Lord thy God am a jealous God, visiting the iniquity of the fathers upon the children unto the third and fourth generation...." [5]

I had always wondered about this: was that fair? Or like a loving God?

But now in the light of the revelation about my fear and Grandmother Sarah, I saw that the Exodus verse was simply stating a fact of life. And I *was* the third generation from my grandmother to be beset by those petty fears.

As is often the case when we are being taught something, this matter of sins being passed down from generation to generation seemed to be everywhere I looked in the Bible.

We are accustomed to the idea that we pass on to our children a physical inheritance—color of eyes, color of hair, even certain diseases: tendencies toward gout, diabetes, certain skin diseases. Handing down a material inheritance is such standard practice that the laws of every country make careful provisions governing wills, probate, death and inheritances taxes. I began to ask myself, is it possible that our spiritual inheritance is as real as the others?

It soon became apparent that just as we can inherit either a fortune or debts, so in the spiritual realm we can inherit either spiritual blessings or those liabilities (unabashedly called "sins" in Scripture) that hinder our development into mature persons. These blessings or liabilities do not come to us solely by heredity. Obviously they are also passed on by example and by teaching—conscious or unconscious.

For instance, I think of a mother with a habit of keeping an untidy bedroom; her daughter now fights a continual losing battle with cluttered closets and drawers.

I've a friend who can scarcely go to sleep at night without reading herself to sleep; her father before her had the same habit, as do both her grown sons.

My husband Leonard dislikes tomatoes, sweet potatoes, liver, broccoli; so do sons Chester and Jeffrey. My grandmother used heaping teaspoons of sugar in her coffee or tea; my father did too, and also my brother.

These are trivial matters. Above this lowest level, more serious bequests are handed generation to generation....

A man whom I'll call Sam found himself hindered by a terror of any emotional involvement with other people. At an office farewell party for a secretary who was moving to another city, the girl began to weep as she opened her gifts and read the enclosure cards. Even though she was weeping from gratitude and fond memories, Sam was still uncomfortable and found himself sidling out the door. "But this is silly," he told himself. "Why am I doing this?"

It was a pattern he had repeated over and over—this ducking out of emotional scenes. As he pondered this fact, a picture came into his mind.... It was a dinner table scene in his boyhood home. Angry over criticism directed at her, his mother had jumped up from the table and flounced out of the house. For a minute or two the father just sat in his chair, weary and lifeless. Finally, he left the table to seek out his wife to placate her. The scene ended with husband and wife returning home arm in arm, surface harmony restored. But there would be other occasions when Sam heard his mother crying and saw his father retreat out the back door to sit in the car and smoke a cigar.

Sam realized that these scenes had been repeated over and over through his growing-up years. How he had dreaded them! Whenever possible he had left the house. He sensed that his father had wanted to retreat from those scenes as much as he had. Now he could understand better one of his father's traits that had long puzzled and annoyed him, a sort of peace-at-any-price stance in any situation involving disagreements.

About three months after this revelation, Sam was caught up in a mild argument with his wife. He did not know that she was unusually tired from a difficult day. When she burst into tears, they were both startled to see their shy six-year-old son hastily leave the living room and run up the stairs. Sam followed the child. He found him in bed rocking his body rhythmically back and forth in the way he had comforted himself as a very small child.

"Oh no!" the father thought as the significance of the chain reaction now into the third generation was borne in upon him. His son knew nothing of the similar episodes in his father's life when he had fled from emotion. Nor of his grandfather's tendencies along this line. Yet here was the child acting out the emotional hang-ups of his father and grandfather. It was uncanny! As he sat on the edge of the bed comforting his son, then and there Sam vowed to find the way to break this particular inheritance; surely this bondage to the fear of negative emotion had harassed his family long enough!

Intellectually, Sam knew that many of life's greatest experiences take place in emotional confrontations involving people. Yes, the man knew that, but the little boy still in the man remained terrified of all emotion.

Up to that time in Sam's life, he had had little use for religion. Yet one day at the noon hour, impulsively he slipped into the back of a church. There were several other worshipers sitting throughout the sanctuary. He could feel growing within him a desire that seemed ridiculously emotional—to stand up, walk down that long aisle, kneel at the altar railing and say, "God, I need You."

But he could also feel rising resistance. What if he got to that altar and actually shed tears? These people sitting there...if they saw him kneel weeping at the altar, would they not think him some kind of exhibitionist?

A deep instinct told Sam that this was a true crisis point in his life. Here he was, again backing off from emotion.

Knowing that the answer had to be "yes" if that vicious chain was ever to be broken, resolutely he got to his feet, walked down the aisle and knelt. Immediately, he forgot all about the other people. He even shed a few tears, but they were glorious tears, a moment Sam could never forget. The chain *was* broken and though not everything was healed instantaneously, that day in the church was the beginning of a new level of maturity for Sam and his family.

All of this gave me ample proof that the Law of the Generations is a fact—the sins or the blessings of the fathers *do* come down to the children.

It is the nature of sin to divide, to build walls, resulting in strained relationships or estrangement. I wondered if the Law of the Generations might give not only clues to the difficulties between the generations in our time, but even constructive answers. How might we pray so that the negatives could be transformed to positives?

In the process of searching for an answer, I was surprised to find that the last words of the Old Testament have to do with these problems between the generations. They are words of great promise. At the last days, God promised to send another prophet who

> ... shall turn the heart of the fathers to the children, and
> the heart of the children to their fathers.[6]

The date of the Book of Malachi has been placed at about 450 B.C. The writer mentioned Elijah as the forerunner of that "Sun of righteousness" who would "arise with healing in his wings." All these centuries later we know who the Sun of righteousness is, the greatest of all the prophets—the Lord Jesus Christ.

At the beginning of His public ministry Jesus made it clear that He had not come to destroy the Law, but to complete and fulfill it. Jesus would recognize the Law of the Generations, like all other law, as part of His Father's world. But until then there had been that missing dimension, exactly the question I had asked. After we struggle and find that we can't keep the law by our own effort, then what? Is there any hope for us?

It is at that point that Jesus gives us the good news of His Gospel: He who is Truth and therefore is above the Law, will do for us what we cannot do for ourselves. So there is not only hope, but a real answer. We cannot turn the hearts of our children to their parents, but Christ can.

It was my son Peter who helped me to apply these new insights about my fears and Grandmother Sarah at a time several years ago when both of our families were coming to grips with the negatives in the Law of the Generations. No doubt Peter's position in the intertwining generations put him in the perfect position to help me with my fears. We found that our prayer work fell into three parts.

First, having brought into the light all remembered dark heritage from previous generations, I had to forgive all these ancestors and release them from my judgment.

Second, Peter prayed that I be cut loose from these negatives. As I remember it, his prayer went something like this:

Lord Jesus, You have told us that Your Word is the Sword of the Spirit,[7] that it is sharper than any two-edged sword known on earth. Whatever You say to us cuts deep and lays bare even the thoughts and intents of the heart.[8]

You've also assured us that You came to earth to loose all bonds, to set every captive free.[9] Lord, Mother has been captive to these fears that we've been laying out before You. Yet You've declared that where the Spirit of the Lord is, there is liberty.[10]

So now, Lord, I take that Word and claiming it and wielding it as the Sword of the Spirit that it is, in Your Name and by Your power I hereby cut Mother free from every chain and shackle from the past. I release her now to her rightful heritage—the glorious liberty of the children of God.[11] Thank You, Lord Jesus, thank You. Amen."

This powerful prayer led naturally into the third step, praising God for every part of this experience. For we found that the release would not be final unless I received it in faith, and as I had been discovering, praise is the swiftest, surest route to faith.

So now I began to understand how Christ makes the Law of the Generations work for us. It was our friend, the late Starr Daily, who gave me some further insights about what our part is in this process.

For many years Starr, originally an expert safebreaker, had been in and out of penal institutions, finally pronounced hopeless by the judge who sentenced him to prison for the third time. Later, in the penitentiary hellhole, he experienced one of the most dramatic conversions of the twentieth century. After the prison doors opened for him in 1930, he wrote ten books, gave innumerable lectures, conducted hundreds of interviews with youthful criminals.

Out of the totality of Starr Daily's great contribution to prison reform, I'm concerned here with but a single facet of what he learned—how a change in the attitudes of parents can effect changes in a son who is in prison. A number of his examples [12] demonstrated to me that the Law of the Generations works positively in as precise a way as it does negatively.

The father of a twenty-four-year-old prison inmate sought an interview with Mr. Daily one day to ask for help. "I've tried everything with my son," the man mourned. "There's nothing left but God."

"Well, He's quite a leftover," was the dry reply.

Wordlessly, the man handed Starr Daily a summary of his son's record. It looked bad indeed:

...excessively quick and bright in intelligence, but infantile in emotional reactions and responses. Reformatory, jail, and prison record of nine years. Type of crime: sex offenses, burglary, robbery, forgery, confidence games, picking pockets, purse snatching, drug and narcotic peddling.

"Looks hopeless, doesn't it?" the father commented.

"Don't you believe it," Starr told him. "While there's life, there's hope. It's up to you."

"Up to me!" the father almost shouted back. "What do you mean by that? What can I do at this late date?"

The father and mother made no pretense of being "religious"; they went to church twice a year, on Christmas and Easter. The home had always swung between two extremes—great leniency when the parents were in good humor and not busy, and unusual severity when they were out of sorts or rushed.

Starr next prescribed a spiritual rehabilitation program for the couple. "I'm going to be hard on you," he told them, "because I sense that you mean business."

The program was to be carried out in a way that would funnel into it tremendous spiritual power: husband and wife were to be "in agreement" about what they were trying; [13] they were not to discuss it with anyone, keep all of it a secret between them. [14]

Then Mr. Daily wrote out a prescription for the couple. In relating this particular story Starr did not detail the prescription. However, it was not too difficult to cull out of Starr Daily's writings [15] the sort of spiritual rehabilitation program he recommended:

1. Rise early enough to start the day by giving one hour to the program. During this hour, use only the Bible and a notebook and pen or pencil. Start with reading the Gospel of John. Jot down in the notebook:

Any verse or promise about faith.

Make notes about the character traits and attitudes of Jesus, remembering that when you want to know what God is like, look at Jesus.

Together try conversational prayer aloud—no "thees" and "thous," honest straightforward talk about anything that comes to mind.

2. Begin to focus on the fact of Jesus' identification with anyone in need. Keep reminding yourself that He stands at the center of each person's need ready to help, to be the Saviour.

Pick out three situations each day in which you in secret and silently pray for another person, visualizing the Saviour spreading His light within them and their affairs.

Then practice trying to trust other people—not because they necessarily deserve trust, but because you are trusting the Spirit of the Lord in them.

3. For now, do not ask anything for your son. He is God's child as well as yours; God loves him even more than you do. Turn him over completely to that light of Christ within him.

Whenever you think of your son, picture the light spreading as God does His own work within this boy.

Mr. Daily explained to this father that he and his wife were the key to the situation in the sense that the Law of the Generations enabled God to use them as His divine catalyst to change their son.

"As you work on this program," Starr explained, "you'll be reclaiming your spiritual parenthood. You see, God's order for the home is that husband and father must shoulder spiritual along with financial responsibility. In a real sense the man is to be God's representative—priest or prime minister, as you will—for his own household. When the man takes this rightful place, then God promises His protection and blessing for that home."

"My wife's been the spiritual one in our family," the man objected.

"Maybe that's part of your problem. With both parents alive, in God's eyes there's no such thing as the woman being the spiritual head of the house. When that happens, strength and vitality go out of Christianity every time."

"Why? I don't get it."

"When a father thinks so little of God that he leaves any slight gesture toward Him up to his wife, how important are children—especially boys—going to think religion is anyway? Maybe," Starr added gently, "that's part of the problem with your boy."

The father ruminated on that for a moment. At last he said slowly, "Looks like I've got a lot of work to do."

The father left with new hope. But it took him and his wife two months really to get under way with the program Starr Daily had assigned them. Disregarding the initial awkwardness and unreality they felt, they took up prayer separately and together.

Though these parents did not understand why, during these months they no longer worried about their son. Later on, they understood that Starr's prescription had helped them put first things first: they were actually living out the Scriptural promise, "Seek ye first His kingdom of God, and His righteousness; and all these things shall be added unto you." [16]

Three and a half months passed. The father had long since finished the Gospel of John and had gone on to the Acts. One morning he had gotten to Chapter 10, where he was reading the story of the Apostle Peter and the Italian centurion Cornelius. Suddenly, a particular verse leapt out of the page at him:

> God hath shewed me that I should not call any man common or unclean. [17]

His eyes were riveted to the words. An insistent thought

kept hammering on his mind for admittance. Was God
trying to give him a message through that verse?

The story was plain enough. Peter was given a vision of a
huge sheet let down from heaven filled with all manner of
creatures including some that the Jews regarded as unclean. The meaning: Peter was to disregard the Jewish
taboo on certain foods. This led into the larger truth that
Gentiles who wanted to ally themselves with the infant
Christian church did not have to become Jews first. That,
in turn, burst into a truth so big—here the father held his
breath—that it embraced the whole world: God was asking
Peter and all of us to love everything He had made, all His
other creatures and one another. Nothing—no one—is to
be refused the grace and love of God. So that had to
include his son, the boy in prison.

Since God had accepted and welcomed him, the father,
God expected him, in turn, to have the same openness of
heart toward his son.

A warmth the man had never before felt flooded his
heart. Here was a message to him straight from God. He
would hold fast to that and no longer believe the prison
official's negative prognosis about his son. Now he could
receive every thought of his son into his mind with
thanksgiving.

Here is Starr Daily's brief summary of what happened:

> As this father turned from fear of and doubt in his son
> and looked steadfastly at the good with more and more
> praise, the boy began to respond to the new parental
> conviction and attitude. And it was done *"across space"*
> *without personal contact.* When the father visited his son
> six months later, the young man was cured of his
> criminal mind and well on his way to total rehabilitation.

When the parents (and especially the father) allowed
God to become the Head of their home, the immutable
Law of the Generations worked just as Starr had pre-

dicted—from sharply negative, the situation was turned upward to a glorious positive.

I have been fascinated to read about what happened in one entire family where the blessings of the Law of the Generations were joyously fulfilled through many generations.

In her delightful book about "the uncommon union of Jonathan and Sarah Edwards" [18] Elisabeth D. Dodds gives us a composite portrait of the Jonathan Edwards family. Edwards, the Puritan, has been wrongly pictured as an overly serious ecclesiastical sourpuss, remembered chiefly for a single sermon, "Sinners in the Hands of an Angry God." The full picture of him is very different.

Sarah Pierrepont and Jonathan Edwards were married in 1727 after a courtship of four years. Edwards was over six feet tall, towering over most of his contemporaries. His bride was a vibrant brunette with erect posture, gracious manners, and a gift for conversation that put people at ease.

The Puritan view of marriage was not the restrictive and spiritless one usually assumed. Most Puritans had a healthy viewpoint toward marriage, sex, and family life. Sarah's wedding dress was "no white wraith mistily drifting toward some vague spiritual experience...but she wore a pea-green satin brocade with a bold pattern as she stepped joyfully toward her lover."

Sarah and Jonathan were to have eleven children. Edwards believed in rising very early, so everyone in the house was routed out even in the dark winter predawn for prayers by candlelight. The family heard the father read a chapter from the Bible and then ask God's blessing on the day ahead.

Each child had chores. As the child's taste developed, his or her tasks were chosen as largely as possible on the basis of special talents and wishes. For example, Esther gardened, while Mary claimed that she was the champion maker of chocolate. The house functioned efficiently because all these highly individual children were taught to work together.

Courtesy was the rule. The parents approached the discipline of their children united; this may be one reason why the children, in turn, married happily.

One Samuel Hopkins, who spent many months with this family, wrote in his quaint style:

> Sarah carefully observed the first appearance of resentment and ill will in her young children toward any person whatsoever, and she never connived at it.... Her system of discipline was begun at a very early age.... She wisely reflected that until a child will obey his parents, he can never be brought to obey God.

Edwards always gave one hour a day of complete attention to his children. Toward evening, he would take his place in his chair, one with a high back, unmistakably the father's. No one else presumed to sit in this particular chair. During this hour the children could ask questions, get help with lessons, or anything else they wanted.

Today it staggers us even to think about the work involved in such a household. How did Sarah Edwards stand up under this? Her security and fulfillment came from her certain assurance of her husband's love and the place of great honor always given her in their home. Jonathan treated Sarah with total courtesy and serenely expected that each child would follow his example. His wife always sat next to her husband at the table. Their children were able to observe daily the small affectionate demonstrations of their parents' love for one another.

About four o'clock on fair afternoons, Edwards would emerge from his study and suggest that Sarah join him in a horseback ride. The couple would ride together in the hills above the river. Edwards would test the day's harvest of ideas against Sarah's practical intelligence.

Sarah depended on her husband for her own spiritual replenishment. Whenever she felt an acute need of it, she would dive into his study during the day, confident that no matter how intent he was on his writing, he would put down his pen and turn to her with a lighted face. She fed on his leadership in family prayers and on the quiet times she and Edwards spent together on devotions after the children were in bed, a time together that put a benediction on the bustle of the daylight hours.

In those Colonial days, most women lost their looks early. Not so, Sarah. Her husband appreciated her beauty and her style. Everything she did was with flair. She took the trouble to tie her hair with a ribbon for breakfast and found that extra time to arrange bouquets of the daylilies, pansies, and pinks she grew.

Though the Edwardses had little money, Jonathan once spent eleven pounds for a gold chain and locket for his wife. So unusual was this for the time that his parishioners were critical of what they regarded as an overly lavish gift.

On another occasion, Sarah went through a bad emotional time for a number of weeks. Long before anyone had thought of psychotherapy, Jonathan had Sarah sit down and tell him everything she could remember about the weeks past. Using a shorthand system he had invented, he took down her words in full. By promptly reliving the difficult weeks, Sarah was able to put into perspective the pressures which had built up over fourteen years of never-ending household demands. From then on, she sailed through strains that might have sent another woman into bitter seclusion or whining invalidism.

In this family where "the hearts of the fathers and the children" were so visibly turned one to another it is possible to see how God blessed them down through the generations "unto thousands of them that love me, and keep my commandments." [19] In 1900 A. E. Winship tracked down 1400 of the Edwards' descendants and published a study detailing what astonishing riches this family had contributed to the American scene. By 1900 this single marriage had produced:

    13 College presidents
    65 Professors
    100 Lawyers and a dean of an outstanding law school
    30 Judges
    56 Physicians and a dean of a medical school
    80 Holders of public office:
        3 United States senators
        Mayors of three large cities
        Governors of three states
        A vice-president of the United States
        A comptroller of the United States Treasury

Members of the family had written 135 books ranging from *Five Years in an English University* to a tome on *Butterflies of North America*. They had edited 18 journals and periodicals. They had entered the ministry in platoons, with nearly 100 of them becoming missionaries overseas.

The Edwards family is a beautiful showcase of how God fulfills His promises when we do our part. For the greatest blessings that God has to give us are never offered just to the individual. Always, "the promise is unto you, and to your children..." [20] And the early Church held up as the ideal not individual salvation but household salvation, thus demonstrating the outworking of the Law of the Generations in the love and interrelatedness of the Christian community.

God is sending us a ringing call to understand that we cannot escape the blessing or the curse of the generations. If we will allow Him to, our Lord

> ...shall turn the heart of the fathers to the children, and the heart of the children to their fathers....

Here is God's singing, soaring promise of what this could ultimately mean to nations of splintered families.

"The generations" can start to assume their creative function *at any point*. Even if most of one's life is in the past and certain children and grandchildren are acute problem cases, yes, even then God can turn this curse that goes down through the generations into a blessing. Moreover, this redemptive work can even work backwards, as in Peter's prayer for me, when my son was the instrument used to stop the fear inheritance up through an older generation as well as down to the generations to come.

For each of us—no matter what our situation or how we feel we have failed—there is hope.

See, I have set before you this day life and death, the blessing and the curse...

Therefore, choose life.

5

The Joy of Obedience

Have you ever gotten an inner nudge to do something but resisted it? Then later you found out why you should have obeyed the nudge? Most of us have experienced this.

Of course, we are right to be careful about obeying hunches, because they can come from selfish desires or from negative forces outside us. On the other hand, when a person has asked God to take over his life and guide his actions, disregarding the inner Voice can be costly. I have heard story after story dramatizing how the Lord tries to reach us with His wisdom and help.

The latest comes from Nancy De Moss. She and her husband Art,[1] on that unforgettable Sunday night, September 3, 1972, were living in a spacious English Tudor house not far from Valley Forge, Pennsylvania. The De Mosses have seven children.

The week before Labor Day weekend, Nancy received a telephone call from her sister Lynne. She and her husband were going on a short trip for the holiday. Would Nancy be willing to keep their baby? With seven De Moss children in the sprawling house there was always room for one more. Nancy readily agreed. She thought the eleven-month-old Brandon was one of the most beautiful babies she had ever seen, tow-headed with big blue eyes and a smile that melted everyone who saw it.

But this time taking care of Brandon turned out to be difficult. The baby was restless from teething. For two nights the entire household got little sleep. On Sunday Nancy decided to move the baby's crib from the guest room (where it was proving difficult to hear him) to the playroom down the hall.

While the family was at dinner that evening, Ginny, a good friend of Nancy's sister, dropped in. "I've come to take Brandon home with me," she told the family.

When Nancy protested, Ginny explained, "Lynne had asked me to keep Brandon. I was the one who should have taken him. I just know it. But we had something on for the weekend and I let this loom too large in my mind and turned her down. Ever since I've known that was wrong."

"But my sister will be home soon," Nancy said, "and I don't mind keeping the baby a bit."

"I know. But Lynne asked me to keep Brandon in the first place."

When Nancy saw that nothing she could say would change Ginny's mind, she agreed and Ginny drove off with the baby.

Later on that night Art and Nancy had been asleep several hours when they were awakened by violent pounding on the door.

"The house is on fire!" The housekeeper's voice was shrill with fear. "Get out! Quick! I've got the children out!"

Art and Nancy stumbled to their feet. The hallway was thick with swirling acrid smoke. Shouting the children's names, they groped their way to the front door. Figures were clustered on the lawn, orange-red in the light of the flames from an upstairs window. Counting over and over, Nancy at last was reassured—all seven outside, safe.

They crowded around her, all talking at once... "The smoke made me cry, Mummy"... "We got out by the back stairs"...

It was one of the children's statements that sent a sudden chill up Nancy's spine, "When I passed the playroom door, Mom, it was *full* of fire right up to the ceiling."

The playroom!... Nancy looked up to the flaming square of window.

"It seems to have started in there," the housekeeper said.

And Brandon—Brandon would have been in the playroom where no human effort could have reached him.

In telling me the story, Nancy's eyes opened wide at that point. "I still get shaky every time I think, what if Ginny hadn't come—"

I too blinked in realization. "It certainly puts a frightening priority on obeying those inner nudges," I commented.

"Yes, it does—except that Ginny said it was more like a distress signal, then after that like an inner shove. She's been pondering for sometime now how a person gets God's guidance. In this situation the signal was loud and clear. She was restless that particular Sunday afternoon. Her thoughts kept going to Brandon and her refusal to take him in the first place. But the child was obviously all right with us. Then suddenly Ginny had this strong feeling that she *must* go and bring Brandon back to her house.

"She was afraid she would sound silly to us. It could be embarrassing. She tried to shake off the feeling, but by dinnertime Ginny knew she had to obey. Instead of calling me, she left a message with the housekeeper to have Brandon's things ready. She knew that if she came in person, I couldn't turn her away without the baby. And you know, later investigation proved that the fire *had* started in the playroom exactly where Brandon would have been sleeping. So the baby's life actually hung on Ginny's determination in obeying what she so deeply felt."

As I pondered this story in subsequent days, I remembered how often Jesus had told us that we would be wise men and women to obey His instructions. He even went on to say that when we go through great difficulty—such as torrential rain and floods and storm winds beating against our house, it will not collapse and we won't be in real danger—if we obey Him.[2]

Yet how difficult it is for most of us to believe that the obedience God asks of us is for our benefit. A story like Nancy's makes it clear that it is *not* obeying that poses the appalling risk. No wonder Jesus had so much to say about obedience!

Unlike earthly kings, God does not want our obedience out of fear. Our obedience to Him is the fruit of lives growing in the rich soil of love and trust. Our obedience is to be at once both the result of our loving God and also the proof of our love.[3] As with our human love, we are going to be capable of loving only to the extent that we abandon ourselves to another with no reservations.

Nancy's story made me eager to search out Jesus' words on obedience. I found an amazing assortment of riches promised those who learn the joys of obedience:

Salvation is given to those who obey.[4]

When we purpose in our will to obey Jesus and tell Him so, then we shall know whether Jesus' teachings are from God or merely His own.[5]

We become members of Jesus' family when we obey Him.[6]

The Father will come to a man who obeys and make His abode within him.[7]

Jesus will manifest Himself to those that obey.[8]

The Holy Spirit is given to those that obey.[9]

Our deeds will be blessed when we obey.[10]

As we obey Jesus, the Father will shower us and our affairs with His love.[11]

Certainly, these are impressive dividends from obedience. But what exactly are we to obey? Since Jesus often mentioned His commandments, I found it helpful to read the Gospels through, setting down in a notebook the commandments which Christ Himself gave us. There are a remarkable number of them and many are surprisingly precise.

In addition, Scripture clearly points out other kinds of obedience God requires of us:

1. To law and governmental authority.

As citizens of transient earthly kingdoms (along with the eternal kingdom of God) we are voluntarily to subject ourselves to law and the national government over us.[12]

2. To the individual's Christian fellowship—what the Bible calls "the Body," meaning the true Church, the Body of Christ on earth, we are to "be subject one to another." [13] Thus the individual's inner guidance is to be checked against the wisdom of the group mind.[14]

3. To our human family.

Depending upon our individual position in the family unit, God asks of us obedience and responsibility in a chain of Divine Order which He has established. . . . Christ is the Head of each human family.[15]

The husband is under Christ's authority as he assumes leadership of his home and final authority over the children of the household.[16]

The wife is the helpmate to the husband, protected by him from stresses outside the home and even from any abuse from children. God would elevate woman, not plunge her into servitude. Rather, her husband is to honor her with an unselfish love even as "Christ loved the Church and gave Himself up for her." [17]

Children are to obey both their parents "in everything, for this pleases the Lord." [18]

This Divine Order gives us necessary safeguards so that the individual does not mistake the Shepherd's voice. With such solid support, we can relax into the freedom of a living Lord's dealings with us individually. It is when we try to hear Christ's Voice for the daily decisions that we begin to know Jesus personally. Most people are astonished at His interest in the details of this relationship: how well He knows us, all the little things we thought we had successfully hidden; how realistic and relevant are the directions that He gives us.

Substituting a type of superspirituality for Jesus' homespun practicality can be one subtle way many of us try to keep a safe distance between Him and us. C. S. Lewis humorously illustrates this by telling us one way we can "render our prayers innocuous": make sure that they're always very "spiritual," that we are concerned with the state of another's soul, for instance, rather than his rheumatism. [19]

It may turn upside down one's preconceived notions about Jesus to realize that He *is* concerned about rheumatism and not especially interested in the lofty generalities in which we tend to take refuge. The Bible also tells us that He is concerned about the fall of sparrows and the baby's teething and our little habits that have us bound more than we realize.

Insomnia may seem an odd affliction through which to learn the Lord's definition of obedience.

Not long ago I was still one of those unfortunates struggling with sleeplessness. In 1955 my physician had suggested a mild sleeping pill as the best solution. After years of using these, I was aware of the still small Voice on the inside calling the pills into question. But I kept ducking. There was the fear, not even admitted to myself, that if I listened to the inner Voice, He would say something I didn't want to hear.

On those sleepless nights when my churning mind would

not be turned off, wearily I would finally get up to find the cylindrical plastic bottle with the tiny capsules, pink on one half, blue on the other. Sometimes half-aware of a "Stop" on the inside, I would pause even as my hand reached for the bottle. "But I'm so exhausted," would run the counter thought. "Surely this isn't the time to fight spiritual battles. I need sleep to get on with that important work tomorrow." Once again I would take the sleeping pill.

Then one morning in 1972 en route to the airport to catch a plane, I realized that I had left the sleeping pills at home. I thought, "Great! God has a wonderful sense of humor. The joke's on me! So this is the way He's going to give me the breakthrough I've been wanting." Then I asked Him to see to it that I slept naturally.

As usual, His ways were not my ways. That night I did not sleep at all. Dawn found me weary from tossing and from praying in what seemed to be a vacuum and fighting a losing battle with self-pity. But leaving the pills behind had uncovered in a stark way how overdependent I was on barbiturates.

Upon returning home, my prayers took the form of direct questions: "Lord, am I hearing You correctly on this? Is this false guilt I have about something really unimportant, like these foolish little pills?"

When His answer finally came, there was no difficulty about recognizing His voice, "Yes, pills are foolish. But the more important point is, you desire sleep more than Me. Therefore, lay your cherished sleep on My altar. Make this your alabaster box of ointment poured out for Me."

His words rang true, like the notes of a clear bell perfectly in tune. Obviously He was applying to my life His "If you love Me, keep My commandments." I realized then that obedience was going to be the key to some fresh new understanding. I was also to find that this is the way to get understanding rather than by the intellectualizing, library-digging route—obey first, then the illumination comes.

That September afternoon I searched through the medicine cabinet for all the sleeping pills. There was a large supply on hand. Taking a deep breath, I flushed them away and watched as the swirling mass of pink and blue disappeared from sight. Then I told God that I was going to depend on Him alone for sleep.

There followed eight rough days and nights. My dependence on God was real enough but so was my sleeplessness. How was it, I would marvel over and over, that both body and mind could be so fatigued, yet I would be unable to sleep? Isn't it man's natural state to sleep?

Quickly I found that continued loss of sleep was resulting in oversensitized nerves day and night. The slightest noise was amplified many times.... Someone would turn the pages of a magazine and for me it would be a loud rustling flip-flop. A bug would hit the windowpane and I would jump. I would turn over in bed and the freshly laundered sheets crackled in my ears. I couldn't even nap of an afternoon. Something was inhibiting the sleep mechanism.

That God would let the struggle be so brutal came as a shock. Having taken what I fondly considered a positively heroic step in dumping the pills, I had expected my reward: an instant miracle.

I was given one, though not what I had expected. Even in the midst of my deepest fatigue there was no real temptation to go back to the sleeping pills even for one good night's sleep. The set of my will was firmly held by Someone else, astonishing to me because it was not of my doing.

I was learning about the part the will plays in our relationship with God. First, there is that period of initial struggle of the will when we know full well that a decision has to be made. God won't force it on us; it must be entirely our choice.

Once the struggle is resolved to the point of saying "Yes" to Him—especially when it's accompanied by some irretrievable step such as the pill-dumping—then the struggle in the will subsides. Grace is given an individual at that juncture, at the point of the decision previously made. God regards it as a binding contract. It's as if by saying "Yes" to Him we pick up the ball (the will) and throw it to Him. He takes it then; He carries the will for us.

Even so, during these days I was given no relief on the sleep front. In an effort to understand, I began doing some reading about sleep. Some scientists believe that the brain has both a sleep center and a wakefulness center,[20] much as one's heart action is regulated by one set of nerves to stimulate activity, another set to reduce activity. It is theorized that natural sleep comes through reducing the wakefulness center's activity partly by withdrawing nervous impulses to the brain. Artificial sleep from pills comes through a chemical that enters the blood stream and may depress or inhibit the waking center's activity, thus changing the brain's chemistry. So for me, long use of even mild sleeping pills obviously had knocked my sleep mechanism all askew.

The nights seemed endless. I would hear a dog barking somewhere, then the electric refrigerator clicking off. There would be the sound of a train in the distance, the five-after-two-in-the-morning freight. The engineer was blowing his whistle for that long straight stretch just before town.

The long periods of wakefulness required sharp disciplining of thoughts and emotions. I had had a lifetime tendency to let my thoughts sink to the bottom every time I let my mind go fallow. Now a new level of obedience was being asked of me where negative or critical thoughts, doubting and worrying must be turned off immediately. After a few nights I noticed that I could take more authority over the negativism. This then, was another bonus of obedience.

I was also having to battle another byproduct of barbiturates. These drugs tend to inhibit dreaming. In sleep experiments [21] those deprived of dreaming begin to show

nervous and behavioral disturbances. Since much of my
dreaming had been inhibited, conflicts and tensions had
been building up in my unconscious.

It was a great night when I got three to four hours' sleep.
When I did sleep, my dreams seemed continuous and wild
and persistently pointed to two deep anxieties—rejection
and danger. In an effort to understand, I wrote down the
dream of September 23rd:

> I am the preacher's wife in a church in which an
> elaborate wedding is being solemnized—more gala than
> solemn. There are tickets to present at the church door
> and a fashion show is also to be part of the affair.
>
> I am acutely aware that I am not part of the "in" group. I
> seem to have arrived late and am incorrectly dressed.
> There is some discussion as to whether I am to be
> allowed into the church without a ticket. Fashionably
> dressed women are milling all around me looking at me
> curiously.
>
> The dream ends without my knowing whether or not I
> will be admitted inside to see the ceremony.

There were also many dreams in which there was actual
danger:

> A group of us have been told that something important
> (unidentified) is missing. We are asked to go and get it.
> We have to walk a long way—uphill and down, through
> several houses, in one door, out another. I feel
> threatened. Some of the women argue with me, some are
> belligerent.
>
> There are even physical threats—one especially vivid
> one: as we pass through one house near the front screen
> door, the man of the house warns, "Look out! Pull your
> hat over your forehead. And watch the angle that you
> open that door."

On the porch a rifle is mounted on a stand to the left of the door. It is connected to the door like a booby trap, so that when the door is opened to a certain angle the gun fires.

I wake up shivering with fear.

Sometimes resentment would rise in me. "All right, Lord," I would protest, "I obeyed You and look where it's gotten me. I've been miserable ever since."

Eventually the answering insight came, "When you obey, I do more than handle one little thing. You've been demanding an instant miracle for sleep; I want a healing of the whole woman. You've been asking for *one* blessing; obedience is the door through which I plan to flood you with blessings."

Following that, on the eighth day came the first breakthrough. After the worst night of all, I slept a little toward dawn and awoke with a single clause in my mind, presented to me in an authoritative and luminous way: *Blessed assurance, Jesus is mine.*

I recognized it as an old gospel hymn, one I had not thought about for years. When I looked it up and got all the words, God's message to me was plain and oh, so welcome:

> Blessed assurance, Jesus is mine!
> Oh, what a foretaste of glory divine!
> Heir of salvation, purchase of God,
> Born of His Spirit, washed in His blood,
> This is my story, this is my song,
> Praising my Saviour all the day long.. .[22]

This came as if in direct answer to the rejection aspect of my dreams. Obedience had helped me identify and face the rejection. Here was God's reassurance of His love and care for me, as if He was saying in terms of sleep, "You may fall tranquilly asleep any time you need to, for I love you."

So obedience in the little area of pills had led to the beginning of this deep healing of a basic need. The last line

of the hymn pointed me to the next step in the healing—
praise. That now-familiar way of praise—the open door to
God!

After that, the threat-fear aspect of my dreams diminished, then disappeared altogether. In their stead delightful
dreams of promise surfaced. Such as the one on September 30:

> I am wandering from room to room in a large house. In
> the spacious dining room is a large and beautiful rug, and
> on it an intricately designed carved mahogany table, with
> portraits on the walls. An air of mustiness pervades
> everything as if these rooms have long been in disuse.
> Though I have never seen such a room, in the dream I
> have the impression that it is mine.
>
> Going on to the adjoining room, I stand looking at tall
> cupboards with glass doors all around. They are filled
> with china and glassware that I recognize as belonging to
> me, but these possessions have not been used in a long
> time. I stand staring at all of it wonderingly, thinking how
> beautiful it is and what happiness to know that it will now
> be used again.

Whatever else this meant, certainly there was implied the
picking up again of joyous activities that had somehow
been set aside. The quantities of china and glassware
suggested entertaining as a reactivation of human relationships in a creative outgoing way and an end to the
unconscious mind's conviction of rejection.

The ninth day saw real victory, the wonderful feeling of
sinking blissfully to sleep without fear and resistance.

Now, all these months later, I can say, "Yes, it's natural
to sleep." And how great not only to be free from the chains
of dependence but to know that lifelong problems are being
healed.

Yet the road to freedom had to be through that low door
of obedience. Best of all is the closer fellowship with the
Lord that always follows obeying a specific He asks of us.

After such an experience the Shepherd usually allows us a plateau for rest and refreshment. Then we learn that this obedience is a steady daily discipline and that the discipline is for life. But being fickle creatures, we use our freedom of will sometimes to take back what we've already handed over to the Lord.

It took my friend Pat Baker several years to conquer the cigarette habit. But finally breaking the habit was the least of her rewards. She was given insights about her own personal motivations, about the difference between real and counterfeit sacrifice, about how important it is to let God design the blueprint for obedience rather than trying to fabricate it ourselves.

After many tries, Pat had at last achieved a four months' conquest of the smoking habit. The victory had come through a simple step of obedience. For weeks Pat had been feeling God's inner "Stop" each time she reached for a pack of cigarettes. There came a day when she said "Yes" but added, "If I'm going to have to quit, You'll have to do this for me." Lying on the dresser before her was a pack of cigarettes. Deliberately, she left them there. Every time she was tempted to pick one up, she would think, "If this were my idea to stop, I'd already have a cigarette in my mouth by now. But it's just not me at all."

She found it exhilarating—the most joyful experience of her life. Then one evening she and her husband Dick had an argument. In a spirit of rebellion, Pat fled the house and drove around town trying to dispel her anger. All at once, she found herself reaching for a pack of cigarettes her husband had left on the front seat. Even as she did so, she was saying on the inside, "Lord, I know You've told me to stop. And I really will stop—but not quite yet."

For a year after the argument with her husband, Pat found herself waging a losing battle in her struggle with tobacco. She asked prayers from all and sundry friends. Some of them suggested that one way of tackling the problem was to probe why she had started smoking in the first place. Yet Pat could find no answer to the question.

At last she got to that point of desperation I knew so well. "O Lord, I want to be free. I really do. And I won't take the cigarettes back this time." There was no immediate answer.

Then one Sunday afternoon she felt as if she was coming down with a cold. She decided on a nap. When she awakened she instantly recognized that there was something not of herself in the clear thought in her mind, "Get up. Get dressed. Go down to the Bethany Church."

Pat was inclined to argue, "Lord, that's a wild church. I'm an Episcopalian. I've never been in that kind of place—" Then more humbly, "Lord, if this is really You and this is what I'm supposed to do, would you please let Dick agree to it?"

Ordinarily her husband Dick would say in a situation of this kind, "Don't be ridiculous. You've been out three nights this week. Be sensible and go back to bed."

This time however, when she told him of this strange nudging, he answered, "Go ahead, I think you should."

When Pat got to the church she found that some sort of evangelistic services were going on. She slipped into the back hoping that she wouldn't be noticed. After all, this was a small town. What would her fellow Episcopalians think of her attending this kind of church?

Then the preacher's words caught her attention. He was speaking about Cain and Abel and about Abel's "more excellent sacrifice."

"Perhaps," the young preacher said, "Cain never had liked the idea of killing innocent little lambs as a sacrifice to Jehovah. Why would Jehovah ask them to do that? Wouldn't it be better to wait until he understood why, and then obey?

"Meanwhile, if God wanted a sacrifice, how about that beautiful mound of fruits and vegetables he had grown! Those perfect bunches of grapes! Those luscious pomegranates and figs! Surely Jehovah would like those!

"You see, the problem with Cain," the young preacher

summarized, "was that he was offering a sacrifice all right, one that he had thought up, but *not the sacrifice God had asked for.*"

Sitting there listening, Pat thought of all her multitudinous church and civic activities, of her generous giving of time and money, of her sacrifices during Lent. But the clear counterthought came to her, *None of this is any good unless you do the particular thing I'm asking you to do.*

"O Lord," Pat answered in her thoughts, "I hear You loud and clear, but I can't do what You're telling me to do. I've tried. I just can't."

Now the evangelist was giving an altar call, but it wasn't the usual one. "All those," he said, "who came here expecting God to do something for them, come forward to receive it."

That sounded the right note to Pat. She knew that being there hadn't been her idea in the first place. "But," she struggled with herself, "I'm just not going down there. I know that young man will shout like those other evangelists do.... Lord, do they *have* to be so loud about it?"

Moments later she was astonished to find herself kneeling at the altar rail. The evangelist made his way to her first of all. Without saying a word, he knelt quietly on the other side. Pat looked across the rail at him, surprised at his quietness. Finally he said, almost whispering, "The Holy Spirit never gives one of us a message for another person in order to hurt or embarrass them. The message is always given to help another. Do you understand that?"

"Yes, I do," Pat replied, marveling at the way the young minister was speaking directly to her thoughts.

"Would you like to hear what God has for you this afternoon?"

She nodded.

"Well, He's ready to deal with you about your problem with nicotine."

Pat stared at him in astonishment. How could he possibly

know that? She listened wide-eyed as he began telling her when and why she had started to smoke. "It started when you were a teen-ager and it grew out of the soil of rebellion. Even then, God was calling you, but you weren't willing to listen. Now He has a special gift of the Spirit for you, one that He wants you to use in a particular ministry for Him. If you're willing to get rid of the nicotine, He'll reveal more to you of what this is all about."

Then the evangelist told Pat how to get free. "If you will resist the nicotine for three days, the Lord will do the rest. At the end of that time, He promises to reveal something of the particular kind of work He's calling you to."

As she drove home that night Pat thought, "Well, I suppose I can do anything for three days." But she was to find even three days so much more difficult than it had been the first time. Now it was a moment-by-moment battle.

On the third day, a friend whose marriage was in trouble came to thank Pat for helping her find her way out of darkness several weeks before. Immediately, Pat realized that she had allowed her bondage to cigarettes to interfere even with helping other people. She had been so preoccupied with herself and her hang-ups like smoking that there had been no time or mind-space for anyone else. The impact of her friend's gratitude brought Pat tears of remorse followed by a surge of joy and a strong resolve that bolstered her resistance.

From that point, Pat found herself free of the desire to smoke—when she was awake! But strangely, she began to dream of smoking.

The dreams were so vivid! She could taste the cigarettes and smell the smoke, and would wake up with the knowledge that she had been fighting the desire to smoke on unconscious levels. Out of this experience Pat learned that we have to be of one piece—not divided between the conscious and the unconscious—before a prayer can be finally answered. In her case, Pat had been delivered from smoking on the surface; now a deeper work was going on in her unconscious.

Dreams by night and insights by day revealed to her what the evangelist had suggested: the smoking had started through insecurity during her courtship days. Now she was able to remember what had goaded her to start smoking—nothing more than several paragraphs in one of Dick's letters. He was then at the University of Florida and, to tease her, he had written glowingly about another girl.

Pat had overreacted with anger and jealousy. Wanting to rebel against Dick and her whole life, she chose cigarettes as the best symbol of rebellion. Hadn't her mother always made *not* smoking a symbol of virtue? Before she and Dick could resolve the quarrel, Pat had started smoking.

The battle of the cigarettes is four years behind Pat now. Depending on the Lord (instead of cigarettes) in moments of friction and stress has brought Pat not only joy, but a steady stream of deepening insights to help other people with their problems.

When Jesus says, "Follow Me," not a one of us is going to drop his fishing nets to leave all and go after Him—unless he feels he can trust Him. One memorable sentence quoted by the Quakeress Hannah Smith sums it up, "Perfect obedience would be perfect happiness if only we had perfect confidence in the power we were obeying." [23]

So we're back full circle to the only basis there is for obedience—love and trust. It may seem hard to be asked to have this kind of confidence before we have had personal experiences of God. But He also helps us out of that dilemma. The moment we "purpose in our heart" to obey Him, at that instant He comes to help us. His incomparable gift is the ability to obey, to move out into what usually looks like uncharted and dangerous country.

That's the way it was for Abraham long ago. The Lord had told him to uproot himself and his family: "Get thee out of thy country, and from thy kindred...unto a land that I will shew thee...and I will bless thee...and thou shalt be a blessing." [24]

There was the word of command. There was the promise of blessing. There was no option to ask "Why?" or "Please explain everything to me." Always and always the understanding comes after the obedience.

So Abraham obeyed. "He went out, not knowing whither he went." He did not need to know because God knew. And the result of this "blind" obedience has blessed uncounted millions down all the generations.

6

"To Sleep!
Perchance to Dream..."

I dreamed last night...

> *In a living room I saw a pedestal-stand about two feet tall. On it had been placed the head of a woman. From a distance it looked like one of those marble busts that one sees in palaces or museums.*

> *But this bust was different. It had been severed from the body of a living woman and placed atop the pedestal.*

> *In my dream as I looked on, a female figure appeared in the room. She looked at the bust as she passed within a few feet of it. Then she uttered just two words, "It stinks."*

I keep wondering, what is the dream trying to tell me? Seemingly gruesome in imagery, I was to learn later that it held a potent spiritual message.

Few of us attached importance to dreams until the rising influence of psychiatry began to pique interest in the

subject. Even those who have never been near a psychia-
trist's office now know that patients are asked to take their
dreams seriously enough to capture them on paper and
consider them.

Even so, the average person wonders from time to time if
dreams have anything rational and constructive to say to
us. Or are they the result simply of eating too much pizza
or of something one saw on the Late Late Show?

On the other side, I have heard of instances where
scientists or inventors, unable to finish an experiment or a
project because of something eluding them, decided to
"sleep on it." And somehow as they slept, the unconscious
served up the solution needed—sometimes directly upon
awakening, sometimes in a dream.

Yet most have regarded these experiences as flukes.
What about the bulk of dream material? Isn't it mostly just
garbage-pail residue of daytime experiences?

Clearly, psychoanalysts do not think so. It was in 1900
that Sigmund Freud published his book *The Interpretation
of Dreams*, for the first time connecting dreams with the
unconscious in an empirical study. Among physicians and
the public in general, Freud's book met with contempt: it
took eight years to sell the 600 copies of the first edition.

As time went on, dream interpretation came to be an
accepted part of psychotherapy. Even so, I could uncover
little on the subject in Christian literature. The Church for
the most part was ignoring the subject. This was strange
when we consider the thread of dream material all through
the Bible. I had no sooner become interested in the subject
than I realized that the Bible is a veritable storehouse of
dreams. How had I previously overlooked this! Jacob
dreamed of a ladder from earth to heaven; another time of
spotted he-goats mating with the flock. Joseph dreamed of
his brother's sheaves bowing down and worshiping his
sheaf; later, he interpreted the Pharaoh's dreams. The child
Samuel's dream; Amos's dream of a plumb line; Isaiah's of
his lips touched with the live coal from the altar; Ezekiel's

dream of the valley of dry bones. The book of Daniel—full
of dreams. Such an amazing amount of material!

The gist of the Bible's message is that God frequently
uses dreams as a medium of revelation.

> If there is a prophet among you, I the Lord make myself
> known to him in a vision, I speak with him in a
> dream...in dark speech.[1]

Nor is there any diminution of this emphasis on dreams
in the New Testament. We see the Wise Men being warned
in a dream not to go back to Herod but to return to their
country another way; Joseph told in a dream to take the
young child and his mother and flee to Egypt. We see
Pilate's wife frantically sending her husband the message,
"I have suffered many things this day in a dream because of
him [Jesus]."[2] A major tenet of the early Church was
turned on its head by the Apostle Peter's dream picture of
the sheet let down from heaven with all manner of birds,
reptiles, animals—clean and unclean—in it. And the last
book of the Bible, Revelation, is almost entirely dream and
vision material of John, then an old man.

Why does the Church in our time pay so little attention
to dreams? For a number of years, Freud's viewpoint that
the unconscious was concerned mainly with sexuality
dominated the field. Perhaps the trouble was that, blinded
by Freud's emphasis, the Church could not find a connection between the Scriptural emphasis placed on dreams as
the vehicle for all manner of messages—dreams thus being
one way of God speaking to man—and the Freudian
doctrine of sexuality.

As the years have gone on and Freud's dream theories
have been amended and enriched by the works of Alfred
Adler and Carl Jung and others, as well as a decade of work
in sleep laboratories,[3] I discovered that a few men here and
there in the Church have been constrained to take another
look at the Biblical emphasis on dreams. Two of them,

Morton T. Kelsey,[4] and John A. Sanford,[5] both Episcopal priests, have experimented, often successfully, in helping troubled people make use of dream material. (At the time I discovered this, little did I realize how much this was shortly going to mean to me personally.)

It's a big subject and generalizations are dangerous. Those who worked in the field warn that we must not try to work out pat formulae to help us interpret our dreams. The point is that the psyche, the total mental and psychological structure of a person, is not just the repository for dead memories but is living and fluid; it will not be pigeonholed any more than the Spirit of God acting upon the psyche can be pigeonholed.

Having warned us, they nevertheless come to our aid with some helpful suggestions.... The unconscious usually "thinks" or translates thoughts into pictures. These pictures usually take the form of either parables or cartoon-like story material. The parables are in many respects reminiscent of the stories and symbols Jesus used in His parable-stories; in other dreams they are akin to the kinds of stories in the folklore of all peoples. Often our dream cartoons or parables are woven into a story or playacted out on an inner stage while we sleep.

The unconscious mind does not think analytically, but symbolically or pictorially. Dream symbols are provocative in their wide variety and above all, in their originality.

We've only to take note of a few of our dreams to know that with our conscious mind we never could have put together such highly original imagery. In some images, there is great simplicity, but the originality is in the way the dream uses them. Here are some symbols from my own dreams and those of others close to me:

> The dreamer is in a rose garden eating rose petals, but carefully; eating the petals will make him intoxicated.

> A child's wicker toy basket is turned upside down over a flame to quench it.

A flight of newly constructed stairs has no place to set one's feet because all the treads are missing.

My house is burning, but is not consumed.

A snowstorm of small squares of fresh white paper falls from the sky.

A toilet is made of several huge shells.

A large pair of scissors is used as a murder weapon.

I see a baby in a tiny boat on a rushing stream.

We wonder where such highly original imagery comes from. In part, the experts say, from conscious sights, impressions, and thoughts passed on into the 90 percent of the psyche below the level of consciousness, then screened, condensed, and translated into dream images.

But beyond this personal area, Freud, Jung, and others believed that the unconscious draws its material from the race mind—what Jung called "the collective unconscious." It is at this point that many dream figures and images connect us with the symbolism used by Jesus, the folk stories of all peoples, and the world's fairy tales.

It reminds us of that memorable little statement inserted in the Gospel of John. "He [Jesus] knew what was in man." [6] Therefore, it shouldn't surprise us that He deliberately chose to use symbolism which would speak to both the conscious and unconscious levels of men of all nations in every century. Notice how Jesus used objects in the external world to teach us truth about the internal world even as our dreams do:

A candle covered by a bushel basket.

A plank sticking out of a man's eye.

Pearls being thrown before hogs.

Digging up a treasure in a field.

A minuscule seed growing into an immense tree.

A woman hiding starter-dough in a barrel of flour.

Fishermen with a dragnet pulling in unimaginable varieties of fish.

A serpent lifted high on a stick.

Though some dream symbols come out of this collective unconscious like visions replete with sights and sounds wafting out of some far country where we were once at home, our dreams are often intensely personal and self-reflective. Something deep within seeks to give us a message. Different characters in our dreams are usually parts of our own being.

Aspects of our personality we have ignored or even cast out of our consciousness now seek to be heard. This is so even when the dream figure is of the opposite sex from the dreamer. Psychology teaches us that every man carries within his dominant masculine psyche some largely unconscious feminine traits, what Jung chooses to call "the anima" just as every woman possesses some masculine traits, "the animus." Thus a feminine figure in a man's dream may be trying to point him to "anima" qualities of sensitivity, of the emotional life, of the willingness to love and be loved.

The kind of help our dreams can give us is as varied as people's temperaments and needs. Pat Baker [7] fighting her cigarette problem for example, found that dreams helped her become a believer in a personal God who could comfort and guide her. Married at eighteen, Pat had become pregnant almost immediately. Throughout her pregnancy, she had been deeply troubled, feeling in no way ready for the responsibilities of motherhood. She had a hunger for faith, yet doubts about a personal God. During all those months, the cry of her deep spirit had been, "How can I rear a child when I myself have no answers to what life is all about?"

During childbirth, while Pat was under anesthesia, she

had a strange dream. She was sitting in the audience in a theater with a large stage before her. The figures who appeared on the stage looked like cartoon characters come to life. Mrs. Baker described every vivid detail of this dream:

> On stage right appeared a woman slowly pushing a baby carriage across the stage. The baby, a girl, was sitting up in the carriage with knitting needles and a ball of yarn trying to figure out a knitting pattern. The baby's face was tense and worried trying to understand the pattern.
>
> As the mother pushed the carriage on, the baby was making progress: another part of the pattern would be finished. The scene before me was so huge that I could clearly see the knitting in the baby's hands. By the time the carriage was almost across the stage, all the pattern was figured out except one stitch. Then the whole tableau—mother, carriage, baby and all—fell off the end of the stage.
>
> Watching, I could feel the drop—kerplunk! in the pit of my stomach. I heard myself saying, "Oh no! God, You can't let that happen. You can't let that poor baby die without figuring that pattern out."
>
> Then I heard a male voice offstage chuckling reassuringly, as if to say, "Don't worry about it. I've got it all figured out."
>
> I then also understood that the baby would know that she wasn't going to be left with that one stitch of the pattern missing. I felt inside myself a relieved, "Oh! Thank God!" as a great peace swept over me.
>
> Then as though to dramatize before my eyes the truth of the reassurance, almost immediately the stage came back into view. There was another mother, another carriage, another baby like the first scene, only this time the baby was peaceful. No strain on her face.
>
> I saw the same knitting in the baby's hands, but now with the missing part of the pattern figured out and an

additional one added. This time the mother and baby did
not fall off the stage.

Before this, it had never occurred to Pat Baker to take
dreams seriously. As if to make certain that she would not
discount her dream because of the anesthesia, she was
given a detail-by-detail repeat of this dream two more
times—once while still in the maternity ward, and then
again after she returned home from the hospital. This was
the confirmation she needed.

The dream's first gift to Pat was peace of mind. It also
helped her to believe in the existence of God in a way she
never had before. At a deeper level and after meditating on
the dreams prayerfully, Pat realized that the baby in the
carriage was a part of her being: *she* was the one who in the
first dream couldn't figure out the complicated "knitting" of
life; she was the one afraid she would fall off the stage of
life.

The second time across the stage, she had figured out
life's pattern and she did not fall off. Thus the new mother
was given total assurance that the One whom she could not
see but had heard as the Voice offstage, knew what was
going on in her life and had everything under control. With
His help, she and her husband would be able to rear their
daughter.

In those rare instances when dreams do warn of a coming
event, the purpose is never to frighten or discourage us.
The Creator's work through the unconscious, as elsewhere,
is affirmative, directed toward a constructive end. Therefore the dream warnings present possibilities we are meant
to avoid, seldom actualities.

Dr. Glenn Clark told of how Stella Holbrook, a Minneapolis woman,[8] dreamed that she saw her best friend, a
Mrs. Simpson, walking back and forth in a room holding

her head between her hands. She had gone insane. Horrified by the dream, Stella was unable to sleep for the remainder of the night. Early the next morning, she telephoned the friend saying that she had to see her. When they met, Stella told her, "You are in deadly peril. You must see a doctor immediately."

"But I've never felt better in my life," the friend, Mrs. Simpson, remonstrated.

"No matter. I plead with you to see a doctor. I've never had a dream so real."

As much for her distraught friend's peace of mind as anything, Mrs. Simpson made an appointment with her doctor. He found a brain tumor located where it would probably cause insanity without prompt surgery. Mrs. Simpson was stunned. Her friend had dreamed the truth after all. But it was the rest of the dream that made her recoil in horror. In Stella's dream, Mrs. Simpson was stark raving mad. So wouldn't it turn out that way—surgery or no surgery?

With this double burden of fear heavy upon her, Mrs. Simpson stopped off to see Dr. Clark on her way to the Mayo Clinic. His advice to her was first, to clear out superstition. "There's no power," he told her, "in the psychic realm of foretelling the future that can stand against God's power. You must vigorously reject any form of superstitious attachment to this dream."

Then he added that *the dream warning had been given so that the event foreseen would not have to come to pass.* "To foresee a thing in time," he suggested, "is just like foreseeing a thing in space. You would not run head-on into it, would you? You'd make a detour around it."

Having agreed between them how to make a detour by means of prayer, Mrs. Simpson went on to Mayo's. The earlier diagnosis was confirmed. They were preparing for the operation when it was decided to ask both Dr. Judd and Dr. Will Mayo to examine the patient. Dr. Will was one of those doctors who studied the person along with his symptoms. In conversation with Mrs. Simpson, he discovered the quality of her faith.

The great surgeon seemed to withdraw into his own thoughts. After a moment of silence, he spoke slowly, thoughtfully. "Any brain surgery is drastic, carries its own risk. There's one other way to proceed. You're the sort of person who may be capable of this other way. The human body is a marvelous creation. When helped by faith and prayer, sometimes it can take care of its own problems. I wonder?" He paused and looked at her long and hard. Mrs. Simpson almost had the impression that he was listening.

"Yes, I believe this is the way. My advice is, let's not operate right away. Mrs. Simpson, I want you to go away for three months. Live quietly, in as healthful a manner as you know. Apply all the faith you have during this time. Then let us here at Mayo see you at the end of three months."

So Mrs. Simpson went to a mountain cabin and devoted herself to a three-months' prayer journey toward health. Day by day she sought, on the one hand, to close every separation between her and God; on the other, to open every facet of her being to healing.

In September she returned to the Mayo Clinic. New X-rays plus carotid angiograms left the specialists puzzled; the tumor was no longer there. Yet in June it had been as big as a hen's egg.

Other doctors were called in, including first, Dr. Judd, and then Dr. Will Mayo. After Dr. Judd had studied the X-rays and exhaustively examined the patient, he seized Mrs. Simpson's hands in excitement. "This," he exclaimed, "is a great miracle." Dr. Will was equally joyous. "I think this calls for a celebration," he said.

About the time I was realizing how pinpointed dreams can be, I met the Reverend Morton Kelsey, Episcopal priest and Notre Dame professor. I then read some of his books and asked if he would be so gracious as to give me help in learning to interpret my dreams.

He replied that he would be happy not only to give me his thoughts on specific dreams, but also some general principles of interpretation. I was to send him eight or ten dreams written out. We would then agree on a date for a long telephone conversation.

The telephone conference was eventually set up for three o'clock on the afternoon of July 18, 1973. With Professor Kelsey's permission, I recorded our forty-five-minute conversation. Morton Kelsey was speaking from South Bend, Indiana.

"First," he commented, "let's put any work with dreams in this framework.... The only way anyone should go into the unconscious is, first, to ask Jesus Christ for His power and direction and protection. Personally, I find that without Him I'm in danger even going to the grocery store without His direction, let alone trying to teach a college class.

"Then some general guide lines:"

Ninety-five percent of dream material refers to the dreamer rather than to the one being dreamed about.

Realize that the process of dreaming is, in itself, therapeutic.

One of the greatest dangers in dream interpretation is thinking that you're getting guidance for other people. Almost always it's about *you*.

When one dreams of a husband or wife, it may not necessarily refer to the mate, rather what one is "married to" emotionally and spiritually.

An often helpful procedure is:

Write down your dream immediately upon awakening; if necessary, interrupt your sleep to write it down. Keep a pencil, pad, and flashlight by your bed for this purpose.

Later, write down the main events happening in your life just then and any major fears or worries. You will need this framework for interpretation of your dream.

As your will consents to taking dreams seriously, you'll be able to remember more and more of them. The more dreams we write down immediately upon awakening, the more the unconscious will serve up.

After writing your dream down, talk it out with some trusted person. Let his reflection add wisdom to interpreting your dream.

Third, turn your attention to a study of symbolism, analogies, and images. A good place to begin is to review (perhaps with notebook in hand) the Bible's rich symbolism.

Most of us soon find that our thinking and training has not been in such directions: when we were young, we probably read too many Dick-and-Jane-type stories about going to the supermarket, the dentist, or helping the nice teacher change her flat tire, so now our imaginations need reawakening and nourishment. A deliberate return to the reading of the mythology and fairy tales of all nations and of books like *Hiawatha, Gulliver's Travels, Alice in Wonderland,* C. S. Lewis's[9] novels will help to reconnect us with an important part of ourselves and also assist us in interpreting our dreams.

Take the significant insights or questions into your prayer life. This will provide material for meditation.

During meditation it is helpful to confront the other person or persons in your dream (almost

always part of you) and enter into imaginative
dialogue with "them." Then invite Christ into
this three-way dialogue for His thoughts and
directives.

Following these general guide lines, I was eager for
Morton Kelsey's observations about my dreams of rejection
and danger during the sleeping-pill crisis. "Your dream of
September 23rd and the one following[10] are both classics,"
the voice on the phone had a quality of joy, even laughter.
"The first one involved an elaborate wedding. How often
Jesus spoke of weddings! A wedding is the union of
opposites. Nothing about a real mating of opposites was
possible for you until after the pill-dumping.

"Your dream wedding included a fashion show. It is
reminiscent of the prodigal son on whom the father placed
the 'best robe.' The wedding, you wrote, was 'more gala
than solemn.' God is not dour or grim-visaged about His
religion; His grace takes from us the burden of 'oughtness'
and duty, releases us to worship Him joyfully as a feast, a
banquet, a celebration. When He has a wedding feast, He
does it in top style!

"You were 'incorrectly dressed'... you didn't have on
the right wedding garment. Remember that on September
23rd you were still working through the aftermath of the
pill-dumping. You were not quite ready for the celebration.
So the dream ended without your knowing whether you
were admitted to the wedding scene."

Then Professor Kelsey went on to discuss the dream
involving physical danger.

"'We had to walk a long way,' you wrote. In late
September with acute insomnia still with you, the road was
seeming very long indeed.

"The rifle on the porch is a reference to the sleeping pills,
I feel sure. The dream's gun booby trap was meant to be a
warning. Your victory was not yet complete. By returning

to the pills you could fall back again. 'Look out: Watch it! This is a life-and-death matter,' the dream was saying..."

"By September 30th, you had won your victory, so this is a dream of promise. The house is a typical dream symbol representing one's total being.

"The dining room is for feeding people. What have you done in your writing except to feed people! You wrote, 'a carved table' on a 'beautiful rug'... 'portraits on the wall.' You are going to feed people beautifully.

"'The tall cupboards... filled with china and glassware' unused for a long time. The years of the sleeping pills had cut you off from part of your own being. Now you can use a lot of content and rich creativity in your psyche you had even forgotten you have.

"I'll make a prediction, Catherine.... What you write in the future may have more significance than what you've written in the past."

"Morton," I answered, "I hope you're right!"

A little later I switched the conversation to the Head-on-the-Pedestal dream.[11] "I have some ideas about it," I said, "but I'm very curious about yours."

"All right," came the voice over the telephone. "First, a random comment. The female figure's 'It stinks' reminds me of Martha's almost identical statement at the tomb of her brother Lazarus.... Also, do you know C. S. Lewis's *That Hideous Strength?*"

"I have a copy," I replied, "but haven't read it yet."

"You'd better!" Again the chuckle came over the phone. "In the first chapter an Englishwoman dreams of a French prisoner visited in his cell by a rather coldly cynical man. The visitor unscrews the man's head and carries it away."

"I'll start the book tonight."

"All right. Now first, most dreams want us to look inward. Therefore, the head on the pedestal is your head. And the female figure is probably also another part of you.

"Now one or two questions to you, Catherine. Have you

had trouble with always wanting to *understand* before you step out in simple obedience?"

"Always. Most definitely. In relation to healing and lots of things about the Holy Spirit, thinking I need to understand has been a real stumbling block."

"Second question, which do you value most, the intellectual process or the emotions?"

"The mind—far and away. I think the emotions can really lead us astray."

"True in part," Morton Kelsey retorted. "Well, I think the dream was issuing you a stern warning. It was saying, 'The head needs a body to be whole—not just the emotions, but the *entire* person.' You see, Christianity is the world's earthiest religion. Centuries ago even very spiritual monks knew that working with their hands—gardening or erecting buildings, working vineyards or even wine-making, copying manuscripts, whatever—was as much a part of true worship as prayer. The use of the whole person, you see."

"Then the dream was saying that I am wrong to place the head, the intellect, on such a pedestal?"

"Correct," came the voice over the phone.

"And that when we sever the mind from the rest of us, the end result is that we die—even intellectually—and so begin to decay? And"—I paused—"stink."

"Right. Your prayer-meditation on this dream could include at least two questions: first, at what points are you resisting the real thrust of the Holy Spirit in your life because of an overemphasis on the mind?"

"Ouch! Now you've put your finger on one of my hang-ups with some aspects of the Holy Spirit Movement."

"A lot of us have the same difficulty.... Now, ask yourself the second question: 'Lord, what must I do to get my head back on my body, to begin functioning as a whole person? What is my first step in that direction?'"

I was beginning to see what he meant. "My dreams are providing lots of material for meditation."

"Not just for you personally either," Professor Kelsey replied. "For instance, hasn't the twentieth century created a society where the head rules—education, science, and technology supreme? We thought we could cleave the head from the body—divorce, 'put away' the spirit, the conscience, the imagination, and emotional life and get a Utopia. Maybe instead we have a civilization that could be summarized with a quite inelegant 'It stinks.'"

Dream therapy of a poignant nature was given to Tom Dowling, whom I met in 1967 at the first *Guideposts* magazine Writers Workshop. As the background for Tom's dream, it is necessary to fill in certain details of his life....

The Dowlings lived in California. In September 1958 Tom had taken his wife Babs to Hawaii on a vacation trip to help her recover from a spinal fusion operation. The young couple had left their four children in the care of Tom's father. On the fourth day tragedy suddenly struck: Babs suffered a severe cerebral hemorrhage and after the necessary brain surgery was unconscious for thirty-five days. After consciousness slowly returned, it became apparent that the young woman was paralyzed. Sight and hearing were left to her and she could on occasion speak a word or two. That was all. In the agony and shock of what had happened to her, Babs was in such desperate need of love and reassurance that Tom stayed by her bedside for the first fifty days, even sleeping there in a chair at night. Often, so often, he would reach for her hand or pat her cheek, and the gratitude in her eyes spoke volumes.

In November the paralyzed woman was flown back to a hospital in San Mateo County. Babs lived for just over two years, never recovering from the paralysis. Part of the agony was that her mind was so sharp. She knew what was going on around her. Yet since she couldn't move even a finger, existence became a living death, like being buried inside one's mind. Babs' dark brown hair turned to white.

During the two years there were three major operations and twelve minor ones. Shouldering all home responsibilities and the care and rearing of their four children along with his job, Tom managed to spend forty hours a week at his wife's side. Sometimes he would lift Babs into a wheelchair and take her to the hospital roof so that she could feel the sunshine on her face. Occasionally on a Sunday afternoon he would take her home for a few hours to be with the children and to see that home was being kept ready for her.

When death came to Babs, Tom was holding her hand, whispering a prayer of benediction into her ear. It seemed a merciful release for her and for him.

But Tom soon discovered that he had no release. He was tormented by a dream that kept repeating itself. Though Tom remarried in 1961 and was happy with his new wife, Ginny, the dream recurred sometimes twice a week. Soon he developed serious insomnia. Here is Tom's version of the dream that refused to be turned off:

> I am hurrying to the hospital. When I get there I cannot find Babs' room. Frantically, I go from floor to floor, room to room, calling her name. My panic and frustration grow by the minute because I know how much she needs me.

> Finally I stumble into the right room. There she is as always, unable to move, sobbing my name.

> Then I awaken in a cold sweat, tears on my face. The nightmare has drained so much emotional energy I can hardly get out of bed and go to work.

Then came the 1967 *Guideposts* Workshop. Tom Dowling was one of twenty-four writers out of 1200 applicants chosen for the week at a country estate on Long Island Sound, a scene of many religious gatherings. In this relaxed setting, companionship and a deep level of communication grew among the five *Guideposts* staff members and the writers from all over the country.

Although most of the time was spent on developing writing skills, there was an early morning prayer time for those interested. Each participant was asked to pick two people from the group to pray for. They could keep the names secret if they wished. Later on, Tom found that a writer from Texas, Dot Main, had chosen him because she sensed that he had pressing needs, though she had no idea what they were. Tom never told anyone at Rye about his nightmare problem.

Looking back, I see the hand of God in almost everything that happened that week. One of the Workshoppers' big discoveries was that writing grows out of life: get the life set right and enriched and creative production rises to new heights. Beyond that, how better to summarize what happened than to say that the Holy Spirit was there that week in fullness and power? Prayers were answered, problems resolved, lives changed.

At the end of the Workshop, Tom left for California feeling that this had been the greatest week of his life. When his wife Ginny, met him at the San Francisco airport, she took one look at him, saw a new calmness on his face, and exclaimed, "Tom, something wonderful must have happened to you!"

A few nights later Tom dreamed again..

As so often before, I am hurrying to the hospital. (Strange! I always know I am dreaming, but can do nothing about it.) *Oh God! Not again—please. Don't let it begin all over again.*

But this time when I reach the hospital there is none of the usual frantic searching. I go directly to Babs' room. She smiles up from the bed and oh, joy! extends her arms to me! She is no longer paralyzed!

She takes my face in her hands and calls my name and great waves of joy, unimaginable joy, rise up in me.

She asks me to put her in the wheelchair as I'd done so often before. I start pushing her toward the elevator to the roof thinking she'd like to soak up some sunshine, but she says, "No, not the roof. Take me in *there.*"

I turn in the direction she is pointing and find a room full of people. It's the library at the retreat house on the Sound where my little Workshop group met each day.

As I wheel Babs into the room, the people come to greet her. Great rays of light, love-light, radiate from her as she holds out her hands to each of them!

My happiness is beyond belief. There are tears of happiness in my eyes. Yet there's much more joy to come.... When Babs has greeted each Workshopper, she says, "I want to stand." And suddenly she's on her feet!

Then the scene shifts to Oakland, where Babs was born. We're walking beside Lake Merritt as we used to long ago. She's laughing and twirling like a girl full of life and happiness. Then she puts her head caressingly on my shoulder—and the dream ends.

Tom Dowling added, "When I awoke, I bolted straight upright in bed. My usually heavy heart felt feather-light, gay. There was the unmistakable feeling of having been in God's presence. The messages of the dream were so plain:

Babs was no longer paralyzed and was extremely happy.

God had let me know that He loves me.

There is an assurance—a knowing—that I'll never have the nightmare again.

And Tom never has, from that time to the present. The deep wounds to his emotional life and his psyche reaching into the unconscious that Tom had sustained from Babs' terrible illness had been healed—permanently.

Let's suppose the Church and its leaders want to return

to the Scriptural view of the importance of dreams. How could we of the laity play a part?

One experience from a Fellowship-Prayer Group in Chappaqua, New York, provides some hints.... One of the members, Jean Nardozzi, shared with the others her desperate feelings of exhaustion and her difficulty with sleeping. Because she is a kindergarten teacher with two separate groups of 30 five-year-olds each morning and 30 each afternoon, Jean called herself "a walking disaster area."

For two Wednesday nights the group prayed for Jean. On the third Wednesday, Jean told her friends, "I had a strange dream last night. I'd like to know what you make of it...

> Some people were holding a baby and indicating that it was mine. In the dream I acted astonished because I didn't know I *had* a baby. The child had been totally neglected, was pitifully thin and undernourished.
>
> Then the dream gave me a message over and over, "The poor thing needs milk."

Two people present gasped simultaneously and both started to speak. Then it came out that in prayer during the interim week (with no communication between the two), each had been given identical guidance for Jean: "She needs milk."

In addition, one of the two, Elizabeth Sherrill, recalled that the morning she had been given this message, she had also been pointed back to Numbers 12:1-10, the story of Aaron and Miriam's criticalness of Moses, particularly to verse 6:

> Hear now my words: If there be a prophet among you, I the Lord will make myself known unto him in a vision, and will speak unto him in a dream.

As events turned out, Jean was led to travel to Boston for

an appointment with a specialist, a nutritionist. Among other findings the nutritionist discovered serious calcium deficiency in Jean's system. In passing, the doctor remarked that calcium is one of nature's best soporifics, adding, "The old folk remedy of warm milk at bedtime has that basis in fact." The patient left with diet lists along with necessary supplements.

Within a short time Jean felt like a new person with her sleep improving night by night.

An incident like this reveals that we don't need to be sleep-laboratory researchers or trained analysts to get on with letting God show us how to use our dreams. It is encouraging to recall that our lives are set in the era prophesied by the Old Testament prophet Joel:

> And it shall come to pass in the last days, saith God, I will pour out my spirit upon all flesh. . . . and your young men shall see visions and your old men shall dream dreams.[12]

"All flesh...." It had not always been so. In Old Testament times only the privileged few ever had the gift of the Spirit—only certain prophets, priests, and kings. From this elite group the only true dream interpretations had come. So the Bible's message for our times seems to be: not only will the Spirit of Truth use dreams and help us to understand them, but He is the Interpreter *par excellence.* And His help is available to every one of us.

At first we may be able to interpret only a fraction of the dream material that comes to us. But if we persist in taking our dreams into our prayer life and acting upon what we understand, we will experience an unfolding progression. In the years ahead I believe there will be exciting experimentation on this subject among Christians. God will lead us through our dreams to all sorts of provocative discoveries about our hidden selves in His plan to refashion us into whole people.

7

The Fallen Angel

Is Satan alive and well on planet earth? You be the judge.

It happened a few years ago....In the space of a few weeks incidents of striking similarity were related to me separately by two close friends. One came unexpectedly from Lamar, a man in his early thirties; the other I heard from Jennie, a young housewife, in the middle of a tape-recorded interview with her on another subject altogether. At the time I could never have guessed that this was a door opening, urging me on to investigate a subject about which I had been largely ignorant.

The first incident was in a letter from Lamar.

> ...On this particular Saturday, an acquaintance afflicted with a creeping paralysis so that he was mobile only in his wheelchair had been visiting in our home.
>
> Dick attended services in our church and had been prayed for often at his own request at healing services—with no apparent results.
>
> Dinnertime approached and my wife asked him to stay to

dinner. Ten o'clock came, ten-thirty. Still our guest made no move to leave. By then I had shared everything I knew to share with him.

"Dick," I told him, "tomorrow's another day." Reluctantly, our guest left and my wife and I went to bed.

During the night I dreamed that I was still talking to Dick. This was one of those crystal-clear things; even the words I spoke to Dick. "Have you ever heard a word, Dick, that comes down to us in many churches—'exorcism'? Do you know what it means?"

I woke up with a start and my voice not only had awakened my wife, but she actually jumped about a foot off the bed.

As I opened my eyes, my attention was drawn to a figure standing in the opening of the closet, the door having been left widely ajar. He was tall and lean with the statuesque, stately figure of a young man. His silhouette was sharp because he seemed to be dressed all in black.

But it was his face to which my attention was drawn. He had cropped black hair, high cheekbones, a pointed chin—clean shaven—piercing eyes that were glowering at me with rage. It was a face full of evil. Instantly, I knew this was Satan.

I was chilled and frightened. All I wanted was to get him out of that room. From somewhere deep in me came the words, "In the name of Jesus Christ, begone! Satan, go!"

Even as I stared, within a few seconds he disappeared.

Later on, I went to see Dick and found out that he had been deeply involved in the world of the occult. He even had two spirits whom he called by name and who were now so familiar that they would wait upon him in various ways. When Dick flatly refused to submit to exorcism, I began to see why no amount of prayer effort or caring had worked for him: while he wanted to be healed physically, he did not want to let go his love affair with the occult.

The last I heard of Dick, he had stopped coming to church.

You know me so well you'll realize that I'm not the type given to visions. But this experience has done one thing: since then I've never had any slight doubt about the existence of Satan.

My instant reaction was "How wild!" The experience may have settled the matter of Satan as an incarnate spirit for Lamar, but for me it raised a lot of questions. Was Lamar telling me that he had actually seen a creature— Satan? If I hadn't known Lamar for some years and eaten many a meal in his home, I might have written his "vision" off as the hallucination of a disturbed person. But this particular friend's level-headedness and love for life were in total contrast to the strange, dark, and unappealing world of his nocturnal experience. I wanted nothing so much as to slam the door on that world.

But the very next week while in the midst of a long recorded interview with Jennie (whom I have known well for five years or so) came another story. Here it is as I took it from the tape:

On a particular night I went to bed, then later was awakened by a light coming in my room. At the foot of my bed stood this man about six feet two. He had a black butch haircut and dark features and eyes. He just stood there looking at me.

Now since I came to know Jesus eight years ago, I've had many problems, yet I've never known such an out-and-out fear as I knew it at that moment. Through my mind went the thought, "Oh my God, who is that?"

The thought had no sooner crossed my mind than I knew that Jesus Himself was standing beside me protectively on the right-hand side of my bed. And strange thing, He had His staff in His hand. As if in direct answer to the question in my mind, He explained the dark man standing at the foot of the bed. "He is the personification of Man."

Well, I'd never heard that word before, but I knew what it meant. My immediate reaction was, "I've got to get up out of bed and call someone to pray for me."

That too, brought a response. It was like the Lord saying, "No, you've got to face him sooner or later." Only please understand that this was not in external words—it was all interior.

So I stayed in bed and screwed up my courage to look at the dark man again. He stood there unmoving, radiating—what shall I call it?—the personification of evil. I couldn't have been more grateful for the feeling of Jesus' presence and the security of that staff in His hand. Then Jesus said, "He has to appear to you personally so that you can learn that everything that the devil and man can do to you are not going to harm you as long as you stay close to Me. *Don't ever again let any of his life live in you or have any power over you.*"

As I began letting my mind roam over all the wonderful changes that had come to me in the last eight years and the fullness of my life in Christ, that personification of evil standing at the foot of the bed was instantly gone. Then I went to sleep, peacefully and lovingly.

Two details of my friend Jennie's description struck me especially: the phrase "the personification of Man" and her insistence that in her vision Jesus was holding a staff. I wondered if a staff in His hand had significance in connection with moments when we face evil?

Beyond that, my emotional reaction to Jennie's confrontation with Satan was the same resistance I had felt to Lamar's experience. Still—here were two friends whom I knew to be wise and solid persons. I trusted them completely, yet they had presented me with what I regarded as "far-out" stories.

I had also been noticing that every time I read a book review page or saw the ads, more and more titles of the type of *Rosemary's Baby* were being published. Publishing houses had whole lists of titles on Satan and the occult. Entire stores were being given not only to occult books but to hundreds of items, trappings of the occult such as masks, candles, incense, charms, games, zodiacal highball glasses, napkins, tarot cards, and witches' hats.

"Just a fad," I thought. All of it went so directly against my experience of God as being all-love and goodness that I had decided to keep my eyes solely on Him as my personal answer to the rise of the Satan cults. But when first one close friend thrust the distasteful Satan subject on me, then another, I saw that I couldn't continue to duck it. Having a new respect for the importance of obedience, I realized that I was being asked personally to take a look at the kingdom of evil and become knowledgeable about it.

"All right, God," was my response. "If you're telling me that Satan is real and on the march and attacking today, and that You want me to look at him and hear what You have to say about all this, I'll do it. But please be with me every minute because I'm not looking forward to this."

Up to this time, I had read little about Satan except in the writings of the late C. S. Lewis, eminent Cambridge scholar and convert to Christianity from atheism. In *Mere Christianity,* Mr. Lewis had hit the Satan subject head-on:

> I know someone will ask me, "Do you really mean, at this time of day, to re-introduce our old friend the devil— hoofs and horns and all?" Well, what the time of day has to do with it, I don't know. And I'm not particular about the hoofs and the horns. But in other respects my answer is, "Yes, I do.". . . If anybody really wants to know him better, I'd say to that person, "Don't worry. If you really want to, you will. Whether you'll like it when you do is another question."[1]

Neither of my friends, Jennie nor Lamar, had in any way
sought an experience of Satan. And C. S. Lewis was right,
they didn't enjoy Satan. Still, questions had been raised
and would not be put down. Given a devil at all, I realized
that he must be spirit. Therefore, I resisted the idea of
external manifestations, like horns and a tail and being
dressed in a ludicrous red suit. Satan's appearance would
be of less importance than his character. How was I to
research Satan's character?

The obvious place to begin was to see what God had
Himself chosen to reveal to us in Scripture about Satan and
the problem of evil. I set myself to spend thirty minutes on
this study early each morning before breakfast. Propped up
in bed with a cup of coffee, a clean notebook, a chain
reference Bible and full concordance, I began.

Right away I was surprised. The first reference I turned
to described Satan as a beautiful creature, once a magnificent archangel called Lucifer, "the shining one," or "the
son of the morning." Some Bible scholars surmise that
Lucifer was the greatest of the heavenly creatures who led
all the rest in glorifying God. But the time came when
Lucifer began to covet this worship for himself:

> How art thou fallen from heaven, O Lucifer, son of the
> morning!...For thou hast said in thine heart, I will
> ascend into heaven, I will exalt my throne above the stars
> of God....I will ascend above the heights of the clouds;
> I will be like the most High.[2]

When this shining angel broke his relationship with the
Father, he led a revolt in heaven. The Book of Revelation
hints[3] that Lucifer may have enticed one third of the
heavenly hosts to revolt with him. After all, their angelic
leader still had his superior intelligence, his attractive
persuasiveness, and his power.

At that time Lucifer's name was changed to Satan—
"adversary" or "resistor." I wrote down some of the other

names I found for Satan. The names tell us a great deal about the ex-Lucifer's character:

Enemy
Tempter
Destroyer
Liar
Unclean spirit
Foul spirit
Accuser of the brethren
God of this World

As I thought about it, I realized that God must have known that this awful perversion of His beautiful creation had been possible. Ironically, it was because God had lavished so much on Lucifer that the tragic reversal came about.

But the Lucifer disaster did not dissuade the Creator from His eternal intention to create truly free man. For man He made a special place, the garden-planet Earth set like a blue and green jewel in the gray cosmos.

Man would be perfect physically, equipped with a body exquisitely formed, from the chromosome pattern of each cell to the human eye with its retina composed of seven delicate layers of molecular and nuclear tissue, ganglion cells, and nerve fibers; from the chemical complexity of the blood with its own transport system for bathing and nourishing every cell, to the brain marvelously constructed with some 100 billion neurons and at least two times that many glia. Neuroscientists like Dr. Francis Otto Schmitt have shown the human brain to be so complex that it makes a sophisticated electronic computer look like a child's toy.[4]

But more important than man's incredible body was God's plan that his judgments would partake of the Creator's own goodness and love, so that human beings would know unimaginable happiness and fulfillment.

So God looked on His creation—man—and pronounced that creation "very good." Yet by giving us the attributes of personality, especially a will with which to choose, He deliberately ran the risk that men or angels might reject His plan.

That is exactly what happened. By the time planet Earth had been formed, the archangel Lucifer had already become heaven's rebel. Our little planet became the stage for the fight to the death between Satan and his cohorts and God the Father.

The conflict began in Earth's springtime. God had warned Adam and Eve that if they ate of the fruit of the Tree of Knowledge, they would surely die. Even as Satan had wanted to be like God, so now he sought to transfer the same rebellion to the mind and will of Eve first and then Adam.... God didn't tell you the truth, the serpent suggested, "for God doth know that in the day ye eat thereof, then your eyes shall be opened, and ye shall be as gods...."5

Man decided to take his chances on Satan. The result was tragedy for that first man and woman and for every descendant down the long ages since. For man's decision to eat the fruit of the Tree of Knowledge was to set his will against God's to enthrone himself "as a god" independent of his Creator.

It was as if my right arm "decided" that it no longer needed the rest of the body, so it would separate itself and take up life on its own. The severed arm would die.

But physical death was only part of it. It was man's spirit that made him the crowning accomplishment of creation. *That* was why man was told that he had dominion over the animals, "over every living thing that moveth upon the earth."6 It was because Jehovah had "created man in his own image" that the writer of the Book of Hebrews, echoing the Psalmist, could say lyrically:

> Thou madest him [man] a little lower than the angels;
> thou crownedst him with glory and honour....

Thou hast put all things in subjection under his feet. . . .[7]

That same spirit that enabled man to worship, to make decisions and moral choices, to plan, to remember, to assimilate ideas and store up knowledge, to reason—not only meant that there was a great gulf fixed between man and the rest of the animal kingdom; it also meant that man's spirit would be dependent for its real life on the Spirit of which it was a part. To the Tempter, Jesus said, "Man shall not live by bread alone."[8]

As a result of man's disobedience, death entered life, precisely as God had said it would. Not just the cessation of the heartbeat and the decay of the flesh that marks the end of every man, but all the interim ills that lead up to death—sickness, disease, pain, weakness, accidents, famine, pestilence, plague, fear, loneliness, hatred, jealousy, hurt, cruelty, torture, murder, suicide. Now began the long history of man's inhumanity to man—man now bound tightly, stultified by the fallen divided nature which he himself had chosen. And because God had given man true freedom of choice, He could not and would not forcibly overrule that.

Man might have been left there. The story could have ended as the poet Edna St. Vincent Millay has it in her heartbreakingly beautiful sonnet sequence *Epitaph for the Race of Man.*

Here lies, and none to mourn him but the sea,
That falls incessant on the empty shore,
Most various Man, cut down to spring no more;
Before his prime, even in his infancy
Cut down, and all the clamour that was he
Silenced; and all the riveted pride he wore
A rusted iron column whose tall core
The rains have tunneled like an aspen tree....

> Whence, whence the broadside, whose the heavy
> blade?...
> Strive not to speak, poor scattered mouth; I know.[9]

But it did not end that way. God's love yearned over His deluded creatures. "God's impossible Love," as C. S. Lewis called it in one of the most brilliant, witty, and penetrating books on Satan ever written, *The Screwtape Letters*. He puts these words into the mouth of the influential demon Screwtape as he instructs the underling tempter Wormwood:

> "... He really loves the human vermin and really desires
> their freedom and continued existence...."[Then,
> catching himself and realizing that this is heresy in the
> underworld's theology]... "The reason one comes to
> talk as if he really had this impossible Love is our ut-
> ter failure to find out that real motive. What does he
> stand to make out of them? That is the insoluble ques-
> tion...." [10]

Out of God's "impossible Love" a rescue plan was evolved, surely one that only the three Persons of the Godhead together—Father, Son, and Holy Spirit—could have conceived: Jesus would leave for a time that perfection of communion and communication that He had always enjoyed with the Father and the Holy Spirit, and come to earth clothed in flesh, born of a woman like all the sons of Adam. Jesus would be God revealed, the God-man walking the earth demonstrating what the Father is like—His love and compassion, His reverence for all life, His power to unbind, to set free, to remake.

The plan became fact at a specific moment in time, thus dividing all history into two parts—B.C., "Before Christ" and Anno Domini, "In the Year of Our Lord." The God-man's teaching was incredibly impressive, had the sure touch of One who spoke "with authority." His miracles, even His enemies grumbled, had the world following after him.[11] It is at that point that people reading the Bible for the first time are in for a surprise. The writers of Scripture insist that the real point of Jesus breaking into human history was neither His teaching nor His miracles; rather, that Jesus came to earth for the purpose of dying and being resurrected to life on the third day.

Thus His death and resurrection was the Master Plan to win back for man all that he had lost in Eden. As the last Adam, Jesus would mount His cross taking all of us, Adam's heirs, with Him into the death of the old, now-spoiled creation. Thus He would accomplish a perfect exchange. As Derek Prince, British-born Greek scholar and author, has summarized it in a single memorable sentence, "Jesus took the evil that was due to us and the entire Adamic race that we, in return, might receive the good that was due to Him by eternal right."[12]

Jesus went to His cross as the willing agent of the divine plan. Nevertheless, His agony in Gethsemane shows us that humanly He shrank from the torturing hours ahead. All His growing-up years in Nazareth He had seen crucifixions. When Jesus was about twelve, He could scarcely have helped seeing the crucifixion by Varrus, Prefect of Syria, of 2000 rioters after the death of Herod the Great. The field full of 2000 crosses would have made an indelible impression on any sensitive boy. How well He knew that the nails used in crucifixion (square, one-third inch on each side) were real enough, as real as the pain and the agonizing thirst, the cramps, and the ultimate asphyxiation. Even so He considered that "to this end was I born, and for this cause came I into the world."[13] Therefore, He was "obedient unto death."

The victory was God's, for on the third day Life poured back into the dead and mutilated body of Jesus. The crucifixion and resurrection are history's watershed. Those who speak of some sort of "spiritual resurrection" are missing the point. For the first Adam or the last Adam or for any of us sons and daughters of Adam still in the flesh, nothing short of the resurrection of the flesh would have been any victory at all. Satan would not have been deceived; Jesus' surprised, incredulous disciples would not, and neither would we.

Satan knew defeat now. Henceforward any man or woman could look at the Tempter unflinchingly and say, "You're a liar, a defeated foe, a bluffer, and a washout. I stand here in the name of Jesus—the Christus, the Victor —and on His finished work. Begone—." There is nothing for the Tempter but to slink away.

Thus the Bible nowhere teaches us to believe in Dualism, the philosophic premise that two equal and independent powers—one of them good, the other bad— eternally vie for supremacy in the world. It is easy even for the Christian to attribute more power to Satan than he has and thus fall into heresy. Rather we are told that our earth is enemy-occupied territory. The Rightful King has landed and has already won the decisive victory. But we are still living through the mopping-up stage of the battle. The time will come when Christus, the Lord Emmanuel, will finally ring down the curtain on all remaining pockets of rebellion and guerrilla warfare to establish His kingdom openly for all to see.

Satan still has one ace card to play. If he can keep any man from believing the truth about Jesus Christ—who He is, the Life He holds out for mankind, the fact of his (Satan's) defeat—Satan can then keep that man in bondage to his dark kingdom. For though I have a million dollars in a bank account in my name, if through some chicanery I am persuaded that I do not have it and make no overt move to use it, the money in the bank does me no good at all.

Thus the Accuser of men employs unbelievable craftiness and resourcefulness, artifice and deceit to keep mankind from knowing the truth and acting upon it. With him the technique of lying has been honed to a fine art. His ways of camouflage and duplicity are almost limitless. After all, this was Lucifer, the magnificent archangel, with his great intelligence, only now turned totally to negative designs.

Nor does Satan give up on us even after we become followers of Jesus. He never gives up so long as we inhabit these vulnerable bodies in this uncertain life. After we become Christians, his aim is to oppose and stymie us so that our spirits will be stunted short of maturity. He also wants to keep us ineffective so far as spreading to others the good news of freedom in Christ Jesus.

Satan cannot create anything new, cannot create anything at all. He must steal what God has created. Thus he twists love and God's wonderful gift of sex into lust and sadism and myriad perversions. He disfigures the heart's deep desire to worship God and persuades us to bow before lesser gods of lust or money or power.

"But," the protest rises within us, "if Christ won the victory, then why isn't the war with Satan over? Why doesn't God simply wipe Satan out?"

It's a valid question. God's luminous answer was given me one morning: "Because the Father is determined that all the sons of Adam will, for as long as possible, have a second chance to reverse that decision made in Eden." Jesus bought this second chance for us. The Father is determined that His Son's tremendous sacrifice will not go for nothing.

C. S. Lewis in his book *Mere Christianity* expresses the same thought in different words:

> ...Christians think He [God] is going to land in force; we don't know when. But we can guess why He's delaying. He wants to give us the chance of joining His side freely.... I wonder whether people who ask God to interfere openly and directly in our world quite realize what it will be like when He does. When that happens, it's the end of the world. When the author walks onto the stage the play's over...."[14]

So it is as if nothing had changed since that moment eons ago when man was presented with his stark choice: would he believe God or Satan?...Which one had his happiness at heart?...Would he let go his connection to Life in God and set up on his own? Time is still holding its breath for our answer now. Which way will each man, each woman, decide now?

"But," some may protest, "I never consciously made any such decision." We do not need to. That is the state we are all in just by being born of the flesh into the race of man and inheriting our father Adam's nature just as surely as we inherited the color of some ancestor's eyes. And it would be just as useless to protest that inheriting a sin-disposed nature seems scarcely fair, as to protest the color of our eyes or the race that dictated the skin's color.

The truth is that whether we are millionaires directing a financial kingdom or youthful idealists in revolt against a materialistic world, or quite ordinary citizens content to live self-centered lives of quiet mediocrity, until such time as we grasp our second chance, reverse the fiasco-decision made in Eden and get reconnected to Life, we remain vulnerable to Satan's cunning approach and to his designs. When I understood that, then I could see why the phrase which had been given to my friend Jennie, "the personification of Man" was so appropriate. Satan remains the personification of adamic Man even as Jesus is the Personification of the new Man. Each of us can escape the bondage of Satan's kingdom for the freedom of Christ's kingdom only when he resolutely sets the rudder of his will so to do.

That's why the moment of decision for Christ is so vital. That's why the angels themselves rejoice when even one lost lamb is brought back on the shoulder of the Good Shepherd.

As my morning study progressed, I began to see why God

had insisted on this distasteful chore. A good hard look at evil as it is presented in the Bible and an obedient following through of the whole story left me with one overwhelming impression—a great feeling of confidence and victory. The Bible story of the conflict between good and evil is not downbeat at all, but upbeat; it is the story of the total defeat of evil because of the absolute power of Christ.

But God had wanted me to study this subject for myself until I was not only aware, but fully persuaded of the reality of the kingdom of evil. Sooner or later a lot of tough experiences, doubts and temptations were going to be thrown at me (and at other people close to me) and it would be essential that we know how to fight them.

An additional reason why we dare not pretend that Satan does not exist is that God has deliberately placed Himself in the position of depending upon us human beings to tell His good news and to spread His kingdom on earth. We cannot get on with this task without being hindered by Satan at every step of the way. Satan's tactics fall into many categories, among them higher spiritual temptations, sexual temptations, and what we might call his harassment techniques.

An endlessly used Satanic weapon in his spiritual arsenal is that of discouragement, often interlocked with a degree of self-pity and depression. During our early years in Washington when Peter Marshall often battled discouragement, I remember our quoting at one another one of Hannah Smith's favorite maxims: "All discouragement is of the devil." Of course the remedy is to realize the source of the depression and to remind oneself that spiritual reality can never be gauged by feelings.

Other strategies of the devil include presenting sin as a virtue; the old ruse of exhibiting the bait and concealing the hook; suggesting "you aren't accepted by God, else you wouldn't continue to be tempted"; keeping Christians musing on their hang-ups and sins; using the seduction technique—good to bad in tiny steps.

Satan sometimes lays the groundwork for sexual sins by encouraging self-pride in a leader and his achievements. This then is followed by the leader being flattered by "opportunities for service" and overextending himself. Family relationships suffer in the wake of too much travel for meetings and speaking engagements. As the home life deteriorates, then the Tempter at times arranges "a plant" such as an immensely attractive married woman in deep distress who comes seeking the leader's help. When a liaison follows and becomes public news, the disastrous side effects of this situation always cause great rejoicing in hell. Among them, groups of disillusioned people who leave the church—"If that's Christianity, I want no part of it"—as they judge the church by the fallen leader rather than by Christ and His perfection.

The third category of Satan's strategem dips into the realm of the bizarre. For instance, on a day when a well-known evangelist was preparing to preach one of his rare sermons on Satan, he was dictating notes into a recording device when, suddenly, the machine caught fire. We might be inclined to think, "Wouldn't the machine have caught fire if the minister had been dictating on say, 'God's love'?" Perhaps—except it gives us pause as we go on to experience this sort of harassment over and over whenever we are about to unmask Satan by writing or teaching or preaching.

The following list is taken from the experiences of Christian leaders, all of whom I know:

> The living-room chimney of a house catches fire the last day before a book manuscript on Satan is to be delivered to the publisher.

> En route to a Christian meeting there is trouble with impossibly bad traffic and with the car. In addition to time delays, the leader loses his peace of mind, becomes irritated, and loses effectiveness.

> Mechanical difficulties are notorious. Tape recorders

and amplifying systems often go wild or cease to function.

As the time for an important talk or service approaches, the minister's family grows irritated and edgy. A spirit of contention enters the home. There are minor accidents.

Usually, these vexations are not serious trouble, more like a sort of nasty bullying. Even a few experiences with such obstructionist tactics, however, and we begin to see that the warfare spoken of in the Bible is absolutely real:

> For we are not fighting against people made of flesh and blood, but against persons without bodies—the evil rulers of the unseen world, those mighty satanic beings and great evil princes of darkness who rule this world; and against huge numbers of wicked spirits in the spirit world.
>
> So use every piece of God's armor to resist the enemy whenever he attacks....[15]

In the thick of battle a soldier needs to be able to identify the enemy. In the old days warriors were identified by their uniforms or by a standard held aloft. So how can we Christian soldiers learn to identify the enemy Satan? From my study, I was able to draw the following antithetical lists to help us know what God wants for us against Satan's aims. Lining it up like this enables us to see it more readily....

Satan	Jesus
Seeks to do his own will.	Always obeys the Father's will.
Aims to bind and blind men.	Yearns to free men and open our eyes to see.
Lies interminably.	Is the Truth.
Takes himself very seriously, cannot bear taunting or levity.	Often uses the light touch.

Satan	Jesus
Wants us to live in darkness and hide portions of our life from others.	Wants us to live in the light.
Wants us to doubt and disbelieve God's word.	Longs for us to have faith that He always keeps His word.
Works to make us ignore, disbelieve, or choose for ourselves what to believe in the Scripture.	Steadily assures us that the Scripture is the Word of God.
Pushes us to disobey God.	Says, "If you love Me, you will obey my commandments."
Urges us to use God for selfish purposes.	Longs for us to be used by God to help others.
Tells us, "My body belongs to me."	Tells us, "The body is the temple of the Holy Spirit."
Wants sickness and disease.	Wants wholeness of body, mind, and spirit.
Spares no effort to bring us sorrow and grief.	Wants our joy.
Desires our death.	Eagerly bestows life stretching on into eternity.
Condemns and accuses us.	Assures us, "I came not to judge the world, but to save the world."
Pushes us toward self-contempt.	Assures us that each man is of infinite worth to Him.
Fosters discontent and grumbling.	Urges contentment and praise in all situations.
Urges us to think that we can get virtue in one big slug for life.	Desires that we depend on Him minute by minute for what we need and claim our "daily bread."

Satan	Jesus
Urges us to concentrate on the sins of others.	Tells us to look at the beam in our own eye and remove that first.
Wants us to hang onto resentment and bitterness.	Tells us to forgive others in the same way God forgives us.
Urges us to have our fun now, try to forget about paying for it.	Influences us to pay now in time or effort, then fun later is assured.
Attempts to get us to hide our sins and make excuses for them, thus encouraging their festering within.	Wishes us to run to Him, bring our sins into the light and have them forgiven, cleansed, and forgotten.
Labors to have us believe that temptation *is* sin.	Assures us that temptations rightly handled strengthen us.
Wants us, when we fail, to wallow in discouragement or despair.	Encourages us in failure to ask forgiveness, accept it, rise, and go on.
Aims for us always to wear a mask and act a part; be all things to all people.	Plants in us the desire to be true to ourselves; to let others know where we stand.
Wants our faith always to be for the future.	Wants us to cultivate a present moment faith.
Seeks steady procrastination.	Teaches us that "*Now* is the moment of salvation."
Strives to have us preoccupied with "what ifs?" (what might happen); to be hagridden by the future.	Is concerned with what we do in the present; wants us to offer up the *present* moment to God.
Urges us toward a false, lofty superspirituality.	Wants us to live out daily "Without Me ye can do nothing."

Satan	Jesus
Delights in a "moderate" religion with no extremes.	Wants the total man—"Thou shalt love the Lord thy God with *all* thy heart and with *all* thy soul and with *all* thy mind."
Works for churches to be divided into "clubs" or factions with "party spirit."	Leads us toward unity amid diversity of gifts of the Spirit amongst the people in the Church.
Wants us to see all morality as relative, no final truth or falsehood.	Insists that He *is* the Way, the Truth and the Life; God's laws are absolute.
Labors to destroy all law, God's and man's.	Fulfills the law and the prophets and adds righteousness to it.
Labors for war.	Desires peace, the fruit of righteousness.

I was soon to find out that this period of instruction was not going to be limited to quiet bookwork. Lessons from life were just around the corner.

8

The Unholy Spirit

It was from a pair of hippies, Carrie and Jeff Buddington, that I first heard the term "the unholy spirit." I met Jeff and Carrie in September, 1969 in the small Cape Cod church where my son Peter is pastor. It was a surprise to hear Peter welcoming to the platform to receive into the church such a young couple, "swinging" in appearance, rather than the typical older retired couple of that Cape Cod community.

After the formal part of the ceremony was completed, Peter turned to the congregation. "Because Jeff and Carrie have traveled such an extraordinary route to arrive at this point of commitment, I've asked them to share a little of their story with all of us."

Jeff, tall and broad-shouldered, spoke of how long he had run back and forth across the United States seeking the answer to what life was all about. Carrie, hair flowing to her shoulders, spoke softly of how she had come out of the jungle of drugs to find the reality of God. As they talked, people were leaning forward with interest. I was so intrigued that after the service I asked for an interview. Our two-hour talk together later that week proved to be memorable and revealing.[1]

As I replay today the tape I made of that two-hour conversation, I can still see the scene in Edith's and Peter's living room: the warm afternoon sun streaming through the windows reflecting back from the silver-gray shingles outside; Carrie, hair swinging, sitting on the davenport with legs tucked under her like a little girl: both Jeff and Carrie surprisingly articulate.

The first part of Carrie and Jeff's story parallels the experiences of thousands of today's youth.... They had met in 1968 at a California commune. Jeff was from Massachusetts. After one semester of college, he had restlessly ricocheted from job to job—selling insurance, building pipe organs, designing stage sets, even a circus big top stint. Carrie was a Californian who had gotten hooked on drugs—marijuana, acid,[2] speed,[3] in that order—during her senior year in high school.

At the time the two met, each was on speed. "I found out in a hurry," Carrie explained to me, "that speed makes you paranoid. All of life becomes one big fear trip. It also gives you this delusion of grandeur.

"But where I got hooked was, coming off it, crashing, is so awful you keep staying up because you can't bear to come down. If you ever do, you ache inside. Your guts get really up-tight. Your nerves are on end. You get cramps. You can feel the heat coming off your head—'bzzy-bzzy'—like being plugged into a high-tension wire."

"Drugs do one good thing for kids, though," Jeff added. "They show that there's a world other than the material one. Maybe that's part of the reason so many kids these days have finally let go of two hang-ups of the older generation. First, the kids see no point in trying to accumulate things. Second, they know now that science doesn't have the answers to life they once thought it did. So science can never again be their god.

"Carrie and I had more in common than just thrill-seeking. We were on this big search for some meaning in life. We still thought that happiness meant the way you lived externally, that if things around you were the way you liked them, then you would be happy."

They found very few answers to their big questions in the commune. The forty members (eleven children among them) had erected a large hexagonal lodge of logs on the 240 acres of Oregon woodland[4] where the commune hoped to escape civilization and the Establishment. Meant for a central meeting place as well as sleeping and eating quarters, the lodge had homemade furniture, a cast-iron stove for cooking, even a library of some 500 books. There was no electricity or running water—only the streams in which to bathe and wash clothes. The men dug a well. All possessions were shared.

Carrie added, "It wasn't long until we discovered that we weren't going to eat if we didn't work. And the work wasn't going to get done without a routine." The rule was made that everyone had to work at least four hours a day. They planted a vegetable garden, fished in the river, kept chickens and goats. Since the winters were severe, trees had to be cut and the wood sawed and split for firewood.

Carrie and Jeff started living together in a tepee they had built. "But something was still missing," Jeff explained. "Carrie and I spent hours in that tepee huddled beside a little fire, watching shadows on the slanting walls, trying to figure out what it was that still eluded us. We were like people stumbling around in the Los Angeles smog.

"The reality we continued to seek in the LSD visions was increasingly hideous. Eventually we got tired of seeing ourselves as we were—like people with naked bodies covered with warts and souls all deformed—and we knew it. But we couldn't find any way to change ourselves.

"Then we began having bad acid trips. I remember the first. It was a foggy day. Carrie and I were walking down this hillside and the big old oak trees were dripping—one of those spooky days. I began to feel something evil reaching out to possess me.

"Crazy thoughts appeared in my mind. I kept seeing a kind of crude black basalt male figure with a hawk's head and a male phallus, a coiled snake on his arm, strange hieroglyphics all over him—and I kept having this urge to get down on my knees in front of it. It was as though I was being asked to take part in some ceremony that I knew nothing about. It seemed to me like something very very ancient. I could feel the control over myself slipping away. Something was eroding my will. Carrie felt the same thing."

Carrie interrupted, "It's like this evil power had been there all along, only he hadn't shown himself at first. He waits until you're well hooked; only then does he reveal himself. And he wants you to think that it's O.K. to play childish games with the drug-taking, that it's spiritual and beautiful—the lovely psychedelic colors, all that.

"But it's counterfeit spirituality, and believe me, it isn't beautiful. It's more hideous than anyone can imagine."

Jeff grimaced in remembrance. "The second of the bad trips was at Thanksgiving. The entire commune was crowded into the lodge, taking acid together. That day we were acting out being 'married' into the brotherhood of man. Outside it was raining steadily. There was a fire going, and the rhythm of drums.

"Suddenly Carrie and I had a loathsome feeling about the whole thing. So did one other couple. The four of us left the lodge and went to the tepee. We sat there huddling together, cold, miserable, too drugged even to build a fire.

"That night we knew that the answer we'd seen in drugs was really a mirage, just wasn't there. We knew then why so many kids commit suicide."

The Oregon winter was severe that year and there was sickness. So few could work that firewood almost disappeared. Their one chain saw was broken too. The situation was desperate.

Then came the miracle. One morning out of nowhere several strange men appeared with saws and axes. "We've come to cut wood for you," they said. The visitors worked all day until they had a big pile of firewood.

"Who are you?" commune members kept asking. "Why are you doing this for us?"

"We're Christians," was the answer. "We have our own little community about fifteen miles up the road. We came because the Lord Jesus told us that your firewood was almost gone."

"But why?" they persisted. "How could God care about us and our commune?"

"Because He loves you."

The experience rocked the hippies as nothing else had. Jeff and Carrie and a few others went up the road to find out more about this brand of Christianity.

"It was in this Christian community that we began at last to find answers," Jeff told me. "The key was the Holy Spirit. We'd had some experience of spirits, you see, we'd encountered the *unholy* spirit—"

"Holy Spirit—unholy spirit," I interrupted, fascinated. "I've never heard it put quite that way." I said the phrases again, listening to the sound of them. "How would you explain the difference between the two spirits?" my voice on the tape recorder asked Jeff.

"Well, we found that the unholy spirit does have power in the world, only it's a power each individual has to allow him. Once a person decides to play around with him and opens the door, the unholy spirit can be overpowering. He can perform 'miracles' and has a lot of tricks: power over nature, power over the elements. But it's a power without any love. It wants just one thing, just one—to destroy."

Carrie spoke up. "The Holy Spirit has power too, greater power than the unholy spirit. He too, waits on our wanting

Him. But He's different. He's all love—real love. And
He's—*for* us."

"What's the basis," I asked, "of your being so sure that
the Holy Spirit has more power than the unholy spirit?"

"Because," Carried promptly answered, "He enabled us
to kick drugs when we'd been on them for so many years.
That's a *real* miracle!"

Jeff continued, "Next, He took away the old haunted,
fear-ridden 'me.' Inside each of us was born this new being,
what the Bible calls 'a new creature in Christ Jesus.'"

"It's not a case of trying to be like Christ, to imitate
Him," Carrie went on. "Who has the strength to do that?
Through the Holy Spirit, Jesus comes to live in us and to do
His own work."

"The next step," Jeff went on, "was to find a church. We
remembered one that had occasionally come to our rescue
with a meal or a warm bed. So we went barreling there,
pretty eager, I guess. To our astonishment we found no
sense of life or power there. More than that, they seemed
almost scared of the change in us. They wanted to help us
when we were on drugs and out of work, sure. A change of
clothes, a hot meal, good advice, concern. But real
change? Real power? God really doing what He said? Wow!
They backed off like crazy."

"Tell me about the change," I said. "How did it start?"

"Well," Jeff said, "one day, all by ourselves, we had our
own Pentecost and accepted Jesus. Later we were both
baptized in the creek and also legally married. People came
from everywhere for the wedding—hippies still on acid and
straight people. We spent the whole day telling them all,
'Jesus is the One you're searching for.'"

The Buddingtons spent four months in the Christian
community, learning. "That new person born in us had to
start from scratch and go to school," Jeff said. "But it was so
great! When you go up on acid, there's always that terrible
coming down again. With Jesus, you just keep going up,
gradually and surely. You keep growing and learning step

by step how to meet and overcome your difficulties. There are problems with self-discipline, of course, but joy all the way. It's that 'living water' for sure.

"Other hippies followed us to the Christian community. The big difference between the two groups is this: in the hippie commune they're still doing their own thing; in the Christian community, they're doing His thing."

This was not the end of the story. Christ as the new Life within them led Carrie and Jeff to Cape Cod to teach for a time in a home for retarded children, then on to become part of another Christian community whose calling is teaching, retreats, help, counseling. They've been there ever since—learning, growing, giving.

On July 9, 1970, Catherine Heidi Buddington was born, by the grace of God, a healthy, normal baby. Then on June 5, 1972, Daniel Jeffrey was born; in November, 1973, Ruth Anne, also strong and normal. And still Jeff and Carrie go on from strength to strength as they dig deeper into Christian disciplines and learn to show others the way.

The childish games with which Jeff and Carrie started out to explore evil's terrain are being played by millions of people today. Witchcraft, the occult, Satan worship, sorcery, spiritualism, tarot cards, horoscopes, are currently big business over most of the world. Among the more popular courses currently offered in many high schools and universities are telepathy, precognition, clairvoyance, and other aspects of scientology; spiritism, I Ching, and witchcraft.

There are now an estimated 10,000 full-time and 175,000 part-time astrologers in the United States. Horoscope readings are computerized. Almost every newspaper and periodical in the nation now regularly prints them. In France 60,000 sorcerers are said to be taking in $200,000,-000 a year. A national magazine estimated that in 1970 there were 500 witches in Manhattan alone.

This fascination with the occult climaxed in the early months of 1974 when Warner Brothers released the film *The Exorcist,* producing what *Time* magazine called *Exorcist* fever.[5] All over the United States serpentine lines waited for hours outside theaters to see the horrifying movie about a little girl possessed by the devil. Once inside, audience reaction repeatedly included screams, hysteria (some requiring hospitalization), blackouts, heart attacks, vomiting, at least one miscarriage, and speedy exits. In New York City a boy ran from the theater toward a nearby church, tearing off his clothes and shouting, "Exorcise me! Exorcise me." Longer-range effects included people believing themselves possessed, acute insomnia, nightmares.

Exorcist fever uncovered an American public with a morbid fascination with despair, pain, and gore. William Blatty's book from which the film was taken sold almost 4 million copies (in addition to the 5 million previously sold) in five weeks immediately after the movie was released; the motion picture is, reputedly, going to be the top money-maker of all time, exceeding *The Sound of Music* and *The Godfather.*

Most of this upsurge has come since 1967. A brilliant young Englishman, Os Guiness, whom I met at L'Abri, Switzerland in the summer of 1972, had researched the new interest in witchcraft, the occult, Satan, and kindred subjects. He could find almost no major works on these subjects for the last two hundred years. History books treated black magic and the occult as curious extinct phenomena: the Enlightenment following the Renaissance, together with the rise of modern scientific knowledge, had effectively silenced witches and laid the ghosts.

Then in 1967, like the cap blown off a volcano after centuries of molten churning underground, there erupted into the open a torrent of publications on Satan, Satanism and all kindred subjects. The underworld's debris has been spewing up ever since.

"Why 1967?" I asked Os Guiness.

"I don't know," was his cautious reply. "Except perhaps that year was, in some strange ways, evil's 'fullness of time.' Between June 5th and 10th occurred an event clearly foretold in Scripture [6]—Israel's six-day war when Old Jerusalem and sacred sites such as the Wailing Wall were repossessed."

"But what connection——? I don't see——"

"Scripture prophesied that event as the beginning-of-the-end times—an accelerating warfare period between good and evil, God and Satan."

This conversation later gave me much food for thought. We are living in a period when evil is getting more evil while good is no longer satisfied with pallid goodness. In the last ten years a movement of the Holy Spirit has swept through the Catholic church and most branches and denominations of the Protestant church. It may well be that the rising popularity of Satanic activities is the unholy spirit's terrified counterattack against the moves of the Spirit.

Other thought-provoking facts about 1967 have been given me by knowledgeable educators. In the United States at least, autumn, 1967, was remarkable for two phenomena: a widespread, dramatic upswing in drug experimentation among the young and the real start of the campus revolution.

Be that as it may, I marvel that so many moderns, particularly the young, can be taking witchcraft and devil worship seriously. As Andrew Greeley, a Roman Catholic priest teaching sociology at the University of Chicago wrote: "What the hell is going on? God is dead but the Devil lives." [7] One answer must be that this generation has revolted against positivism. They no longer believe in religion, humanism, or even the imperialism of science that claims to be the only valid form of knowledge. In the words of one graduate student,

Let's face it, science is dead. While the newspapers and

magazines were giving all the attention to the death of God, science was really the one that was dying.

The second reason why so many moderns now "believe in" Satan may be that large numbers of people have been simply bored with life, seeking a costless thrill, and unsuspecting that there was any real world of evil or of good either. Having been taught the doctrine of relativism (that is, that there is no real or final good or real evil) they expected their exploration to end in fantasy. It came as a shock but also a strange relief, to discover that evil is real. A relief in the sense that people in this machine age were beginning to wonder if anything was real except our machines. One student expressed it in this question, "Is there anything so powerful that it can even make us real? I mean *really real*."

Professor Mircea Eliade of the University of Chicago defines the sacred almost in the precise words of the student: "That is exactly what the sacred is, the really real."

It should come as no surprise that the modern existentialist is not interested in second-hand philosophy or theology. To him, the "really real" is what he or another person experiences first-hand. Thus if some come to a belief in the reality of the world of the spirit via the negative underside (as the Buddingtons did in order to get to the God-ward side), at least we can be grateful that they *are* finding reality.

History proves that there are two sets of experiences which will flush out the power of evil and make Satan surface—one is to reconnoiter deeply in evil's territory; the other is to become a follower of Jesus.

So long as we remain secularists—whether just conventionally good members of society, or even church members who deny the supernatural aspect of religion—then probably we shall give no particular thought to Satan. If we consider the devil at all, we are likely to dismiss him as an outmoded, nonsensical symbol. Incidentally, Satan, like any other saboteur, would prefer to keep it that way. Disbelief in his existence is his best camouflage. If I have a mortal enemy who is intent on destroying me, my ignorance of such an enemy only makes my danger greater.

But I had learned Scripture's observation that Satan is not only real, but that each human life is in dire danger from the unholy spirit.

> Be sober, be watchful: your adversary the devil, prowls around like a roaring lion, walketh about, seeking some one to devour....[8]

And Jesus, speaking to the Pharisees:

> Ye are of your father the devil, and the lusts of your father ye will do: he was a murderer from the beginning....[9]

Moreover, our danger from Satan is to our physical bodies,[10] our families,[11] our possessions,[12] along with the eternal part of us—our spirits.

Meanwhile, my eyes were progressively being opened to substantiation of these Scriptural lessons by events all around me in contemporary life. Occasionally we can catch the Destroyer in the very act of trying to destroy.

Derek Prince, whom I know well, recently related such an incident.[13] At a preaching mission in Chicago, Mr. Prince had emphasized the dangers in playing around with the Destroyer's toys—ouija boards, tarot cards, going to fortune-tellers or mediums—even when we tell ourselves that we are taking none of this seriously.

He had commented that something like going to a fortune-teller just for a "joke" is quite like entering a lion's cage to count the lion's teeth for fun. Where there has been such dabbling, the speaker urged repudiation with a prayer for cleansing and if necessary, the Church's ancient rite of exorcism.

After one of the services, a woman approached Derek Prince, confessing that she had been a medium, and asked him to pray with her. As he looked into her eyes, he sensed duplicity. Knowing that his prayer for her would do no good unless she was ready to make a clean break with Satan, Derek suggested that she was not yet ready.

A day later she came again asking for prayer, this time insisting that she had changed her mind about spiritualism and had repented. Though Derek found himself nagged with doubts about her sincerity, finally he agreed to pray with her. But he found it hard going, like a series of obstacle courses all the way. After a few moments, he told the woman that he wanted to take a little rest, so he withdrew a few steps away and was leaning against the altar rail, thinking and asking for God's direction.

Suddenly he was jerked out of his reverie. A loud, clear voice of a different timbre from the one the woman had been using made him whirl around. He saw her pointing a finger at him. "I see you in a car and it's wrecked against a tree."

Derek Prince's reaction was trigger-quick. Recognizing now what he was really up against, with great firmness of voice he said, "You spirit of divination, I refuse to accept that from you. That's Satan's lie. I will *not* be in any car that's wrecked against any tree."

Later, telling of this incident, he concluded by saying, "Had I not been on my guard, had I begun to believe this woman, I would have been in real trouble. The woman was seeing and describing Satan's destiny for me. By admitting this idea into my mind, I would have submitted myself to Satan's plan."

The Bible not only spells out the peril of Satan's life plan for us, but goes on to give us a plan of defense. For our reassurance, God has made us sure promises of help and deliverance....

> Submit yourselves therefore to God. Resist the devil, and he will flee from you. [14]

> ...God is faithful, who will not suffer you to be tempted above that ye are able; but will with the temptation also make a way of escape, that ye may be able to bear it. [15]

> And Jesus...spake unto them, saying, All power is given unto me in heaven and in earth. [16]

Thus reassured that God has made us "a way of escape," what are those defense tactics?

First, it's a blessed relief to learn, as Carrie and Jeff Buddington discovered through hard experience, that while "the unholy spirit does have power, it is a power each individual has to allow him." That freedom of choice God gave man is so real that the unholy spirit cannot violate it. He must therefore persuade or deceive us.

Satan can call God a liar, he can flash before our dazzled eyes all the supposed sin-fun imaginable, but if we do not agree to his blandishments, give him the nod, he remains helpless. Although the divine part of man—the inner core of him, his spirit—is sacred, nevertheless God has made each man the keeper of his inner castle. We do not therefore have a built-in protection against evil. But we have been given truly free wills. That is why it is possible to hand over so much to Satan and why to do so places us in such jeopardy.

When we understand the factuality of this free will, then we'll be more likely to perceive why it's so dangerous to hand over to Satan any ground in our life on which he can stand. What I have come to call "the beachhead trick" is a favorite one of the enemy.

During World War II the term "beachhead" came into popular usage. A beachhead is that first landing on an island or a shore on which the whole battle may depend. Once that toehold on land is secured, it is usually only a matter of time until the rest of the island or country or even empire falls.

Just so—my life, my body, my affairs are as an island empire that the unholy spirit hopes to win en route to his ultimate objective of my eternal soul. To do that, he too must first gain a beachhead in my life. With that toehold, then he can take his time about gaining control of the rest of me and my affairs—yard by yard, decision by decision. But the analogy breaks down at one important point. In war, through physical overpowering, the victor can force his opponent to bend to his will, whereas God has kept from the unholy spirit the ability to force any human being against his will. Either Satan has to be granted permission by God (as in Job's case), or we have to give Satan the beachhead voluntarily, else he can't have it.

But who in warfare would be foolish enough voluntarily to give a beachhead? We do. We're foolish enough. How often we fall for the Destroyer's beachhead arguments, finding them amazingly appealing....

A little sinning is a good thing, the father of liars suggests to us. Not enough to sink us, of course. Just enough to be easier to live with and more socially acceptable. Anyway, who wants to be Mr. Goody Two-Shoes?

Another day, another approach. Don't we realize that a civilized person doesn't want to be "narrow" in morals, ethics, or religious belief? True, we agree, it is a sunny day on the beach, sparkling sand, fluffy clouds floating in a blue sky. Spiritual warface? What made us even think about such a thing?

Then comes the whispered argument, "All of life has to be a compromise." We can even take it from there for Satan. Of *course* a little ground here and there, not be rigid about everything. How else would conflicting points of view ever reach agreement on anything?

Then there's always "moderation" and "normal"—such reassuring words when compared to "fanaticism" and "extremist." Above all, who wants to be tagged "religious fanatic"!

Thus we succumb to Satan's beachhead strategies. Once he has this bit of ground, then he uses it to stand on for further assaults. I have received tremendous help by keeping this picture of the tempter's beachhead strategy in my mind's eye. It reminds me how dangerous is the initial bit of sinning on any given front.

We are creatures of habit patterns for good or ill. In other words, we do not make a series of equal and independent decisions, rather one decision leads to another. Unfortunately, the natural inclination which we have inherited from our father Adam toward making the wrong choice means that this phenomenon works more easily downward than upward. Any parent or teacher concerned with children knows this well. For instance, it is easier to let a child be sloppy and to allow careless habits to develop than it is to fight uphill toward his becoming an ordered, neat person.

Moreover, each repetition of a downbeat choice makes the next one easier and bothers us less as sin's inevitable deadening process sets in. Even after collaborating with the enemy by handing over the beachhead, we think ourselves still in control, able to call a halt to the enemy's advance any time we choose. Instead, Jesus warns us that "whosoever committeth sin is the servant [or slave] of sin." [17]

Notice how clear-cut Jesus was about His own total refusal so to collaborate with Satan (Jesus is speaking here to His apostles at the Last Supper):

> Hereafter I will not talk much with you: for the prince of this world cometh, *and hath nothing in me*.[18]

Jesus had given no ground because He knew how deadly playing with Satan is. Just as a physician would not dare ignore or underestimate the malignancy of a few cancer cells, even so in God's eyes there is no harmless little "white" evil.

The second defense God has provided for us is what Scripture calls "the armour of light." [19] So long as we stay in the light we're safe because Satan cannot endure light and will not come near it.

A true incident has become an unforgettable symbol of this for me. Some years ago *Guideposts* magazine editors received a short manuscript in the mail. The writer, whom I'll call Mary, was married to Bill W., a traveling salesman, and was the mother of three children, the youngest a baby girl. She and her husband were both active in their local church, where the couple had met and grown fond of an attractive young man, John Ames. On those Sundays when Mary's husband was out of town on one of his frequent business trips, John would give her and her children a ride to church.

Nothing was wrong with that, except that soon it was becoming a habit. Mary found herself looking forward to seeing John and thinking of him often.

An inner warning signal went up for her as she remembered Jesus' words about lust beginning inside us—in the thoughts and the will. "I'll duck this," she decided. She and the children went early to church to get there ahead of John's proffered ride.

The strategy worked the first Sunday. But on the next one when Bill was out of town, John started early for Sunday School too—and picked them up.

On both sides the attraction was intensifying. Even sitting across the room from one another in a group of people, Mary was acutely conscious of John and of his eyes often on her. An electric sexual attraction was developing between them, no question about it.

One night Mary forced herself to face the issue. "I made myself think through the end results if John and I kept on the road we were going. A romantic interlude, nothing more? To think so would be kidding myself. Rather, probably a broken home. My husband's life cruelly hurt and twisted. Worse still for our children. And tawdriness as my reward. On the other side was the frightening intensity of the electricity between John and me.

"In desperation, I dropped on my knees. 'Oh God! This is too much for me.' It was a cry wrung out of me. 'I can't fight any more. I turn this battle over to You.' That night I slept calmly."

The next day with her husband still out of town, Mary spent the entire day cleaning closets, drawers, cupboards, windows. In some way, it must have been symbolic.

That evening after the children were in bed, John Ames appeared at the front door. "Bill's not home," Mary told him. But he came in anyway.

Mary didn't ask her caller to sit down. She remained standing in the center of the room bathed in a cone of light from the electrical fixture overhead. There was an awkward interlude during which John Ames made persistent small talk, his eyes fastened on Mary. As she concentrated on Jesus as represented by that light, she felt herself becoming less aware of John and more and more aware of the enveloping light of God all around her.

Finally her caller noticed the baby asleep on the sofa. "Don't you want me to carry her to her crib?" he asked.

Mary nodded, but did not follow John into the darkness of the adjoining bedroom. Somehow she knew that she must not. There in the darkness John's arms would reach for her as inevitably as—No, *she must stay in the light.* As long as she stood in the light, the values she really cared about—her marriage, the home she and Bill had made together, their children—would be safe.

John remained in the bedroom for what seemed like an eternity, waiting for her, Mary thought. At last he emerged. For a long moment he stood looking at Mary, indecision written on his face. At last reluctantly, he left.

"Then I understood," the author wrote, "the truth of the

Scriptural teaching that there's nothing wrong with being tempted. It's what we *do* with the temptation that matters.

"My tumultuous feeling for John Ames did not disappear overnight. But as I prayed more about it, the entire episode just faded from my emotions, leaving no trauma, no scars, no regrets—just praise to God for delivering me from a serious temptation."

Mary had found for herself the reality of "the armour of light." That protecting armour is, of course, Jesus Himself as prophesied in Isaiah's beautiful words:

> The people that walked in darkness have seen a great light: they that dwell in the land of the shadow of death, upon them hath the light shined.[20]

So, as His disciples, we are urged:

> For ye were sometimes darkness, but now are ye light in the Lord: walk as children of light.[21]

We walk as children of light when we insist upon transparent openness and honesty, no dark secrets, no duplicity, lies, or double-dealing. It was from my spiritual mentor, the Quaker Hannah Smith, that I learned the valuable lesson that hidden sin—no matter how carefully denied, glossed over and secreted away—will give Satan his beachhead and result in our inability to stand victoriously before the enemy or any of his cohorts.[22] The emphasis here is on any accursed thing being tucked back in our lives, hidden out of sight. We may have almost forgotten about it, but Satan never forgets. For us, the result will be failure every time. This is the reason that Jesus had so much to say about the necessity of light and our coming to the light. When men's deeds are evil, they love darkness rather than light.

But he that doeth truth cometh to the light, that his

deeds may be made manifest, that they are wrought in God.[23]

So it helps to stay aware of this principle: whenever we prefer to keep something secret or hidden, tucked away in the darkness, we do well to question our real motives.

Truth is the name of a third defense against the Destroyer pointed out by Scripture. The cynic would always echo Pilate's sarcastic question to Jesus, "What is truth?"—the assumption there being that all truth is relative, so there is no final clear-cut truth. But this is Satan's position, not Christ's. Jesus' words echo down the centuries, "*I* am the way, the truth, and the life."

Naturally, Satan could never agree to clarity. The saints of all ages are in agreement that the unholy spirit delights in fuzziness. He would have us believe that we are being properly humble when we intone, "I hope my sins are forgiven"... "Well, Yes, I think I'm a Christian. I try to be." Jesus wants us to *know* that our sins are forgiven and that we are Christians.

Thus one of our greatest weapons is not just defensive, but offensive: the use of Scripture as truth hurled in Satan's teeth, wielded as the "sword of the Spirit." Jesus' repeated use of "It is written" in His wilderness temptations is a vivid example. Of course, in order to use Scripture in this way, we have to get the habit of reading it so that the truth cast in the cadences of the great English of the Bible sinks deeply into heart and mind. I have found that when I do my part, then the Holy Spirit can do His. So often it has happened! It is as if the Helper searches through the library stacks of my unconscious where all manner of information has been filed away (much of it long since forgotten by the conscious mind) and produces the particular "It is written" needed for the moment of battle. Always Satan flees before this. He flees because the unholy spirit has final respect for the authority of Scripture. Though the Destroyer loathes truth, he recognizes it, thus tipping his hand about those eons spent in the presence of God. Certainly this should give us pause at a time when the authority of the Bible has been so generally called into question.

Satan and his lackeys always recognize and must bow before Jesus, who is our Deliverer. Long before even Jesus' apostles recognized that He was more than an exciting Teacher and Healer, the unclean spirits (demons) who had taken up abode in human beings recognized Him as the Son of God. So over and over in the Gospels we hear an unclean spirit crying out, "What have I to do with thee, Jesus, thou Son of the most high God? I adjure thee... that thou torment me not." [24] Each time Christ was able to cast out the unclean spirit because He is the only One who has never given any ground to Satan.

Usually we think we deserve a "little fun" by a fling into sinning when life has handed us some injustice or when we have stuck faithfully through some protracted trial. A degree of self-pity joins the blown-up pride of our self-congratulation at having been so patient and reliable. Many of us have found out to our sorrow what a deadly brew this is. Our eyes are completely off Christ and on ourselves. Out of this little mess Satan has worked some great triumphs.

But what if we are already in the middle of such a mess? What if one's life is snarled up by habit-patterns, bad human relationships, fears that one can't get rid of, debts, and illness? What then? Is there any hope?

There certainly is! That's precisely the good news Christ brings us....

> So also the Lord can rescue you and me from the temptations that surround us....[25]

> Behold, I give unto you power... over all the power of the enemy; and nothing shall by any means hurt you.[26]

Because thou hast kept the word of my patience, I also
will keep thee from the hour of temptation....[27]

When we bring our misdeed into the light of Jesus' love
and forgiveness and renounce it, we have taken the first
step. The renouncing part is especially important when we
have been toying with ouija boards, spiritualism, witchcraft, fortune-telling, and the like, even though this be
years behind us. In order to belong to Christ, we have to
make a clean break with the accouterments of Satan's
kingdom by renouncing them. Once that break is made,
then we are free to "turn around" and accept Jesus'
forgiveness.[28] Thereupon Satan loses his beachhead and
we are again free.

But Satan, the liar, will throw everything into the fight to
blind us to this final power before which he is helpless—the
finished work of Jesus on His cross, the sacrificial Lamb,
His blood shed for us. God's wish is that no matter what
we've done, we feel guilt only long enough to bring it to the
Light of the World to be dealt with. Satan's aim is to bog us
down through the emotion of guilt, somehow convince us
that *our* sin is too rarefied to be forgiven (an odd form of
inverted human ego!), thus making us feel estranged from
God and inept in serving Him.

The opposite of Satan's lie is given us in a ringing
declaration in Colossians:

> ...he [Christ] cancelled the regulations that stood
> against us...when he nailed them to the cross, when he
> cut away the angelic Rulers and Powers from us, expos-
> ing them to all the world and triumphing over them in
> the cross.[29]

I remember how Peter Marshall once made this truth
real and personal. One evening a friend had questioned
him about God's judgment. Did he really think that there
was going to have to be an accounting for each of us?

"Yes, I do think so," Peter answered promptly. "The Bible makes it quite clear. I think I may have to go through the agony of having Old Scratch, the accuser, recite my sins in the presence of God.

"But I believe it will be like this: Jesus, our High Priest, will come over and lay His hand across my shoulders and say to God, 'Yes, all these things are true, but I'm here to cover up for Peter. He is sorry for all his sins, and by a transaction made between us, I am now solely responsible for them.'"

Suddenly Peter smiled. "And sister, if I'm wrong about that, *I'm sunk.*" [30]

But we're not sunk. Glory be to God!

9

The Enigma of Healing

Most of us feel no need of facing the question "Does God heal directly today?" until we are personally confronted with some physician's blunt finality: "There's nothing more we can do."

Those were the precise words my friend Sandra was hearing so incredulously that night—February 8, 1966. I did not learn of this sequence of events until later when Sandra Ghost (now a close friend. Yes, her name really is Ghost) shared it with me. Arriving at the hospital room where her little son lay, Sandy had encountered Dr. Gallo.

"Mrs. Ghost, there's been no improvement in Kent's condition since this afternoon," the distinguished-looking, dark-haired doctor told her. "No question of the diagnosis—a cerebral hemorrhage. He's still in deep coma."

Over his shoulder Sandra could see the slight form of her two-year-old son, usually unable to stay still for an instant. Now there wasn't a flicker of movement anywhere—from his toes to his blond head.

Dr. Gallo asked gently, "You did call your husband in Louisville?"

"Yes, I did. Bill caught the first plane possible. He should be here at ten o'clock."

"I must warn you.... Kent may not hold on until your husband gets here. Mrs. Ghost, you may go in now." He paused. "There's nothing more we can do."

The words spoken so slowly for emphasis struck Sandra like a physical blow. Their impact detached some part of her mind and sent her thoughts spinning backward to that first day when she and Kent, his hand clinging so tightly to hers, had walked through the front door of the National Institutes of Health on the outskirts of Washington, D.C. What relief she had felt! To think that this great research arm of the United States Government had been willing to take on their son's case of acute lymphocytic leukemia. Why, this place was one of medicine's frontiers. In these vast government buildings they were finding answers. Surely, she told herself, only God could have made the connection between the Ghost family in Louisville, Kentucky, and NIH. Therefore, the fine and compassionate doctors on Two-East (the leukemia unit) would discover the key to the healing of Kent's leukemia.[1]

And in the two months since, the doctors had indeed proved themselves compassionate. In fact, the warmth of everyone around NIH—laboratory technicians, housekeeping detail, clean-up crews, and Mr. Botts, the gentle black elevator operator who "God-blessed" all his passengers—had steadily reassured her.

So how could Dr. Gallo be saying so seriously, "There's nothing more we can do"? For what he meant was, "Kent is going to die and I can't prevent his death. Medicine, science, the best we know, has no further resources to give you."

Her thoughts reeled and staggered. "But that can't be! This is the twentieth century. I—Sandra Ghost—am a twentieth-century woman. I have relied on science. Science can do *anything*."

But she only stared at the doctor, nodded her head, and murmured, "Thank you, Doctor." For an instant she watched the physician's back retreating down the long corridor almost at a trot, as though eager to be away. Then she hurried into Kent's room.

This was Intensive Care with Di-Gi on duty, a nurse whom Sandra had learned to know well during the two months. Every ten minutes Di-Gi was taking vital signs: would Kent respond to the beam of light flashed directly into his eyes? Any sign of consciousness by grip or response? Any change in temperature? Blood pressure?

But there was no visible response—none at all. Her child was so still and so white, his legs so limp. Almost the smell of death was in this room. Was Sandra imagining it? No, this was no illusion; she saw it in the nurse's eyes.

Sandy kept a grip on her emotions through two of the ten-minute periods. Then she broke down, sobbing quietly.

Di-Gi understood. "Some black coffee would help," she suggested, "help me too. Why don't you go down to the Snack Shop for two cups?"

The distraught mother realized the nurse was using psychology on her, but she also knew that some activity would help. "Sure," Sandra agreed, "good idea."

On Sandy's return from the Snack Shop, she was surprised to see Mr. Botts running the elevator; it was rare to see him on night duty, rarer still for her to be the only passenger. As the doors slid shut and the elevator mounted, Mr. Botts asked as he always did, "And how's my little man?"

This time the question brought quick tears to Sandra's eyes. She shifted the sack with its two steaming cartons of coffee to her left hand in order to grope for her handkerchief. "Mr. Botts, Kent's bad. He's—not expected to live." Then from deep inside her came a request that she was surprised to hear herself making, "Will you—would you pray for Kent?"

At that moment they arrived at the second floor and the elevator doors opened. Sandra was no more than three steps into the hallway when she heard Mr. Botts's voice behind her, "Get back on the elevator, would you? Let's pray *now*. Please get back on."

Wordlessly, Sandra obeyed. The elevator doors shut, only this time Mr. Botts left the elevator stationary at the second floor.

"Lord Jesus," he prayed, "I ask you to heal this child as you healed me when the doctors told me I would never walk again. The Church prayed and You heard their prayers, and there's nothing wrong with me now. I ask You to do for this child what You did for me since the Good Book says, 'God is no respecter of persons.'

"Lord, enter this little boy's body. Heal Kent, Lord, and let him walk again. And Lord Jesus, give Kent's mother here Your strength. She needs it so much...."

Was there more of the prayer? Sandy could never remember, only that she was aware of God's love in that elevator as she had never before felt it. And wasn't it odd that during what had seemed to her a long stretch of time, no one had rung for the elevator? Fumbling for words, she tried to thank Mr. Botts. Then she ran left down the corridor and through the double swinging doors to Kent's room. As she went, she glanced at her wrist watch—six minutes before nine.

"Any change?" she asked the nurse.

Di-Gi shook her head. "No change."

As the two women sipped coffee, Di-Gi talked. Sandra discovered one reason for this nurse's special depth of compassion. She had been through trouble too: her mother and her younger sister had died in an automobile wreck just two months before. Sandra wondered why Di-Gi was not angry with God or bitter. She had the feeling that the nurse knew Him.

As they talked, two sets of vital signs were taken. At the third, Di-Gi seemed startled and made no attempt to hide it. "His blood pressure! Coming down fast, toward normal."

Almost immediately, Kent stirred in the bed. His eyes fluttered open. Recognizing his mother, he turned toward her, "Mommy, I'm thirsty."

Di-Gi restrained her excitement long enough to finish taking all the vital signs and recheck them, then she ran for the doctor on duty. He made it to Kent's room in record time.

By the time Bill Ghost arrived from the airport, Kent was fully conscious, sitting up in bed, sipping a soft drink through a straw, anticipating his Daddy's coming.

During the night hours Kent continued to improve. The next day, February 9, Dr. Robert Gallo appeared to be in sharp disagreement with a battery of neurologists. Though the parents at NIH are always considered a part of the "medical team" for their own child, the Ghosts were surprised to hear the physicians openly discussing their differences: Dr. Gallo could not possibly have been correct in his diagnosis, the neurologists insisted; no patient could recover from a cerebral hemorrhage as quickly as Kent Ghost had.

Dr. Gallo stood his ground. Yes, he reiterated, his diagnosis had been correct. He had performed the requisite spinal tap. Nor had a vein been punctured during the tap, thus accounting for blood in the test tube.

Finally the neurologists would not be appeased unless they performed another spinal tap, so Kent was wheeled away to a treatment room. There Dr. Gallo was vindicated: yes, the little boy had had a brain hemorrhage.

Two days later, Kent was riding the rocking horse in the playroom at NIH, unaware of the doctors and nurses who kept drifting by the playroom door, staring at him.... "Can you believe that's Kent Ghost?" Between his turns on the rocking horse, he would ride Mr. Botts's elevator up and down, down and up, and each time a jubilant Mr.

Botts would pat "his little man's" head, make gleeful
remarks or hum under his breath, all the time looking as
though he possessed a secret too marvelous to contain.

My first reaction to Sandy's story was joy. My second
was, then why doesn't God always come to our rescue as
He did to Kent Ghost's? Here is a query asked not so much
by non-Christians nor even by the Christian who has never
admitted healing into his understanding of the whole
Gospel, but by those of us who have long struggled with
this matter of healing through God's intervention.

I first asked the question in 1943 when, because of a lung
condition, I too heard the doctors say, "Sorry! Nothing
more we can do right now. Just lie in bed and rest."

So I was bedridden during 1943, 1944—winter... spring
...summer...into autumn. During the long, tedious days I
was doing a lot of praying and thinking. Since the birth of
modern scientific inquiry, men had come to rely on the
orderliness of nature, what science calls "the uniformity of
natural causes." I could see how Christians had picked up
this concept and applied it to Christian thinking. An idea
can often be as catching as a virus. Such was the case with
an idea that surfaced in the late 1930s and was verbalized
from thousands of pulpits through the decade of the 1940s.
It could be summarized like this....

"We are accustomed to the fact of physical laws—
discoverable, definite, immutable. When we drop an object
from the top of a tall building the object always drops
because the law of gravity always operates. In the spiritual
realm too there are laws just as discoverable, just as precise,
always operative.

"Therefore, the way to get on with spiritual research to
find out how prayers are answered and healing effected is to
discover these spiritual laws and apply them. The results
will then be just as certain as in the realm of the physical
laws."

It was an exciting concept. Many of us had turned to it

with relief. It had given us a way to go. It was like having in our hand the latest AAA strip map for our spiritual journey. If we followed the directions carefully from point A to point B and then C and D, our destination was assured.

Lying in bed feeling half-alive, my need was great. I set out eagerly to find those spiritual laws governing healing. After studying the New Testament, I would then delve into what I could uncover from human experience as recorded in books and in any sort of verbal contemporary sharing for which acceptable proof was offered.

So methodically, I started searching out each of Jesus' healing miracles and analyzing them. I was groping for some common denominator in these healings by which I could uncover the principles or secrets I could apply to my situation. Thirty-seven miracles are detailed in the gospels in addition to thirteen separately recorded times when Christ healed "many" or "multitudes" or "great multitudes."

In order to make a comparative study of Jesus' dealings with the sick and the afflicted, I ruled wide sheets of paper into seven divisions, like this:

The Case of	The Trouble	Means Used	Time	Patient's Part	Others' Part	Christ's Instructions
The deaf man (Mark 7:32-38)	Deafness and severe speech impediment	Jesus' touch on afflicted part with saliva and His word of authority	Immediate cure	None	Friends brought man to Christ, begging that He lay hand on sufferer	Forbade man or his friends to tell others about it

My conclusion from this study could be summed up like this.... Jesus came to earth to reveal His Father's nature and His will for mankind.[2] Jesus saw sickness and disease as intruders in His Father's world, part of Satan's work,[3] thercfore evil all the way. Consistently, He fought disease just as any dedicated physician fights it.[4]

I could find no Gospel record that the Master ever refused anyone who came to Him and asked for healing, though He did, upon occasion, select one to be healed out of a group—such as the man at the Pool of Bethesda [5]— thus obviously, leaving other sufferers around that Pool unhealed.

He did not once say in regard to health, "If it is God's will." [6] There is no beatitude for the sick as there is for others like the bereaved, those who suffer persecution, the peacemakers.[7] Nor did there ever fall from Jesus' lips any statements that ill health would further our spiritual growth or benefit the Kingdom of God. Rather, He not only wants to heal our diseases, He also wants us to stay healthy.[8]

So I asked myself the question, "Then did Jesus intend for these healings to go on after His ascension—even into our own time?" According to the New Testament, He certainly did! How else could we interpret His words, "Verily, verily I say unto you, he that believeth on me, the works that I do shall he do also; and greater works than these shall he do because I go unto my father." [9]

All of this added up to what seemed an unassailable "yes" on the side of healing through the direct action of God today.

Yet this study, including that wistfully well-ordered chart of Jesus' healings, were disappointingly frustrating in uncovering any rules or methodology for healing through prayer. At first glance, faith on the part of the sick one or his relatives or friends (such as Mr. Botts for Kent Ghost) seemed to be necessary. But closer scrutiny told me that while sometimes Jesus placed great emphasis on faith, at other times faith was never mentioned. For instance, what about those crowds whom Jesus healed? [10] Did every person in those crowds have faith? It isn't likely.

Perhaps going to Jesus and *asking* for healing could be

put forward as a rule? No, because many were healed who never asked, like the man with the withered hand [11] or the sufferer at the Pool of Bethesda. [12]

Well then surely, I thought, some degree of goodness must be necessary? Not a bit of it! Here Scripture's message is resoundingly clear: all humankind is born into this earth life with the same stain. "All have sinned, and come short of the glory of God." [13]

And this "coming short" is such a great gap that it can never be filled by human effort: "Not for thy righteousness, or for the uprightness of thine heart, dost thou go to possess their land...." [14] "Not by works of righteousness which we have done, but according to his mercy he saved us...." [15]

Jesus healed out of pure compassion because He was ever—and always will be—"The Father's Restorer." True, after Jesus healed the man at the Pool of Bethesda, He told him that now he would be wise to repent and change "or something even worse may happen to you." [16] But the healing came before the man's change and in no way seemed dependent on it.

Though I was learning, I could find no uniform dependable act or attitude on the part of the sick person that would provide certain healing. At that point I began wondering if things of the spirit could really be pigeonholed and categorized in the way that has been such universal procedure in the physical world? I was beginning to doubt it.

Even so, my search went on into the second phase, the area of human experience since New Testament times. Of several such areas I investigated, I'll mention only one—the healings at Lourdes in southwest France. This has been a healing shrine since a fourteen-year-old peasant girl, Bernadette Soubirous, [17] had a vision of Mary, the mother of Jesus, on February 11, 1858. The girl was told to dig in the earth at a certain place where she would find a spring. She was instructed to ask that a healing shrine be built over the spring.

Bernadette obeyed. Digging in the dry earth, she was astonished to find a trickle of water appear, no bigger than a finger. Over the days, the spring grew larger and larger until today it pours out thirty-thousand gallons of water every twenty-four hours. More than forty-five thousand sick people go to Lourdes each year, most of these as a last hope.

Investigation convinced me that there have been healings so remarkable as to fall clearly into the category of "miracle." The first one in 1858 was that of the eighteen-month-old boy Louis-Justin Bouhohartz, a neighbor of Bernadette. Dying from a disease that Dr. Dozous, the local physician, had said "hesitates between meningitis and infantile paralysis," the little boy had intermittent convulsions with high fever, was unable to sit up, walk, or stand. Feeling that she had nothing to lose, the child's mother plunged him into the icy spring for fifteen minutes and took him home with his little body stiff and blue. The next day, Louis-Justin was walking and eating normally.

Dr. Dozous, who had attended the boy and given him over to death, watched the icy bath and its results, and this convinced him. Incidentally, Louis-Justin lived to be a very old man.

Over the years other miracles have followed, stories that fascinated me as I read of them.[18] The distinguished scientist Dr. Alexis Carrel has left us with an impressive eyewitness report, his observation of the healing of the eighteen-year-old Marie Ferrand from advanced tubercular peritonitis between two-forty and three o'clock on a July afternoon in 1903.

At the time, Carrel was on the faculty of the Medical School of the University of Lyons. Born into a Catholic family, he had become first a Stoic, then a disciple of Kant, then skeptical of any belief in a supreme being. All religious concepts had been ground down and finally destroyed by intellectualism, especially the rigorous German system of Higher Criticism. Any attempt to discuss primary causes seemed useless to Carrel; rationalism satisfied his mind all the way.

Out of this background, having heard so many rumors of cures at Lourdes, the young doctor decided to accompany a trainload of pilgrims to observe, analyze, examine, and discredit these vaunted cures. On the train he was summoned to the side of Marie Ferrand, who was apparently dying. He learned that there was a history of tuberculosis on both sides of Marie's family. After examining the girl, Dr. Carrel concurred in the diagnosis of her hometown doctor—tubercular peritonitis too far advanced to risk surgery.

Dr. Carrel examined Marie again after she got to Lourdes and before she was taken to the Grotto. He found her with an emaciated white face, a pulse racing at 150 beats a minute, an abdomen markedly distended with viscera and fluid, ears and nails of a pale greenish hue, her nose and hands cold. He scarcely expected the patient to live long enough to be carried from the Lourdes hospital to the Shrine.

Later on at the Grotto Shrine, Dr. Carrel stayed close by the girl thinking that she might need medical help. As he watched, astounding changes took place: the lines and shadows on her face began disappearing as color returned; the blanket over her distended abdomen was flattening out while her heartbeat was slowing down to a regular pace. One of the nurses offered her a cup of milk which she drank eagerly. Then she began moving her legs without any discomfort.

Still incredulous, Dr. Carrel reexamined Marie that same evening. She was sitting up in bed. Her pulse was now a steady 80 beats per minute. All traces of distension, hard masses, and fluid had disappeared from her abdomen; hers was the flat, slightly concave stomach of an undernourished girl.[19]

Witnessing this case changed Alexis Carrel's life in several respects. Upon his return to the University of

Lyons, he decided that he could no longer call himself truly scientific if he failed to speak out about what he had observed at Lourdes. He was promptly summoned into the office of the Dean of the Medical School. "With such views, sir," he was told, "you can hardly expect to stay on as a member of our faculty."

"In that case," Carrel replied, "I must look elsewhere."

That was why Alexis Carrel left France to come to the United States, first to the University of Chicago, then to New York as a member of the Rockefeller Institute for Medical Research. There in 1912, he received the Nobel Prize in physiology and medicine for his contribution to the surgery of blood vessels.

The Catholic Church—at first as skeptical about Lourdes as was the medical profession—had finally seen the point of detailed medical substantiation. Thus, in 1885 a Medical Bureau had been established for professional examination and verification of alleged healings. Later an International Medical Association (nicknamed AMIL) with five thousand doctors from thirty countries was added to support the Medical Bureau and the scientific study of Lourdes cures.

Of the many apparent healings at Lourdes, only 1200 in eighty-nine years have passed the Medical Bureau's rigid standards, with probably an additional 4000 genuine cures not finally substantiated because of incomplete data in the Bureau's files. Out of the total, only sixty-two have been submitted to the Catholic Church's Canonical Commission, finally to be pronounced "miraculous."

This rigorous medical substantiation gave me in Lourdes an ideal modern showcase to set alongside the New Testament in searching for that common denominator or set of spiritual laws in healings. Yet a careful scrutiny of the Lourdes healings left me with the same confusion as had the Gospel search. Try as I might, the why or the how of the Lourdes healings could not be pigeonholed or categorized any more than the New Testament ones. For among those gloriously healed at Lourdes have been some roustabout sinners all but dragged to the healing Grotto, while others who apparently fulfilled every prayer condition departed with their physical infirmities unchanged.

Some of the ill suffered severe pain at the time of healing; others were healed with no physical sensation.

While persistence on the part of the sufferer often appeared to be a factor, some have been cured at the Lourdes Grotto at their first bath in the springs.

The conclusion from all of this was clear: there was no neat set of spiritual laws, no cut-and-dried pattern I could follow to insure the return of the health I so desperately wanted. But back in 1944 I was not yet ready to admit to such a conclusion. I tried every way I knew: confession and spiritual housecleaning, asking for the gifts of faith followed by collecting faith passages of Scripture, memorizing affirmations, practicing positive thinking—and so on.

Finally, having prepared myself in every way I knew, with all the faith I had, I asked Christ to heal me. Then I waited impatiently for the next physical checkup and set of X-rays, certain that a loving Lord had observed my stupendous efforts and would respond.

The blood tests and X-rays were taken. Receiving the report two days later was always a traumatic experience for me... a racing heart, a pulse I could feel in my dry throat as I picked up the phone and dialed the number.

The doctor's voice revealed no such excitement. "No change in the X-rays; markings just the same. Sedimentation rate, ah—the same. Just carry on!" And he hung up.

No change—after all that! Incredulously, I sank back on the pillows. I had come to the end of self-effort and the sign before my face read DEAD END.

I hit bottom. And there I met God at the place where He had been waiting for me all along: where I knew that I wanted Christ's presence in my life more than I wanted health. Never mind healing, I wanted to be certain that God wasn't dead, that Jesus Christ lived, that He was real, and that I had been received by Him.

I poured all this out before Him, "God, I don't understand You at all. I've tried. You know I have. You told us
that 'Your ways are not our ways.' That's certainly the
understatement of the ages! Even so, I don't understand
why You're so hard to find. But here I am. I want You to
take me over and do what You like with me. I'm no good as
I am, so I'm not giving You much of a gift. But if You want
me to lie here on and on, like a vegetable—all right, that's
up to You."

There was no fine theological language in this prayer and
certainly, no graciousness in the gift of myself. But it was
honest, probably the most straightforward prayer I had ever
made. Finally, I meant business with God. In the years
since, I've learned that our Lord waits patiently until we
stop playing games with Him. The instant we leave off our
childish fooling around, He knows it and responds. It had
taken me eighteen months of trying everything else, but at
last I wanted the Giver more than His gifts.

That did it! The connection was made. At 3:00 the next
morning, I awakened suddenly to a feeling of crackling
power in the darkness. There followed an experience of the
Risen Christ. Since I've described this elsewhere,[20] I shall
not repeat the details here except to say that I saw and
heard Christ with the eyes and ears of the spirit. And my
observations of His personality, of what He said, and of my
replies and reactions, were even more specific than most of
my contacts ever are with my fellow human beings in the
flesh.

The results in my body were observable too. The next set
of chest X-rays revealed healing. Every X-ray thereafter
showed more healthy lung tissue until finally the healing
was complete. Nor has there ever been any relapse.

Surely there is no joy like that first rush of discovery in
experiencing for oneself that the Lord is alive in one's life,
so much more alive and real than any of us. And I had
stumbled into that revelation in the last way I would have

thought logical—through the relinquishment of myself to Him.

At that point I caught a glimpse of God's sense of humor—His revelation of Himself had outmaneuvered logic.

10

The Roof on the House

When one touches a live electric wire, there's no mistaking the instantaneous power that jolts the body. In the same way, when through relinquishment, I had touched the power of the Risen Christ in my quiet bedroom in the middle of the night, it had been as startlingly obvious.

We have Jesus' promise from His own lips that the Holy Spirit will lead us into all truth,[1] including all puzzling questions we need answered about healing. My problem was that often I was not content to have the Good Shepherd lead me into truth; like a rambunctious sheep, I kept running on ahead, nosing around the pastureland, always thinking that the truth I sought must surely lie immediately on the other side of the nearest hill.

That is how I acted back in 1944 after my return to health. In no time, I had all but forgotten about the necessity for relinquishment. In my joy over experiencing the presence of the risen Lord, I rushed to pray for all manner of neighbors and friends who were ill. This included Kenneth Grey, a neighbor on Cathedral Avenue in Washington who was dying of a brain tumor; an appealing small boy in the last stages of leukemia; a friend in our church with cancer.

I hope that my prayers brought comfort to the ill and to those around them. But they had no appreciable effect on the disease of the sufferers. In each case the illness took its course and the sick ones died.

That was deeply discouraging. Once again I had to go to God to ask Him my mistake. "Go back and look carefully at the way I've led you," I was told.

So I studied all the efforts in 1943–1944 that had failed to bring results:

My effort	*God's response*
Tried to find blanket laws.	No methodology; He deals with each one of us as His child, and each case individually.
Tried to make myself worthy.	"All [your] righteousness are as filthy rags to me." [2]
Tried to have faith in faith, and to work up faith by positive thinking, affirmations, and picturing.	He showed me that this is putting faith in a technique rather than in a Person—Jesus.
Demanded healing as my "right" as a child of God who thought she had met the conditions.	"You have no rights or righteousness in yourself, only in Christ Jesus." [3]

I saw that my demanding spirit, with self-will as its rudder, had blocked the answer to prayer.

"Now take a close look," I was told, "at how Jesus Himself handled the problem of will."

I was startled to find that Jesus (before His resurrection and glorification) insisted upon His helplessness:

> The Son can do nothing of himself, but what he seeth the Father do....[4]

> ...I do nothing of myself; but as my Father has taught me, I speak...."[5]

Thus Jesus' helplessness meant a total dependence upon His Father for everything.

But His *will*, what of that? Since Jesus' perfect humanity was as real as His divinity, His would have been a strong human will, stronger than any of ours. Over and over He reiterated that He had handed over that will:

> "For I have come down from heaven not to carry out my own will, but the will of Him who sent me...."[6]

And to His disciples He said:

> "My meat is to do the will of Him that sent me...."[7]

And at the end, He was "obedient even unto death."

Given Jesus' dependence on the Father, together with His laying down of self-will, then I asked myself, "Why didn't Jesus have to go through the process of relinquishment (for most of us a lengthy and agonizing process) each time He wanted to stretch out His hand and heal some sufferer?" Reading between the lines of the Gospel records, I believe He did relinquish His will each time, then immediately looked to the Father for what to do. But for Him it was neither an agonizing nor a lengthy process because He was altogether clear of our sticking points: does God really love the individual as we understand love; does He really have final power to break or overrule so-called "natural law"? Most of us have never settled these basic dilemmas. Jesus had.

So persuaded was He of His Father's complete love, trustworthiness, and Omnipotent power over all evil that He could make these relinquishments quickly. And just as quickly there flowed back from the Father to Jesus the particular Word to give the sinner or the sufferer along with the necessary faith. Thus occurred the resultant miracle healings. With us it takes longer—hours, weeks, sometimes years of trying everything else.

Meanwhile, as though to keep me seeking in the direction of relinquishment [8] and to let me know that this had not been just one woman's isolated experience, instance after instance kept coming to my attention in literature and history, in journals and letters, and by word of mouth. One of the most convincing and dramatic was Maude Blanford's remarkable recovery from what was diagnosed as terminal cancer fourteen years ago. A friend in Louisville, Kentucky, first put me in touch with Mrs. Blanford.

Attached to a brief typed outline of her story was an impressive statement signed by Mrs. Blanford's physician, Dr. Oscar J. Hayes, making it all but impossible to dismiss the patient's recovery as one of those occasional "remissions" as medical men usually speak of them. I was excited enough to fly to Louisville to get the details from the woman herself, now gloriously restored to health.

In the dining room of our mutual friend, we three women sat around the table sipping coffee as I questioned Maude Blanford. There was no trace of gray in her reddish hair, though she is middle-aged now, a motherly type, comfortable to be with.

"How did your trouble begin?" I asked.

"In my left leg," was her prompt reply. "The leg had been hurting me for two years. I thought it was because I was on my feet eight or ten hours a day. Finally, when I couldn't stand it any longer, my husband and I decided that I should see a doctor."

As the Blanfords' family doctor examined her, he became increasingly sober. Her leg was not her only problem. On the patient's lower abdomen there were lumps—large, firm tumor masses.

"I'm going to have to send you to a specialist immediately," he told Mrs. Blanford. The unspoken word hung in the air between them, "malignancy."

The specialist to whom Mrs. Blanford was sent discovered uterine hemorrhaging. Mrs. Blanford read in his eyes the poor prognosis. "I must warn you," he told her, "I suspect that this is extremely advanced."

"But Doctor," the patient pleaded, "there must be some way you can stop it. I'll go through *anything*—radium, surgery—"

"Mrs. Blanford, I promise you I'll do everything I can."

On July 7, 1959, the patient was admitted to the hospital for seventy-two hours of radium treatment in an effort to stop the hemorrhaging—without success. So in August she was given an additional seventy-two hours of this treatment. "The effect of the radium was total misery," she told me, "like having a hot oven inside me."

On September 29th she underwent surgery. Three days later, as she pleaded with the surgeon, Dr. Hayes, for the truth, he admitted, "The malignancy is extensive and we removed as much as we could. Lymph nodes are affected—that's why the pain in your left leg. One kidney is nonfunctioning because of blockage of the ureter. There is an area of metastasis in the liver. I am sorry. I am so sorry."

Maude Blanford was sent home, apparently to die. She was put on strong narcotics and tranquilizers to control the pain, and she was supposed to come back into the hospital for radium at regular intervals. Over a six-month period, she consumed $1,000 worth of pain-relieving drugs—Zactirin, sometimes Thorazine, and morphine.

Meanwhile, the sick woman began reviewing her spiritual resources, not to make her peace with God before death but for His help to continue battling for life. Mrs. Blanford had no church affiliation and no knowledge of the Bible. She did discover within herself a childlike (though untested) belief in the Person of Jesus Christ.

On the first Saturday of January 1960, she suffered a cerebral hemorrhage and remained unconscious for twelve days. Afterwards, she related a vivid image that had come to her. She saw a house with no top on it. The partitions between the rooms were there, the furniture in place, but there was no roof. She remembered thinking, "Oh, we must put a roof on the house. If it rains, all the furniture will be spoiled."

When she came out of the coma, Mrs. Blanford was bewildered. Instinctively, she turned to the Lord to ask Him in prayer what the vivid image had meant. "Christ showed me," she explained almost matter-of-factly, "that without Him as my covering, my body had no protection. Therefore, my life was in danger. But at that time I didn't know how to get the roof back on the house."

But Maude Blanford's fallacy, as mine had been, was that all her attention was focused on her danger, her roofless house. So despite all her prayers between then and July 1960, day by day her condition worsened. Breathing became so labored that she was reduced to speaking in whispers.

Still she kept struggling back and back for the radiation treatments. Then came Friday, July 1, 1960; she remembers it well. As the radiologist examined her, she asked anxiously, "Is it getting any better?"

"No, as a matter of fact——" his voice trailed off. Mrs. Blanford could read pessimism in his eyes. "I dare not give you any encouragement."

A few minutes later as Maude Blanford's son-in-law helped her into the car and she lifted her bad leg onto the seat, she broke down and wept. "For the first time, death looked good to me. Maybe I couldn't fight any more. I just hoped the Lord would take me quickly." It was a complete handing over of herself for God to do with as He pleased.

As He pleased... a bell of remembrance rang in my mind. My thoughts went spinning back to that September night in 1944 when I had ceased my frantic human striving and laid down my will almost in the same words she had. Only my situation had not been as stark as Maude Blanford's. For me, the alternative to healing was just having to lie in bed year after year; for her, it was death.

I leaned forward, eager to learn the result of this Prayer of Relinquishment. Had she made contact with the Source of power?

"That last visit to the radiologist and my turning myself over to God," she continued, "had been on Friday, July 1st. Well, I didn't have long to wait."

Monday, July 4th dawned beautiful but hot. That afternoon Joe Blanford made a bed for his wife outdoors with chairs and cushions. As the ill woman rested, hoping for the relief of a breeze, into her mind came some Scripture which she was not aware of ever having read....

> Is not this the fast that I have chosen? to loose the bands of wickedness, to undo the heavy burdens, and to let the oppressed go free, and that ye break every yoke?... Then shall thy light break forth as the morning and thine health shall spring forth speedily.... Here I am....

As Maude Blanford quoted this, I found myself looking at her in astonishment over the rim of my coffee cup. "But I thought you didn't know the Bible that well?"

"I didn't. I'd never read the Bible and I didn't even know that verse was there. When I was given those verses in my mind, I was also told, 'Isaiah 58.' My husband had to hunt up a Bible that had gathered dust on a spare-room shelf for years. Then I had to search and search to find the part called 'Isaiah.' But when I found the great verses just as I had heard them, even that 'Here I am' on down in the ninth verse, I knew the Lord Himself had spoken to me."

In the next few days the ill woman felt an intense desire—like an authoritative inner summons—to get outdoors and absorb the beauty of the good earth. She found a way to express this to her husband: "Joe, I want to go fishing."

That made no sense to him. Suppose his wife died on the

way to the lake? The back road was rough. His wife would have to be carried down the steep hill to the lake.

Finally Maude Blanford's insistence that God had told her to do this won her husband over. He allowed some neighbors to take her to the lake. That first day she stayed at the lakeside all day until six thirty. Just watching a breeze ripple the water, looking at the clouds and the wheeling birds and the distant hills brought a refreshment of spirit. That night she was relaxed for the first time in many months and slept soundly.

After that, the lake trip became routine. In three months' time, Maude Blanford was climbing up the hill to the road by herself. Then that inner Voice told her to begin walking upstairs slowly, praising God on every step. Still lifting her left leg with difficulty, at each step she would murmur fervently, "Thank You, Jesus."

Following that came the insistent instruction to undertake a few household chores. So she would sit in a chair and dust a mahogany tabletop saying, "Thank You, Jesus. Isn't that wood beautiful! Thank You for giving me the strength to lift my arm."

Then she tried putting a small amount of water in a pail. Sitting in a light chair, she would mop the floor in the area immediately around her, then inch the chair along and mop another spot. "Thank You, Jesus. I praise You for helping me do this. Is this the way we get the roof back on my house?"

Not that all pain or difficulties were over. She was still on heavy narcotics, still experiencing much nausea as the aftermath of the radium.

About this point she commented to me, "I learned a lot about the difference between self-effort which is the result of our human will to live and the self-effort that's obedience to what God tells us to do. We have to cooperate with *what we see God doing,* as Jesus put it."

She was so right. After our relinquishment, when the initiative passes to God, we need to follow willingly, obediently, trustingly. There must be no running out ahead of Him, but also no lying back limp or passive either. Instead we learn to listen and we follow.

About this time Mrs. Blanford was led to another type of nourishment. The doctor had ordered vitamin therapy and iron sulfate. Iron, she learned, is one of the best oxygen carriers to body tissues. After one of her conversations with Jesus, the insistent direction came: to slough off disease, your body's cells need all the oxygen they can get. He directed how much to increase the dose of iron sulfate.

The next morning as she was preparing breakfast for her husband, she said to him, "Honey, I've been healed." He lowered the morning paper and looked at her quizzically as she told him what had happened. His silence told her that he didn't believe her; so far as Joe Blanford could see, his wife looked exactly as before—except happier.

Mrs. Blanford knew that she was being ordered to share this faith with others, rather like those lepers whom Jesus had healed being told to go and show themselves to the priests. To obey, she had to relinquish false pride and risk a degree of embarrassment. Though not a churchgoer, Maude Blanford went to a small Baptist church near her home. The clergyman allowed her to stand in the service and tell her story. "I have no idea how long I talked," she reminisced. "I do remember seeing tears on different faces in the congregation."

Even so, it took time to rebuild her body-house—nine months for her bad leg to be near normal, three years for evidence of the cancer to leave her. As her body created new cells, the vicious malignant ones were sloughed off as waste. The "football" in her side disappeared. Vitality returned.

One problem remained, however. She still had so much pain. In April she went to her family doctor. "Is there anything more you can do for me to kill this pain?"

To her surprise, she saw tears in the doctor's eyes. "No,"

he had answered slowly, "there's nothing more I can do except give you the drug by hypodermic."

Suddenly she knew.... After all her other relinquishments, the one she faced now was the toughest of all: could she let go the drug crutch? Did she have the courage to say to God, "O.K., I'll even take the pain, if that's what You want for me"?

It was going to take a year of struggle to make that decision. On the 27th of April, 1961, Mrs. Blanford was returning on a long bus trip from a visit to her son in West Virginia. At a five-o'clock rest stop, as she popped the pain-killing pill into her mouth, she knew that at last she could say, "Yes, Lord" even to this: it would be her last narcotic pill.

So it turned out. Not that all pain left immediately. But what remained was bearable and gradually it faded away.

Two years passed during which period Maude Blanford had no contact with any doctor. Then when she called Dr. Hayes again over some small unrelated matter, the surgeon shouted in astonishment, "Mrs. Blanford! What's happened to you? I thought you were——"

"You thought I was long since gone." She laughed.

"Will you get in here to my office and let me examine you?"

"Look," she retorted, "why should I spend a lot of money for a complete examination when I'm a perfectly well woman?"

But Dr. Hayes insisted. "Mrs. Blanford, I promise you that if you will let me examine you, this one will be on me."

What the doctor found can best be stated in his own words:

I had lost contact with Mrs. Blanford and had assumed that this patient had expired. In May of 1962 she appeared in my office. That was two and a half years following her operation and her last X-ray had been in

July 1960. She had had approximately one-half of the X-ray treatment usually given, which certainly was well below what would be required for any effect.

The swelling of her leg was gone. She had full use of her leg; she had no symptoms whatsoever.. Her examination was completely negative and no evidence of cancerous disease could be found....

She has been seen periodically since that time for routine examinations.... She is absolutely asymptomatic.... This case is most unusual in that this woman had a proven, far-advanced, metastatic cancer of the cervix (epidermoid carcinoma) and there should have been no hope whatsoever for her survival.

(Signed) O. J. Hayes, M.D.

A follow-up examination nine years later by Dr. Hayes in January 1972 was followed by the same conclusion— "absolutely no evidence of any cancerous tissue."

Dr. Hayes, Mrs. Blanford, and the Record Librarian of St. Joseph's Hospital in Louisville were kind enough to allow me access to the medical data on her case. We lay people with meagre medical knowledge little realize the extent to which we are shielded from abhorrent details. I've no desire to expose them further. It is enough to say that the greater part of this patient's body was in a pre-death, putrescent state, riddled all through with metastatic cancer.

When I expressed appreciation to Dr. Hayes, the surgeon reiterated, "I'm only stating the facts. Truth must be served. Not that I understand it. I've no medical explanation to offer for Mrs. Blanford's return from certain death."

The puzzle in a case like Maude Blanford's is, why relinquishment? Why does God insist on our laying down our wills even when what we are clamoring for also happens to be His will for us?

I believe that the answer lies in this direction.... God is interested in more than our recovery from a specific illness; He is intent on our learning how to obey Him in the totality of life. Back in 1943–1944 my personal desire for health was the focal point of reality for me. Perhaps so much of me had been packed into that eager longing that there was no room for God to enter and do anything at all so long as my myopic thinking was equating "life" with the health I wanted.

Everything turns here on what constitutes life. In the end God's answer was infinitely more inclusive and richer than mine. So long as I was assuming that fullness of life corresponded to what I was striving for, I was actually deifying my own goal. And "Thou shalt have no other gods before Me" had to apply to my personal desire-world. There was nothing for it but to "put away" that most beloved of all idols inscribed "What I want." The scrapping of a treasure is always painful.

Our struggle with giving up self-will goes right back to the beginning of man's history on earth. It is significant that the fruit of the tree that Adam and Eve insisted on eating at all costs was the Tree of the *Knowledge* of Good and Evil.

The temptation to hang onto self-will is tagged "man's autonomy" and the bait is our covetousness for understanding. It is a temptation to which I, for one, have succumbed as often as most people by always wanting to know "Why?" I've even handed myself accolades for that. Doesn't that show that I'm a seeker, even a spiritual researcher? Didn't even Solomon ask for the gift of wisdom?

No, it doesn't prove much of anything except that I'm like my Mother Eve. She could have offered up the same rationalizations.... "And when the woman saw that it was a tree to be desired to make one *wise*...she....did eat."

Wisdom... understanding—all tempting bait. Except for the thoughts God chooses to share with us, it's still forbidden fruit. So long as we wear the garment of flesh, we can never understand the mind of our Creator.

At the time of the Protestant Reformation, men like Luther, Zwingli, Calvin, Farrel, and others kept insisting that the Biblical view of Man's Fall was that every part of Man fell, including his mind. Indeed, once we admit the Fall at all, what other view makes any sense?

Yet the Western world's humanism rests upon the opposite view. Our virtual deification of human intellect goes straight back to Thomas Aquinas (1227–1274), the intellectual and spiritual father of the Western nations who taught that while man's will fell from grace, his intellect did not. This is the same teaching that reached its height in the eighteenth-century Age of Reason.

When we realize that it was the eighteenth-century which gave America her legal and constitutional documents, we can see why the Aquinas views are so deeply imbedded in our thought. His dogma was even accepted almost completely by the Church. Along with the United States, Britain and other Western nations have inherited from Aquinas a mind-set driven to such depth that we are all but unaware of it.

Whenever anyone sets up his reasoning against God's, he is going the Aquinas way of humanistic autonomy, even though he may piously call it faith. The only true wisdom is facing up to what we actually are—creatures—and then yielding ourselves to the love and wisdom of our Creator. This yielding is relinquishment. And as we relinquish our own defective, incomplete human judgment, it feels like death because it *is* death—the beginning of the end of the old Adam in us.

The psychologist Fritz Kunkel has called this "The Crisis"—the major crisis of egocentricity. For many years prior to the crisis the basis of life has been—openly or

secretly—"My will be done." The result has been increasing rigidity, an inability to change ideas or life patterns, and
a decreasing ability to handle life's burdens. The ego
becomes a hard shell around the person, layer by layer,
deed by deed. Now there remains but one way to crack the
shell—exterior circumstances. To the person hiding within, these appear to be tragic, surely the end of everything.

A marriage is in difficulty. Health or financial resources
are lost. There are misunderstandings between friends.
Someone is taken by death. Then

> he comes to realize the deeper meaning of the great
> paradox, "He that would save his life must lose it.". . . It
> seems to him to be a real death. . . for the Self, the only
> form of life that he knows, must disappear, and there-
> fore, he believes its collapse is death. Thus he believes he
> faces the end of his life. . . . It is true, indeed, that one
> must lose that which *seems* to be his life—the system of
> mistaken ideas and values which are embodied in his
> Ego—in order really to live, to release into life the
> creative, enriching, productive powers of the true
> Self. . . .[9]

Yet. . . doesn't this complete laying down of one's life
seem to be a denial of the need for faith? After my book
Beyond Our Selves was published, I began receiving letters
like this:

> . . . you mentioned in your book that we must give in to
> God's will. I am confused. . . . Does relinquishment mean
> that we can never be sure about praying for any definite
> thing? If so—how can that be faith?. . .

Indeed, many stories of healing in the Bible seem to
indicate that just the opposite of relinquishment—an insistence on life—was the key to Christ being able to heal. In
the cases of the woman with an issue of blood [10] and the

palsied man carried by four friends and let down through
the roof,[11] healing apparently had nothing to do with
relinquishment; rather there was an intensity of desire in
both cases.

Though the importunate widow in Jesus' parable on
prayer [12] was not seeking healing, she was trying to make
contact with the Source of help. Clearly, Jesus was here
praising the strength of the widow's determination.

And in the instance of Marie Ferrand on the train to
Lourdes? The girl was too ill to be struggling with relinquishment or anything else except her next breath.

These people were not "relinquishing" in the usual
sense. They were, instead, going to incredible lengths to
insist on healing, letting nothing discourage them.

It was the extraordinary experience of our friend Virginia
Lively that shed great light on this seeming contradiction.

I've known Virginia for nine years. She's a housewife
(now a widow) in Belle Glade, Florida who does her own
cooking and cleaning, saves grocery stamps, and has to
watch her weight. She and I have had dozens of meals
together, visited back and forth, gone on retreats and
prayed together often. Virginia has a homespun quality
including a sense of humor that bubbles up in an infectious
laugh. She is about the last person I would expect to have
any far-out spiritual experience.

It happened in 1950 after her father Roy Wolff had been
in the Tampa Tuberculosis Sanatorium for seven months.
The sixty-three-year-old man's illness had been discovered
almost by accident. A casual visit to the T.B. truck going
the rounds had revealed three cavities about the size of
silver dollars in the top of his left lung.

That was bad enough. But Mr. Wolff's condition did not
respond to treatment and he was losing ground. The crisis
came in October. Mr. Wolff's latest X-rays gave a grim
prognosis. INH (Isoniazid), almost a miracle drug for many

tuberculosis patients, had effected no change in the patient's diseased left lung. The three cavities had enlarged into what looked like a figure eight. The physicians at the sanatorium dared give the drug for only six more weeks. The patient was too old to undergo surgery; they could hold out little hope.

Virginia and her mother and sister were together when they got the news. At that time not a one of them knew how to pray. Roy himself had little use for religion. He had not attended a church service all his married life because as a boy he had been "churched to death."

True, Virginia and her husband were church members, active at fund raising, church committees, and bazaars. Civic-minded church activists, neither husband nor wife had even taken subjects like prayer or healing into serious consideration. It would never have occurred to Virginia or her mother or her sister Doris to ask God to step into Roy's case and change medical facts.

One night soon after this discouraging hospital visit, Virginia was driving home from a PTA meeting when suddenly, she began to cry. She realized that she was under pressure as head of the Halloween Carnival that year, but it wasn't really the Carnival. She knew that. A deep intuition told her that the tears were for something much deeper.

Tears, more tears, floods of tears, started over again that night and then the next morning. The crying jag lasted for four days and three nights. Virginia was convinced it was the start of a nervous breakdown.

But on the morning of the fourth day, after her husband Ed had left for the bank and the two children for school, all at once she felt power in the air around her. The atmosphere in the quiet living room seemed to hum and crackle as though she were standing in the center of an electric storm.

As she sat in a high-backed chair, through the window she saw a ball of light on the eastern horizon. The light was moving, traveling toward her with incredible speed. It appeared white, yet from it poured all the colors Virginia had ever seen.

Then it was beside her. Although it seemed impossible that anything with such energy could hold still, it took a position at her right shoulder and stayed there. As she stared, she started to smile. She smiled because He was smiling at her. She now saw that it was not light, but a Face.

Even now Virginia finds it hard to put into words a description of that beautiful countenance. His forehead was high. His eyes exceptionally large. But she could never fix the color of His eyes any more than she could have the color of the sea.

More than individual features was the overwhelming impression of life—unhampered life, life so brimming over with power and freedom that all living things she had seen seemed lumps of clay by comparison.

Not for a moment did Virginia hesitate to call this Life at her side Jesus. And two things about Him struck her most. The first was His humor. She was astonished to see Him often break into outright laughter. And the second was His utter lack of condemnation. He knew her down to her very marrow—knew all the stupid, cruel, silly things she had ever done. But she saw that none of these things, or anything she would ever do, could alter the absolute caring, the unconditional love that she saw in those eyes.

It was too immense a fact to grasp. Virginia felt that if she gazed at Him for a thousand years, she could not realize it all.

She did not have a thousand years. She had three months. For as long as that, the face of Jesus stayed before her, never fading, never withdrawing.

For the first two weeks of this great experience, Virginia had given little thought to her father. She felt so joyous and free that there was no way she could have recaptured the previous mood of fretful grief.

Just after lunch one day she was lying on her bed reading the Bible. Growing drowsy, Virginia turned on her side, intending to take a nap. She was looking at a patch of sunlight on the wall thinking of Him, of how wonderful He is. That crackling vitality! When He'd said that He was Life, she smiled to herself, thinking, "Is that ever the understatement of the ages!"

Suddenly her train of thought was interrupted as an X-ray picture of lungs three times larger than life appeared in the middle of the sunlight. Unmistakably, her father's X-ray; she would have recognized it anywhere. There was the unusual figure-eight cavity and the single dollar-sized one at the top of the left lung. There were the same shadows and areas of scar tissue she had seen so often on the hospital X-rays.

Could this be an odd quirk of tree or cloud shadows? Virginia turned to look out the window. No, nothing.

As she turned back to puzzle over the picture on the wall, a white line about three inches wide moved slowly up the wall. As the white line passed the lower lobes of the lungs, it left behind healthy lungs with the scar tissue gone. As it traveled upward over the diseased portion, it left behind healthy tissue—no cavities.

Virginia stared incredulously. What was going on anyway? She hadn't even been thinking about her father, much less praying for him. As if in answer to her perplexity, the entire episode began again. A second time there was the enlarged picture of Roy Wolff's X-ray on the wall, all the familiar and distinctive markings. Once more the same white line appeared at the bottom and traveled slowly up, leaving behind it the shadow print of two perfect lungs.

"Then Dad's well!" Virginia whispered.

In the Face at her side she was suddenly aware of a new dimension of joy. He threw back His head and laughed and the laughter filled the room.

Virginia found herself crying again, only this time it was for gratitude. She wanted to fling herself on her knees to thank Him. For some reason it was the kitchen where she knelt as the torrent of praise poured from her.

She never knew how long she spent there, the linoleum cold against her bare knees, but she does remember that as she got up she looked at the kitchen clock. Twenty minutes after two.

From the wall phone in the kitchen she spoke to her mother. "Mother, this is Virginia. Daddy's well!"

"Yes, honey, his spirit's been wonderful."

"Mother, not like that. Really well. Daddy's healed."

"Yes, dear." Her mother's voice sounded flat and tired. "We mustn't let ourselves be discouraged."

Virginia stifled her exasperation. "Mother, when are the next X-rays?"

"Next Wednesday."

"Then I'll call you Wednesday evening," she said. "But remember that I told you, Daddy's well." And she hung up.

The minute Virginia heard her mother's voice on Wednesday night, she knew that the truth had begun to surface. "Virginia, the most annoying thing. They got the plates mixed up! Poor Dad's got to go back for more X-rays tomorrow. Why, they sent down pictures of someone who never even had T.B.—"

Virginia almost laughed. "Mother, Dad's O.K. No matter how many X-rays they take, they're not going to find anything wrong."

And of course the next set of X-rays showed no sign of disease either. The sputum tests were negative; the culture test was negative.

By then the doctors were puzzled. Perhaps they had X-rayed from the wrong angle. More chest studies were made, this time from every conceivable angle. No sign of disease in the lungs.

A week or so later Virginia and her sister Doris stood beside a doctor at the sanatorium looking at the latest set of X-rays. "Where are the cavities?" Doris asked in pretended innocence.

A frown creased the doctor's forehead. "Well, I'll tell you—Hmmm...Well, there aren't any cavities."

"How do you explain that?"

"I haven't any explanation," the physician admitted. "There are times—. Well, what can I say?"

The sisters left the doctor's office for a long visit with their father, who was still being kept in bed because the hospital couldn't quite credit their own tests. That day the sisters heard the patient's side of the story....

"It happened one day at my nap time—"

Virginia remembered the kitchen clock. "Excuse me, Dad. When do you take your nap?"

"About two—few minutes before, few minutes after—"

Then that was about the same time I was lying in bed, Virginia's thoughts went. *Because twenty minutes later I was in the kitchen—*

"Well," her father continued, "I was just lying here when all at once there was the strangest feeling—like something draining from my body out of my feet. At first it frightened me."

"But there wasn't much time to be scared because the draining sensation was followed by a swoosh of well-being that filled up my whole body. I felt warm and cared-for. Loved—that's it. Loved. Never felt so well in my life. No reason to be here now. I'm going home."

It was soon apparent that Roy Wolff's healing was not just physical. His attitude about Christianity was totally changed. For the rest of his life he was a happy man in love with His Lord. Almost every time the church doors were open, he would be there. He started a Sunday School class to share his growing faith with other men. He was always seeking people out to talk about Jesus. Moreover, many chores he had always disliked—like mowing the lawn or gardening—were now a delight to the new creature Roy was.

The tuberculosis never returned, and Roy lived out his life in thanksgiving to God.

After that Virginia has gone on to a remarkable healing ministry. It is quiet but well-grounded. The healing always includes any sickness of the spirit and the deep mind along with the body. Virginia is given such amazing insights into the depths of human personality that recently professional men—doctors and psychiatrists—have been consulting with her about specific patients.

"And every time," Virginia told me, "I learned the same thing I'd learned with my father—that when healing comes, it's because our eyes have been on Jesus one hundred percent. We can get our attention so firmly fixed on the problem or even on the general topic of healing that we get our eyes off the Healer."

This was where Virginia's story showed me that what I had thought was a contradiction between relinquishment and faith was no contradiction at all. In each of the cases mentioned earlier the sufferer was rushing to Jesus as the Source of help. Each one had faith in *Him*. It was His robe they wanted to touch.

Yet Virginia, like the rest of us, is still groping her way with many questions about healing unresolved. If in our early Christian search we pour forth glib and ready answers, in later years we dare not do so. With the earthly loss of two grandchildren still vivid to me, I know there are no easy, simple answers as to why some are healed in this life and some are not.

But we have learned that God's objective is whole men, wholly dependent on Him. So His Spirit will counteract each time we try to tag, categorize, and pigeonhole Him—for instance, in the direction of rules for healing. Obviously, we are to worship Him rather than a set of spiritual laws.

We resist that because laws are pat and predictable, whereas people are not. Since this is true with human persons, then how much more so with God!

Even as Jesus advised us to begin by taking the lowest seat at banquets, so with healing we are well advised to begin with the lowest place.... "Lord, what would You like to tell me about this situation? How do You want me to pray? What do You want me to do?"

Relinquishment and such a seeking prayer will always bring His response. Often it is a surprising response that we could not possibly have anticipated.

The twenty-three-year-old daughter of a close friend of mine had been treated for years for attacks which the doctor tentatively diagnosed as myoclonic seizures (often linked to *petit mal*, a form of epilepsy). The girl's mother was told by the Spirit, "Ask the doctor for a blood sugar test." It turned out that extremely low blood sugar (hypoglycemia) had been responsible for the trouble.

In another less serious case, a woman's leg and back pains were submitted to Jesus. "Your white sandals, look at them," she was told. The left sandal had a strap across the instep so tight that it was interfering with circulation. "Throw the sandals away," came the simple, practical order. She obeyed and the pains were gone by the next day.

Does this seem too simple, too obvious even to mention? Not when we understand that our Lord was a carpenter who wore sandals and who knows all about the mundane details of our lives. Often we miss the wisdom He seeks to give us because we are so intent on the high-flown superspirituality of our preconceived image of Christ.

Through all of this we need to be careful not to confuse what the old egocentric self wants—to succeed, to get well, to be loved—with that positive, trusting, obedient attitude that wants only God's will for us...

> Self will turns the eyes on self and what self strongly wants.
> Faith turns the eyes on Christ to ask Him what He wants.
>
> Self will worries about the results.
> Faith worries only about obedience, then leaves the result to Jesus.

Until we have heard His directives regarding a given

situation, we would do well not to assume healing "on general principles" and run out ahead of the Lord trying to claim healing anyway. If we do, we'll be guilty of the sin of presumption, and not even Jesus—the Son of God—ever dared presume on the Father.[13]

Then how can we tell the difference between presumption and faith? Presumption assumes something to be true in the absence of God's proof to the contrary. Faith hears and receives God's word first-hand via the Spirit speaking to our spirit, and moves forward only on that word.

Jesus meant it when He said, "The Son... does only what He sees the Father doing." [14] Notice the word "only" in Jesus' statement. That's altogether different from doing something because God hasn't said not to do it. The latter road is a tangled maze of errors, mapped out by Satan. When we run out ahead of God, an element of daring God and of boldness bordering on impertinence, even unbelief, enters the situation.

But then when we *have* gotten His directives and obeyed them, we no longer have to carry the responsibility for the results. Jesus is the Healer. The results are His.

There will be times when the results are not what we yearn for: not all for whom we pray are restored to health. Honesty and honest sharing is necessary here. The skeptic has a point when he accuses some Christians of sweeping negative experiences under the rug. True, but I have never known a hospital to shut down because it lost some patients. Despite disappointments, the Christian is obligated to pray for the sick because we are bidden to do so [15] and because the crumb of our caring is but a morsel broken from the whole loaf of the Father's infinite and tender love.

With our eyes fixed on Jesus we go forward, knowing that the time will come when the whole person—body and spirit and mind—will be presented unto Him faultless, without spot or blemish.

11

The King's Treasury

Some years ago a physician's wife took issue with something I had written about daring to trust God for material and physical needs. "That's being selfish," she remonstrated, "and self-centered prayers just aren't answered. I don't think we have any right to pray about anything but *spiritual* things. Besides, the Bible says that God knows what we need before we ask Him, so why should we ask?"

The God I know does not want us to divide life up into compartments—"This part is spiritual, so this is God's province, but that part over there is physical, so I'll have to handle that myself." If we are to believe Jesus, His Father and our Father is the God of all life and His caring and provision include a sheepherder's lost lamb, a falling sparrow, a sick child, the hunger pangs of a crowd of four thousand, the need for wine at a wedding feast, and the plight of professional fishermen who toiled all night and caught nothing. These vignettes, scattered through the Gospels like little patches of gold dust, say to us, "No creaturely need is outside the scope or range of prayer."

The experience of Edith and Francis Schaeffer beautifully illustrates how material, physical, and spiritual needs are all part of a whole. I first became aware of this couple through reading Francis Schaeffer's *The God Who Is There* in 1971, followed by Edith Schaeffer's *L'Abri*.

In 1945 Dr. Schaeffer, theologian and philosopher, was a pastor in Grove City, Pennsylvania, when he was asked to go to Europe to make a study of the condition of Protestant Christianity. He visited thirteen countries in thirteen weeks, encountering such need as he had never seen and finding this a searing spiritual and emotional experience. Dr. Schaeffer was more deeply stirred by Europe's postwar spiritual devastation than by the shell holes and bombed-out buildings.

Then in August 1953 he became convinced that God was calling him and his family to a higher level of giving, working, and sacrifice; to give up the security of a fixed income for an uncertain, nonstructured work in Europe, possibly with a Swiss base.

After reading Edith Schaeffer's account of all this and pondering it, what interested me was that as the Schaeffers moved on to that higher level of obedience and commitment, God's supply started to work in their lives in a different way—what I choose to call supernaturally. I wondered if I wasn't glimpsing an important principle here.

With a wife and four children to provide for, Dr. Schaeffer knew that this had to be a family decision and a family commitment. As the spiritual head of his home, Francis Schaeffer laid out before his wife Edith and their children all the alternatives. The decision was unanimous—they would say "Yes" to God's call and depend on Him to supply the $1800 the six of them needed for the boat fare to Europe. However, circumstances had created a deadline; if the Schaeffers were to go, they would have to have all of the $1800 in just three weeks, by September 9th when the boat sailed.

Their daughter Priscilla painted a big thermometer on a

poster. Within a few days the poster was beginning to show a red line depicting the money received. Opening the mail became the most exciting event of each day. Checks began arriving from the most unexpected sources, most of them for small amounts. The red line on Priscilla's thermometer kept rising. God was giving the Schaeffers a foretaste of what was to become a way of life for this family—trusting the "God who is there" to supply whatever they needed.

Years afterward, Edith Schaeffer would explain this more fully:

> What happens when you pray? God is all-powerful in every realm.... One way in which He works is to "move" in the realm of men's minds.... God can cause someone to feel a strong "urge" or "conviction" to do something. So when we pray for a certain amount of money, God can cause one person to reach for a checkbook and send that amount, or He can cause a dozen people to send odd fractions of that amount, causing the total to be exact. ... When that kind of thing happens, you know that you have contacted a *Person* who has replied.[1]

In those days of late August and early September 1953, God the Person replied. During the three weeks, all of the $1800 arrived. It was the opening door to the work that became L'Abri (meaning "the shelter"), a Christian evangelical community in the tiny village of Huémoz high in the Swiss Alps.

In reading *The God Who Is There*[2] I had been intrigued by two strong features of Dr. Schaeffer's approach not usually found in the same person: he is a conservative, committed evangelical who stands upon all the major tenets of the Christian faith, yet his appeal is to the intellect rather than to the emotions.

The notion that we must throw away human reason for leaps of faith in the dark is anathema to Francis Schaeffer. Did not the God who is there create man's intellectual equipment—the ability to think, to reason, to plan, to will?

If this seems to be a flouting of the danger of going the Thomas Aquinas route of deifying reason, Dr. Schaeffer's answer is that when Christ redeems us, He redeems the mind along with the rest of us. We have exchanged our fallen intellect for that mind "which was also in Christ Jesus." [3] After that, we are not to belittle or throw away the intellect but keep it subject to Christ who nourishes and upbuilds it, and to His truth revealed in Scripture.

Extremely knowledgeable about the world's major figures who have molded philosophic thought-forms—such as Aquinas, Calvin, Kant, Rousseau, Hegel, Kierkegaard, Barth, Jaspers, Sartre, Heidegger—Doctor Schaeffer speaks especially to the young, who so often these days are not aware that any intelligent educated person can believe the Bible to be true. Emphasizing "content" (one of his favorite words), he is fond of saying that "honest questions deserve honest answers" rather than the usual dodge, "Don't question, just believe."

I kept hearing that the L'Abri community had become one of the favorite haunts for agnostics, atheists, scientists, and intellectuals, seekers of all nationalities and types— especially the young. But in just fifteen years how had it grown from this one family with no material resources into such a world-renowned community? In the summer of 1972 my husband Len and I decided to find out for ourselves.

That August we flew from New York to Geneva, planning to go on to see the Schaeffers the next day. But even before we got to L'Abri, we had a foolish little experience that pointed up in a ludicrous way a larger truth we would learn later on.

We started out from Geneva for L'Abri in a rented Fiat on a very warm afternoon. All along the road we passed bicyclists and back-packers. I wondered if many of them were also going to L'Abri. If so, how had the Schaeffers handled and supplied so many transients all those years?

With Geneva an hour behind us, Len, quite thirsty,

spotted a filling station with a row of refreshment machines
and turned confidently into it.

"Swiss francs?" He held out his hand and I dutifully
supplied several coins from the envelope marked "Switzerland" out of the packets of foreign change we had purchased before leaving New York.

Len put a coin in the dispenser, then looked puzzled
when no drink appeared. He pushed levers, fished around
in the coin return, pounded the machine with his fist.
Nothing. He shrugged, put in another coin, and tried
again. Still nothing. Glowering now at the bright-red
machine, he gave up and walked over to seek out the
station attendant.

Len said a few words in English, gesturing toward the
offending machine. The attendant first shrugged, then
scowled and began whipping the air with his hands as words
in French poured from him. *"Voilà—mais Monsieur,
naturellement cette machine marche—"*

"Marche? Not on your life! That machine isn't marching.
It's not going anywhere or doing anything. It's broken."

"Brok-en? *Ah, non, Monsieur. L'inspecteur l'a verifié
hier. Vous vous êtes trompé."*

"Trompé? That's what I feel like—tromping on it." Then,
taking a new grip on his patience, Len said slowly, "Now
look, I put in a franc just like it said."

"Montrez-moi les francs dans votre main—"

Len held out the Swiss coins. The man took one look.
"Mon dieu!" He raised his arms heavenwards. *"Monsieur,
c'est la France. Vous—êtes—en France."*

"France!" Len looked incredulous. "I thought this was
Switzerland. How can we be in France? We weren't
stopped at any border."

The man merely grinned as he turned the palms of his
hands outward. *"Oui,* Monsieur, France. *La machine ne
prend que de francs français."*

Len grinned too—weakly—and we drove off, two
thoroughly cowed and still thirsty Americans. Sure

enough, there on the map I saw that a corridor of France ran for forty-five miles along the southern shores of Lake Geneva. French officials simply didn't bother to check passports in and out of this small section of their country.

The absurd experience of the Drink Machine that Wouldn't kept nagging at my mind. Then in simplest terms I saw it: thirsty, we had needed a drink. Not realizing what country we were in, we had sought to buy what was needed in the coin of another realm.

Just so, many of us—even Christians—not realizing that we are living in the kingdom of God on earth, try to buy the fulfillment of our needs with the coin of another realm—earth's coinage, not God's. It doesn't work, any more than the stubborn red drink machine would work.

The Schaeffers seemed to be living in God's kingdom using the coin of that realm. I was eager to see with my own eyes what the coin was and how it worked.

By the time we reached Ollon, now back in Switzerland, the road had begun to climb. Suddenly we were in the tiny remote village of Huémoz. All around us were sparkling sunshine and brilliant flowers cascading from balconies and windows of Alpine chalets. A sharp turn up a steep driveway and we were at Chalet les Mélèzes.

It was a surprise to see that Dr. Schaeffer, born an American, had become so European in appearance, rather like some philosopher-hermit out of the Middle Ages. Not a tall man, his gray hair is casually cut and he wore a trim gray goatee. Kindly intelligent brown eyes dominated his face. He was fond of wearing baggy Swiss tweed knickerbockers, long woolen socks, and brogue-type shoes that should by all rights have been ornamented by a silver buckle.

Edith Schaeffer was a more vivacious, gregarious version of her philosopher-husband. Her mind, her speech, and her body seemed ceaselessly active. As individualistic as her husband, she wore her long dark hair combed straight back, loosely twisted into a chignon. More often than not she was a study in browns—her deep brown eyes set off by one of the brown dresses she is fond of wearing.

Their community consisted of one small church and a series of chalets scattered throughout the village. When Len and I attended the Sunday morning service we saw first-hand what a world crossroads L'Abri really is.

To the pealing of myriad church bells across the valley, we arrived at the church thirty-five minutes early. Even so, we were fortunate to get a seat. The interior was paneled with honey-colored wood; there was a large stone fireplace and a Flentrop organ. Wide windows opened inward to reveal a panoramic view of the Rhône Valley with the peaks of the Dents du Midi in the distance.

When all seats were taken, worshipers sat on the floor before the platform. There were boys and girls in dungarees with knapsacks beside them, together with little girls in fluffy white dresses. A man from India cast off his sandals before he sat on the floor cross-legged alongside a woman garbed in an expensive green pants suit.

With seemingly every inch of the floor covered with bodies, I sat there wondering how the preacher would ever make it to his pulpit. By then the balcony was filled with those who would listen through the open windows. People were even sitting on the platform floor.

Dr. Schaeffer entered and began carefully threading his way between the people, pausing to pat the heads of children, beaming on the hippies and jet-set types, obviously delighted with what he saw. The service was simple, joyful; the message, a penetrating look at Christian commitment.

Our first few hours at L'Abri provided the initial clue as to how God provides material resources for those living in His kingdom on earth: the Schaeffers' part was a total self-giving with every inch of space, every scrap of food, every last franc, every quarter-hour and vestige of strength.

Dr. Schaeffer still had no office, nowhere to work privately
except the bedroom.[4] It is a rare night one finds no
youngsters sleeping on Mrs. Schaeffer's kitchen floor.

That Sunday, as usual, Edith Schaeffer herself cooked a
three-course meal for forty-five people. We were seated at
tables so crowded that the plates of food had to be passed
overhead, then from hand to hand.

During that Sunday meal we heard incredible human-
interest stories of how so many different individuals had
gotten to L'Abri. This is a working out of the second of the
four prayer principles on which L'Abri is grounded: that
God will bring the people of His choice to the community.
This too depends on prayer alone; L'Abri had never put out
any advertising leaflets.

The four principles are:

1. Financial and material needs will be made known to
God alone, in prayer, in lieu of sending out any pleas for
money.

2. That God will send the people of His choice to L'Abri
for work and study.

3. That God will plan the work and unfold His plan day
by day. (This is in place of planning for the future in the
usual "efficient way," such as committee meetings.)

4. That God will send the staff and workers of His choice
for the community rather than L'Abri seeking them
through the usual channels of solicitation or pleading.

Here then, was a most important coin of the kingdom—
giving God and His ongoing work priority in one's life.
Jesus stated it like this, giving us a command followed by a
promise:

Seek ye first the kingdom of God and his righteousness;
and all these *things* shall be added unto you.[5]

An example of how magnificently God fulfilled His

promise by handling the Schaeffer family's needs is the story of their acquiring the Chalet les Mélèzes. In 1955 they needed $7,366 by May 30th for the final payment on the chalet. Eight days before the deadline they had exactly $4,915.69. Once again Priscilla had made one of her thermometers. The family felt that God had led them to this particular chalet, though speaking humanly (in dollars and cents) purchasing it seemed impossible. Yet each mail brought them unsolicited checks so that the red line on the thermometer kept rising.

There were times when it seemed that the suspense would be more than they could bear. Many a man who has lived by faith has testified that though God moves slowly, He never moves too late. Nevertheless, by breakfast on May 30th, the day the payment was due, the family still lacked over 800 Swiss francs. The last mail was due at eleven o'clock in the morning. Dr. Schaeffer would need to take the two o'clock bus in order to make the required payment. In that last mail there arrived fifteen gifts. When letters were opened, the total filled in the gap on Priscilla's thermometer—exactly $7,366. God had done it again! Jubilantly, the family went to their makeshift living room to pray their thanksgiving.

When Dr. Schaeffer caught the yellow bus for Aigle that afternoon, he was lacking only the notary's fee, and he did not know how much that would be. As he arrived at the Notary's office, he found a special delivery letter awaiting him. Thinking how extraordinary it was for a letter to be sent there, he tore it open to find a letter of encouragement from Mr. X—along with the last check: "Enclosed is something that will give me a small share in the purchase of the house today." That gift was the precise amount of the notary's fee—300 Swiss francs.

In Edith Schaeffer's own words to me, "The miracle was the exactness and the timing and God's arithmetic."

After the family was settled in the Chalet les Mélèzes and had time to appraise what had happened, the totality of it seemed even more remarkable. Over a two-month period, 157 gifts had been sent from all over the world. No giver had any way of knowing how the amount of his gift would fit into the total needed. The smallest gift had been one dollar; the largest, $225, with the exception of a single check for $1,000. Yet the total was so exact and the timing so perfect even though many of the gifts had come from far-flung places. Not only that, but after May 30th the gifts stopped as miraculously as they had started. Not another gift came for the house.

Francis Schaeffer would be the last one to say that he and his family are living by faith in order to prove something to the world about God. The God who is there has no need of vindication by His creatures. Rather, for the Schaeffers it has been a matter of obedience: this is the way God has called them to live.

Why had God chosen to ask this of the Schaeffers—and then proceeded to supply their every need? Here is the heart of their prayer-miracle of supply: they could ask and confidently expect *because they had given everything in advance.* After a few hours at L'Abri, one realizes that Edith and Francis Schaeffer have long since laid everything on the altar, even their privacy.

Why? In Dr. Schaeffer's words, "What we seek supremely here in the L'Abri community is to exhibit in some poor fashion the love of God and the holiness of God simultaneously in the whole spectrum of life."

Even in our short visit Len and I felt God's love as all feel it at L'Abri. We sensed Edith and Francis Schaeffer's deep concern and interest in the young people, especially the hippies and the floaters. They care passionately, totally, with utter self-giving about those who don't know what to believe, who have lost their way in life. That there is truth to be found in the Scripture, that God will see to it that we have that truth—that is the fire in their souls, the light in their eyes, the ring in their voices.

As Len and I were leaving, we witnessed a little scene

that remains in my memory as a miniature parable of L'Abri. Walking along with Dr. Schaeffer as he waxed eloquent on some point of homiletics, we were stopped by a little boy outside one of the chalets. He was crying over his tricycle; a wheel had come off. Instantly, the child had Francis Schaeffer's full attention.

First, some comfort tendered by one obviously on the child's wave length. Then a careful examination of the wheel. "Matthew, come here and let's talk about it," Dr. Schaeffer said, drawing the boy into his arms. "Now, I want to show you. I've put the wheel back on, but see this end here?—it's not going to stay on. See, you've lost a part— right here. Understand that?"

The child nodded gravely.

"Now, Matthew, the minute your father comes home this afternoon, you show him what you and I did and ask him please to fix the wheel so it will stay. Will you do that?"

"Oh, *yes!*"

"So, Matthew, ride very carefully now."

Exhibiting the love of God in the whole spectrum of life.

A s we take our first timid steps in God's kingdom, we will begin to find the principle of God's supply working for us too.

"But," most of us think, "I'm not as committed as the Schaeffers." True, but we have to begin where we are.

As long as we have a low threshold of expectation limited to our needs and those of our immediate family, we probably won't turn to God for help in this area; our own efforts will handle it. But when we, in obedience to God, decide to be totally His person at His disposal and take on some enormous task He requires of us, then we are going to find ourselves thrown upon His unlimited supply.

Negative situations throw us upon God's supply when we have made a mess of our emotional or financial or material situations. Perhaps we have abused our body or our relationships; perhaps we have family problems, are in debt or some other sorry predicament. In this plight we long to know how God's unlimited supply can start flowing in our direction.

How God supplies is spelled out for us in Scripture. Beyond that, we have the accumulated wisdom of men and women who have tested out those Scriptural principles and promises over the centuries and can provide us with so many illustrations of how faithful God is.

The first step is to get our eyes off our own need, to look instead at God's unlimited supply. One of Christ's fundamental premises was that God the Father controls all of earth's material resources. Simple words, but what a tremendous assertion! Most of us do not really believe this at all. Yet the Bible emphatically declares it:

> The earth is the Lord's, and the fullness thereof.... [6]

Then we are assured that we are beloved children of this King:

> Behold, what manner of love the Father hath bestowed upon us, that we should be called the sons of God.... [7]

Since we are His children and all the world's riches belong to the King, it follows that He can and will take care of our physical needs:

> But my God shall supply all your needs according to His riches.... [8]

So if we really believed that we are children of the King and that we can trust Him to supply all our needs out of His unlimited supply, there would be no reason for a greedy storing up of things. There would be no fear about inflation or money shortages, for fearing would be a sure sign that we did not believe God's ownership of earth's resources. It would be wrong to have a "poverty complex," because to think ourselves paupers is to deny either the King's riches or to impugn our being a child of that King.

To call our Father in heaven a King, in my opinion, is to understate the truth. Consider the prodigality of the Father's world. He did not create a single kind of fern, but some 10,000 kinds; not one type of palm tree, but 1500 different palms. Not one insect, but 625,000 and more that scientists have not yet named. Astronomers now estimate that there are a hundred billion galaxies of stars in the universe, of which earth's Milky Way is but one: There are a million galaxies inside the bowl of the Big Dipper alone.[9] No poverty complex in the Creator of such infinitude!

The magnificence of His handiwork is seen in the tumbling seas, in a sunset slashing the Grand Canyon of the Colorado. Ride to the top of the mountain at St. Moritz, gasp with awe at the snow-covered panorama of rugged peaks spread out at one's feet. Or see the turquoises and blues in the waters around Moorea and Bora-Bora in the South Seas, colors so intense that no painter could capture them on canvas.

How much of this beauty we bring into our homes and our lives is limited only by our appreciation and desire for it and our faith in the King's ability to supply us. Yet always, this must be a personal discovery. The second step in discovering how to become a good receiver of the King's bounty is to invite Jesus into our need. As we see our situation through His eyes we begin to understand how intensely practical God is in dealing with us, His carnate creatures.

Reflecting that practicality, Jesus' directives to us are always specific, never vague and generalized. He would not allow those who came running after Him wailing, "Lord, have mercy," to stop there; He was forever forcing them out of this "general blessing" area by asking questions like "What do you want Me to do for you?" [10] In other words, "Use your mind, my son. Make up your heart. God is not the Father of sloppy thinking. Nor is He the Lord of generalizing."

At first glance it may seem odd that the more extensive our need, the more important it is to get God's guidance on pinpointing where and how He wants His supply to come to us. It's as if once we find the first right thread to pull, the whole of our tangled problem begins to unravel.

On a certain December day in 1931, an Oregon schoolteacher, Rebecca Euland, found that key thread to pull for her migrant pupil, Billie. It seemed to Miss Euland that the undernourished girl was the victim of more deprivation than any child she had ever known. She thought of that no-breakfast morning when Billie had fainted. Why, the child even lacked shoes. Into the teacher's mind came a picture of the girl's high-laced canvas shoes, 50 cents at the dime store, worn winter and summer. Billie had never slept on a bed, just on a pallet in the family tent beside eight other members of the family. Tangled hair told her that the camper-child was lacking a comb; she also, the teacher suspected, was without a toothbrush.

"What can *I* do?" the teacher wondered. "With my small salary, how can I make a dent in poverty like that?"

The answer came that same day when Miss Euland noticed Billie squinting over her English book. All at once she was reminded of herself at about the same age. That realization was like a light going on in her mind. Yes, she knew what to do.

That weekend she took Billie to a nice restaurant for lunch, then to an appointment with her own eye doctor. A few days later, Miss Euland pressed into her pupil's hand shiny eyeglasses in a handsome case.

"But I've no money for glasses," Billie protested.

"You don't need to have any," came the reply. "Sit down and I'll tell you a story.... When I was your age I needed glasses too. So a kind neighbor took me to lunch, then for an eye examination, just as I took you. She told me that someday I was to pay for them by getting glasses for some other child. So you see, Billie, your glasses were paid for long ago. Some day," she concluded, "you will pay for the glasses of yet another little girl."

The future would underscore what Billie realized even then.... Her teacher had given her not only eyeglasses but an even greater gift: her faith that Billie would not always be a subpoverty camper-child, that some day she would be in a position to give to others.

How right Miss Euland was! After some forty different schools near migrant camps, Billie graduated from East Bakersfield (California) High School in 1941, then from Drury College, summa cum laude. Much of the work on her doctorate has been completed. As an author, a lecturer much in demand, an educator, Billie has seen seemingly impossible dreams become reality. The one closest to her heart is the fulfillment of Miss Euland's prophecy, "Some day you will pay for the glasses of yet another little girl."

In 1961 Billie and her husband George Davis were led all the way to Central America to find that particular little girl. Her name was Gloria, a tiny seven-year-old from Costa Rica. The child, born of banana pickers on a plantation near Golfito, weighed only 29 pounds. Her teeth were bloody from malnutrition.

Gloria was legally adopted by the Davises, and it has been Billie Davis' joy to pass on to her not only educational advantages, but also her strong conviction about the power and fulfillment implicit in giving.

Recently, over lunch in our home, I heard Mrs. Davis describe her new adventure as Director of the High School Equivalency Program (HEP) under the United States Department of Labor. In this role, she has become one of the government's Lady Bountifuls to give opportunities for education and job training to many young migrants. Not even Miss Euland could have imagined such glorious fulfillment of giving for her pupil!

Today, looking back to that 1931 turning point Billie Davis realizes that her teacher's faith in one child's future was really part of a larger dimension: faith that the King means for each one of His children to have the fulfillment of becoming a "giving person" with riches of mind and spirit and substance to lavish on others. Once we have that faith, then we are ready to begin using the coin of God's kingdom. He told us what another important coin is: *to receive, one must give, even out of poverty.*

> Give, and it shall be given unto you: good measure, pressed down, and shaken together and running over, shall men give into your bosom. For with the same measure that ye mete withal, it shall be measured to you again.[11]

This is not only a promise, but a fact of the Father's world, part of the rhythm of the universe. In the last century every farmer knew it as he primed the pump by pouring a bucket of water in to start the water flowing. We feel it each time we stand on an ocean beach and feel the tugging rhythm of the tide washing the sand beneath our feet. We experience it when we step out on God's promise and to our astonishment discover that our Father will never allow Himself to be in debt to any child of His.

Here is an exciting principle for all those in life's holes. Of what do we have a shortage? Money? Household possessions? Ideas? Friends? Love? Prayer-power? Creativity? Strength? Health? Whatever it is, when we, under God's direction, give away out of our shortage, like the tide returning we get back abundance—"good measure, pressed down, running over."

There was a time back in 1964 when Ellie Armstrong would have said she had nothing to give—least of all money. With faith and almost no cash she had attempted to buy a $64,000 motel on U.S. Route 6 in the rolling hills of western Pennsylvania.

Ellie knew the truth, that when we set our eyes on Jesus and in obedience attempt a big task for Him, we can trust

Him for supply. It was in that framework that she was praying for this motel.

The dream she was given was a motel where Jesus would be the Host. There weary travelers could find a spiritual oasis in their travels. More importantly, people who might not have heard about Him and would not go near a church could meet Him there.

I have visited the Port Allegheny Motel, read the inspirational literature Ellie puts in the rooms, and heard story after story of travelers helped and healed of problems and hang-ups and physical ailments as incredible dividends to their good night's sleep. Each of the fourteen motel units has been dedicated to God for a specific purpose, such as a room for healing, a special room for honeymooners, one for alcoholics, another for the mending of broken relationships, the happiness room. When each traveler checks in, Ellie asks the Host which room He wants them in, then asks Him to be present in that room to meet the guest at his point of need.

But for Eleanor Armstrong, it took many a time of testing, many a crisis situation before her dream about the motel could be fulfilled. She had to learn to live in a state of financial dependence as constant as that of the Schaeffers. When Ellie acquired the motel, one of her prayer-requests had been that she would never fail to meet a mortgage payment on time. One midwinter a $300 mortgage payment was due in a few days and she had only $50 to her name. To make it worse, this was off-season and for five consecutive nights not a single car had stopped at the motel.

Ellie began to pray. At last an inner voice seemed to tell her: "Send the $50 to Dave Wilkerson in New York for his work with young drug addicts." Ellie was as startled as any of us would have been. Surely this was not the time to give away money! But the inner Voice had been very clear. She mailed off the $50 that afternoon to Mr. Wilkerson. That same night nine cars came in, one right after another. As she stood behind the hotel register, she shook her head wonderingly as she remembered Jesus' words, "Give, and it shall be given unto you."

The rest of the week the motel was filled to capacity. The mortgage money was paid on time. Ten years of blessings have followed for the Port Motel as a business venture and as a ministry to wayfarers.

Knowing about this second coin of the kingdom, that to receive we must give, helps us to understand the Scriptural admonition to tithe. Tithing was a practice God asked of the Jewish people back in Old Testament times. It means giving to God through giving to others a minimum of one-tenth of one's gross income or harvest or cattle production or whatever. "Minimum" because even as Christ upholds tithing, He also strengthens it by often asking that we give away more than the base ten percent.

In teaching the practice of tithing to the Jews, God was seeing to it that they would have an unending demonstration of how sound the coin of His kingdom is. To buttress this further He gave them—and us—that magnificent promise:

> Bring ye all the tithes into the storehouse, that there may be meat in mine house, and prove me now herewith, saith the Lord of hosts, if I will not open you the windows of heaven, and pour you out a blessing, that there shall not be room enough to receive it.[12]

Notice God's invitation and challenge to each of us to prove Him, to try out tithing. That when we put Him first, we won't have to worry about our supply.

I remember how pointed a challenge this was to me back in early February 1949. In those early weeks after Peter Marshall's sudden death on January 25th, I was still groping to find what God intended the new basis of my life to be. There was that crucial evening when three men had come out to the manse to discuss business matters with me.

"I've worked it all out," the young insurance salesman said, showing me impressive-looking graphs. "From Dr. Marshall's insurance and the Presbyterian Church's pension fund, you'll have a total of $171 a month for the first eight years, then it will drop."

The men were good friends and were trying to be helpful. Yet all that they said that evening added up to a gloomy prognosis indeed: $171 per month wasn't enough to live on in Washington. I had no specific vocational training and uncertain health. They recommended that I sell our car and the Cape Cod cottage. At the end of the evening the men left troubled because they felt I was not worried enough.

They were right. I had heard their words and seen the neat columns of figures and the graphs. Figures didn't lie. Or did they? Deep, deep inside I felt that these three kind men were reckoning without God.

Looking back, I know it was no spiritual strength or virtue of mine that kept me from accepting gloom and doom and sinking into fear. From a few hours before Peter's homegoing to several weeks afterwards, heaven had opened wide and was carrying me over and above all circumstances. That brief experience showed me what it is like to live in the Kingdom of God on earth: it is glory and joy even in pain, and crystal-clear guidance, and oneness with other people, and a giving and receiving of incredible love.

So my guidance was clear, I was to pick up my pen and edit and write. I was to trust God to provide for me and Peter John so completely that, yes, we would tithe even the inadequate $171 a month.

We obeyed, and God provided all right. I did not sell the car or the Cape Cod cottage. Every need was met on time. There were no debts. For Peter John and me it happened precisely as God has promised, the windows of heaven opened and poured out so many blessings that there was scarcely room to receive them.

There is endless fascination in seeing what has happened to individuals who have picked up God's challenge to tithe. A correspondent-friend, Barbara Reynolds, had spent nearly eighteen years in Hiroshima, Japan, as a part of the World Friendship Center ministering to atom bomb survivors and crusading for peace. Meanwhile, Mrs. Reynolds had been offered a scholarship to Pendle Hill, the Quaker study center near Philadelphia. It seemed right to accept. There was only one difficulty: she did not have money for the trip home. It was at this point, she wrote me, that she read Peter Marshall's sermon "Research Unlimited."[13]

I will never forget the challenge that started me on one of the most exciting adventures of my life: "Suppose, for example that a group of Christians decided to experiment with the Lord's exhortation to tithe for one year. What do you suppose the results would be?"

I had never tithed. Quakers don't even pass the collection plate.... Nevertheless, when I finished reading that particular sermon, I felt moved to try.

I began by adding up all the money I had in the world: a few thousand yen in a Hiroshima Bank, a couple of hundred dollars in the United States, and some small change in my purse. I resolved to set aside a tenth in a special purse and the next day, withdrew enough from my bank account to start my Fund for the Lord. I also began to keep a special record of my experiment.

And would you believe it! On January 26th when I began to tithe, I had less than three hundred dollars. When I left Japan two months later (on March 23rd) I was able to turn over, in tithes, more than I had to begin with!

Now, a year later, I can report that the experiment which I began without any particular expectations has developed into a way of life which has opened up amazing and undreamed-of potential.

I'm sure you know that I am *not* speaking of tithing as a

way to get rich quick! No, the amazing effect of my tithing experiment has been twofold: (1) It has completely freed me of the panic fear that used to grip me about being penniless. Now I *know* that my needs will always be supplied. And (2) it has helped me to know the joy of being a channel through which blessings can flow to those around me. The Lord's purse is never empty!

When we give God our unlimited "Yes," then we find in our hands yet a third coin of His realm: *each of us has within himself the clue, the secret, and the potential for everything he will ever need.*

The essence of creativity is to seek Him first, making full use of whatever master coin is yours—to give priority to the Kingdom of God and His righteousness. Then as we begin living in the Kingdom of God on earth, He will show us how to make the best use of our talents. We begin with a seed idea or a seed talent and create something that other people need or enjoy. That plunges us directly into the stream of the Creator's unending creativity and generosity.

This was the truth God was teaching me. When as a widow I was facing what looked like financial extremity, He told me to begin what I had never done before—editing and writing.

The Schaeffers put God's kingdom first by laying lives, time, energy, privacy on the altar to establish L'Abri Community. For over twenty years God has seen to it that all necessary "things" were added unto them.

Billie Davis found that there is no poverty so grim that the King cannot lift us out of it. He showed her how to use even her poverty as her "seed" asset by writing and speaking of it candidly. That sharing of it, such as a *Saturday Evening Post* article[14] now so famous that it is included in English textbooks, led to myriads of opportunities for yet more giving.

Ellie Armstrong was giving God's kingdom and His righteousness priority when by faith, she undertook the motel on Route 6 to minister to wayfarers. For over ten years God has provided the mortgage payments and running expenses and all other "things."

When Barbara Reynolds decided to obey God by tithing, she was taking a first big step toward putting God's kingdom and His ways first. And she has been blessed accordingly.

So I would have to say to that physician's wife who so strenuously objected to any prayer for personal or material needs and to all those who are afraid to pray about money and those other "petty" things—nowhere in Scripture or Christian experience can I find any justification for the idea that prayer should be limited to spiritual needs. So far as I can understand, Jesus taught us quite the opposite.

It is as if God, knowing full well that while we are in these bodies of flesh and blood, we are going to be physical creatures of this earth and earthy, says to us, "There's only one place and one way you can learn of Me, that's just as you are in your present circumstances. Let's deal with your obvious needs and lacks by looking at your assets—no matter how small. I'll show you step by step how to approach Me, how the coinage of My kingdom is put into circulation, how to hand Me your lack and get back My adequacy. What better demonstration of My reality and My love and caring for you could you have? Come, try it.

"Taste and see that the Lord is good. Prove Me!"

12

The Dilemma of Our Rebellion

There they were, six little words, staring up at me from the page of the New Testament: "So do not criticize at all...." [1]

But isn't that a little too easy?, my thoughts went. That would knock out all value judgments, all sifting, all screening. "Do not criticize at all...."? *I don't get it.*

What I really meant was "I resist it." I have always prided myself on my critical ability, enjoying the sizing up and analyzing of people and situations. I did it almost in spite of myself, whether I enjoyed it in a particular instance or not. I identified with the eighteen-year-old girl who recently wrote of her parents and homelife:

We could be called opinionated. Certainly we are a hypercritical family—we don't lavish superlatives on things and places and people. I was raised to look closely, not to accept easily.... I couldn't suspend judgment even when I wanted to: it was as if I went through life with X-ray glasses on, seeing through not just the things I wanted to see through but the things I'd just as soon have believed in too. I was old before my time. . . .

The criticism we applied to everything we encountered we applied to ourselves as well. Never "You are bad," but "You could do better.". . .

The critical faculties my parents gave me have made me more demanding than I should be, given me standards that the real, flawed world can't live up to. . . .[2]

But isn't it good to be observing and analytical, to discuss how things can be improved? I can speak from experience here because I might almost have been this girl. My home training was surprisingly like hers, and for much of it I am grateful. But I have lived a number of years on the other side of eighteen. From my vantage point, I can see the underside—or backlash—of such sharpened critical awareness.

In every situation, this girl and I have fallen into the habit of seeing what's wrong with it, not what's right with it. The good qualities, those things well done, are passed over quickly—in time, scarcely noticed—in order to get on with the critique. All encounters in life, every personality, every institution, every relationship, is a mixture of the good and the bad. When we habitually focus on the bad, we are training ourselves in negativism.

We call it by other names. Looking with such analytical eyes must surely be constructive, we tell ourselves, because what we're really asking is, "How can such-and-such be improved?"

But there is a secret cost in such an outlook to one's spiritual and mental health. In my case, I woke up twenty years into adulthood to find myself deeply schooled in serious negativism. That, in turn, can bathe all of life in emotional gloom. When the habit continues into mid-life or later, the dark glasses of criticalness can lead to long periods of melancholy and even to serious depression.

Exactly this happened to a long-time friend, the author Agnes Sanford. In her case, the depression led to emotional disturbance and thoughts of suicide. In writing of this in her recent autobiography, Mrs. Sanford refers to her escape from this pit of chronic depression as the major healing of her life. But what first caught my attention was her account of how the seeds of the near-disastrous negativism were planted. The setting was Yangcheng in northern China where the young Agnes's parents were Presbyterian missionaries. On any given Sunday, there would be worship at the Union Church....

> But on the long homeward drag, my heart would sink, for I dreaded the Sunday dinner.... The grown people's Sunday sport was the tearing apart of the sermon phrase by phrase and argument by argument. Dr. Harry Emerson Fosdick once preached at our church, and fragments of his sermon were scattered over every course.
>
> Dr. Fosdick preached on Christian love, but he was not *sound* because he did not mention the Blood of the Lamb in about every third sentence. This went on and on until finally I burst into tears and left the table, to the utter consternation of my parents....
>
> What was the trouble? I could not tell them. I did not know. They were good, they were completely Christ-centered...but something was *wrong.*[3]

In Agnes Sanford's words, supercriticalness was "a breaking of the bonds of love." By her teen years, she was beginning to experience the consequences:

> The deep dissatisfaction with life and with God that had begun in me at age eleven was growing. Something was lacking, not only in life, but in me.... I remembered the days when I had come home by the high-road, literally dancing, my feet hardly touching the ground for joy. And thought, "That was the joy of childhood. Grown people never feel like that." Thank God I was wrong!

Yet it was to be many years before Agnes Sanford would be healed of depression and would finally rediscover joy.

The insistence upon picking apart, upon pronouncing judgment, which Agnes recalls from her childhood, is by no means unusual in missionaries' and ministers' families. We Protestants especially belong to a tradition which imposes on every Christian not only the right but the duty to judge every word spoken from the pulpit or printed between the covers of a book. Doubtless this has served as a necessary corrective in the long history of the Church. But the effect of this constant vigilance upon individuals—and whole denominations—can also be a deficiency of love and a lack of joy.

And it is not only Christians who almost from the cradle are taught to be criticizers. It is not only the spirit of the Renaissance and the Reformation in our religion, but the spirit of eighteenth-century rationalism in our politics which encourages every American to be judge of the men and events around him. Our national heroes, the founders of our country, were precisely those men who refused to accept unquestioningly the world as they found it.

The two hundred years since then have trained us that an uncritical populace is a populace in peril. As in religion, so in the secular world: "eternal vigilance" is the price of what we hold dear. From school days on, each citizen must be responsible, must inform himself, must stay on top of issues.

I wonder if we who form judgments of people and issues over our morning coffee realize how unique in the experience of the world is our concept of good citizenship. In most places on the globe even today people are trained in a kind of docile numb acceptance which is the very opposite of the critical spirit.

During a trip to the Middle East, our party of four took a three-and-a-half-hour drive in Jordan with a guide—clearly an intelligent, well-informed man. In the course of the long trip we asked him a single political question, something about King Hussein and an important meeting to be held that week.

The guide's face went as blank as though a sponge had gone across it. "Oh," he said with finality, "I don't think about those things."

He didn't sound like someone who had been intimidated into silence. His attitude seemed merely to reflect that of the society in which he had grown up. "These are not my affairs."

The opposite, democracy's insistence on each citizen's responsibility to be informed and to judge, is accepted throughout western Europe and North America as a positive thing. Yet judging can also have a negative side. Just as the missionary groups in China (which Agnes Sanford knew so well) regarded themselves as knowledgeable "sermon tasters" and experts in theology, so most of us Americans consider ourselves expert armchair politicians. The result is that any man in public office gets sniped at continually by the public and the press. All of us can be grateful for a free press made operative by reporters like the two *Washington Post* newsmen who, in the face of incredible pressure to "let sleeping dogs lie," brought the Watergate offenses to the attention of the nation.

And yet I recall during the years I lived in Washington, especially during the McCarthy era, more than one man's career was ruined by innuendo, character assassination, and blacklisting. Sometimes the news media seemed to thrive on it—not a needed exposé of wrongdoing, but criticism because criticism is one of our national sports. It can be a dangerous sport.

Critics and protestors insist that dissent is for some good end—"for the exploited"—"for peace"—"for liberalizing university rules." Behind that insistence is the conviction, blown up into a philosophy, that insubordination—mild to violent—is the best technique for reform, a healthy process for necessary change. How often I have felt that way as I have agonized over child labor, the living conditions of migrant workers, our inhuman treatment of the insane, the slum conditions of our inner cities.

Sunday afternoons during college days I used to go with a group who visited in the tenements (since torn down) around the State Capitol building in Atlanta, Georgia. My journal reflects my shock and dismay:

> I had dimly realized that places like that existed, but had never seen any before—squalid, miserable, dirty, ill-ventilated. The broken windowpanes stuffed with paper; the sick child doubled up on the dirty bed; the absurdly young mother wearing red ankle socks of which she was so proud, nursing her baby before us; the drunk woman; the crying children....

If protest rallies and sit-ins at legislators' offices had been the style among college students then, I would have been part of them.

Years afterward our family ran head-on into one of those injustices in our society that scream for reform. In 1956, soon after my mother and father retired to Evergreen Farm in Loudoun County, Virginia, Hank Reid, our black tenant-farmer, was caught in a classic loan-shark trap. The manager of the loan company telephoned saying that they would repossess the Reids' household goods unless their debt was paid up within twenty-four hours.

We managed to postpone the immediate crisis, then dug in to appraise the situation. The original loan, taken out two and a half years before, had not been large; incredibly the loan company claimed Hank now owed twice that much. The apparent interest rate was only 3½ percent, but a clause hidden in fine print enabled the loan company to figure the interest charge each month. That made the real annual percentage rate 36 percent. If Hank defaulted a month's payment, the interest for that month was added to the principal and future interest figured on the total. He could never get out of debt.

What was wrong with our laws, I raged, that exempted dishonest outfits of this type from the Small Loan Act and the strict supervision of bank inspectors? Regularly I drove past a cluster of them with flashing neon signs just across the Key Bridge into Arlington. "Quick cash"... "Get your bills paid." The bait dangled hiding the hook.

Hank's plight turned into a family crusade. We made the loan company a proposition: we would pay the total (then take it gradually out of Hank's wages) provided that total was reduced to a fair figure. They refused. We peppered them with letters and phone calls. One morning I was astonished to hear my gentle mother scornfully telling the head of the loan company, "I marvel that you can hold up your head in public, preying on the poor and those who don't know better. You're no gentleman, you're a—a——" Here her vocabulary failed. "Horsewhipping would be too good for you."

Finally the man buckled. We paid, demanding a receipt declaring Hank completely free of debt.

And yet there they were, each time I drove into Washington, those neon signs challenging me: what are you doing to root out this evil from your community? One family had slipped through the net so cunningly laid; how many thousands were trapped for the duration of their working lives unless people with typewriters, an education, with acquaintances in the government, mounted some form of protest? How else, my conscience asked me?

"So do not criticize at all." How are we to understand these words? Criticism, protest, even open rebellion, sometimes seem the only ways that essential change can come about. What about the American Revolution—surely there is an example of great good coming out of revolt?

Or... is it? I remember my first dispassionate look at this touchstone of the American experience. It came during college days when I earned part of my tuition by doing clerical tasks for Dr. Philip Davidson, head of the History Department, as he prepared his book *Propagandists of the*

American Revolution. I remember my surprise at the irrefutable evidence of the extent to which propagandists aided by the Liberty Boys deliberately whipped up the inflamed feelings that led to war with England.

That the American colonies should have received a great deal more understanding and eventual independence is unassailable. The question is, were war, revolution, hatred, and bloodshed the best way to achieve needed goals?

Two hundred years later, may we not still be suffering the results in the American temperament? Perhaps the "good" revolution was not as harmless as we like to think. During the last six years when violent crimes in the United States have increased more than 90 percent, many sociologists and historians have been telling us that the seeds of that violence may well have been planted during the very founding of our country. The National Commission on the Causes and Prevention of Violence asserted:

> Our nation was conceived and born in violence—in the violence of the Sons of Liberty and the patriots of the American port cities of the 1760s and 1770s....

These analysts then went on to point out what a large part violence played not only in the launching but in the expansion of the young Republic westward, in our violent and dishonest ways of dealing with the Indians, in the vigilante groups of frontier society. They cite evidence that America's long training in insubordination of the heart is resulting today in a schism-ridden, polarized society with cracks and rifts all through.

Whether analyzing the steps that lead to the breakup of a marriage, or of the high school student who joins a violent revolutionary group, or even what caused the American Revolution—the process goes something like this.... Criticalness leads to discontent. Discontent expels appreciation and gratitude. Self-pity moves in and turns the attention inward; surely self deserves something better, we tell ourselves, such as happiness, prosperity, that its ideas and demánds be heard and implemented. If what self wants will hurt others—spouse, children, parents, store proprietors, educational institutions, bystanders—well, they asked for it in one way or another. Anyhow, the end justifies the means.

But if rebellion has such built-in dangers, how can necessary change come about?

It is at this point that we can see a clear parting of the ways between the philosophy of dissent and the wisdom of Jesus of Nazareth. How else could we view statement after statement of Christ's? ...

"Thou shalt not kill." [4]

Then said Jesus unto him, "Put up again thy sword into his place; for all they that take the sword shall perish with the sword." [5]

"Whosoever is angry with his brother... shall be in danger of the judgment... whosoever shall say, Thou fool, shall be in danger of hell fire." [6]

"Agree with thine adversary quickly, while thou art in the way with him...." [7]

"If ye forgive not men their trespasses, neither will your Father forgive your trespasses." [8]

"Try to show as much compassion as your Father does. Never criticize or condemn—or it will all come back on you." [9]

Yet no one accuses Jesus of a Pollyanna attitude toward the evil and injustice of His time. His fury at the perfidious money changers was a form of violent protest, no question about it.

Studying Jesus' response to evil I began to see three guide lines. First is the question of motivation. We see into the heart of Jesus' motive in one of the most beautiful verses in the New Testament:

> Thou [Christ] hast loved righteousness, and hated in-
> iquity: therefore Cod, even thy God, hath anointed thee
> with the oil of gladness above thy fellows.[10]

"Loving righteousness," in His case came before "hating
iniquity." Does it, I wondered, in our crusades and causes?
When we go forth to stamp out sin, disease, poverty,
oppression—as He did—do we keep uppermost in our
minds the heart-stirring vision of the world as God intended it to be? Or does hatred of the enemy we are
opposing gradually fill our horizon?

Then second, He gave us the love test:

> "Listen all of you. Love your enemies. Do good to those
> who hate you...." [11]

Here Christ was making a clear distinction between the
iniquity which He hated and the sinner who, even though
his own will was responsible for his sin, was nevertheless
now the victim of it, bound by it. I saw only too clearly why
I could never, relying on my own strength, launch a "just"
campaign against the loan-shark industry: my reaction to
these businessmen falls so far short of love. Indeed, this
command to love our enemies is often not possible for us
worldlings; it is a miracle God Himself has to work in the
human heart.

Therefore, the third guide line follows inevitably. In the
end Jesus chose God's way, not man's, to deal with the
iniquity He loathed. Judas Iscariot wanted his Master to
use the world's technique by rebelling against Rome. Judas,
the classic revolutionary, wanted armed political rebellion
against the godless forces of Rome. Jesus deliberately
refused, thereby telling us for all time, "No, the end does
not justify the means." He chose instead God's way of
changing men's hearts and minds and lives via the Cross.

Certainly we cannot "love righteousness" and "hate
iniquity," then use any of iniquity's techniques. Those who

recognize in Jesus of Nazareth the First Rebel, see equally
that His weapons were never those of unrighteousness. He
will never allow us to do evil with the claim that it's to
achieve justice or right.

Part of the problem here may be that we have not
understood Jesus' way. When I realized that He was
standing against my critical spirit, I felt the need to dig into
the Bible to get its teaching as to what's wrong with
grumbling and revolt. Right away I found the answer to my
questions about that verse which had so startled me, "Do
not criticize at all." I saw too why God regards even the
lowest rung of protest—complaining and grumbling—not
as a petty personality flaw, or even as an offense against
another person, but as serious sin against Him directly.
The Apostle Paul wrote stringent words on this.

> And don't murmur against God and his dealings with
> you, as some of them [the Jewish people] did, for that is
> why God sent his Angel to destroy them. All these things
> happened...as object lessons to us—to warn us against
> doing the same things; they were written down so that we
> could read about them and learn from them....[12]

I found that "all these things" in this passage referred
back to the Books of Exodus and Numbers. We read there
how God had tapped the reluctant Moses on the shoulder,
directing him to lead the Jewish people out of bondage in
Egypt to the Promised Land.

As Moses obeyed, remarkable proof of Jehovah's presence and protection was given to the children of Israel time
after time: the rolling back of the Red Sea so that they
could cross it; a pillar of cloud by day and fire by night to
guide them; the provision of food and water in the desert.
God made them the solemn pledge that if they would trust
Him, He would supply their every need from the smallest
to the greatest.

The Israelites had less than two hundred miles between

them and their goal. That distance could be covered in
weeks. But they did not trust God. From Exodus 14, when
they fled slavery in Egypt, to Numbers 14, in the midst of
their desert trek, there is the record of a series of "murmurings" against circumstances, against their leaders Moses
and Aaron, against the lack of water, the hardships of the
journey, the strength of their enemies. They were dissatis-
fied with the food God provided and longed for the dainty
fare of Egypt. Each time the complaints reached the level
of mutiny, Moses would intercede with God on behalf of
the people. Each time Jehovah would humor His fussing
children and stoop to meet their demands. Miracle followed miracle. But rather than being grateful and praising
Jehovah for these mighty acts, the people would soon begin
complaining again, offering back to God discontented
hearts and yet more grievances.

The murmurings reached a climax as recorded in the
fourteenth chapter of Numbers. This time the murmurings
went too far. The congregation wallowed in self-pity,
lamenting and weeping through the night, "Would God
that we had died in the land of Egypt!"

By then the Israelites had finally traversed the two
hundred miles and were virtually on the doorstep of the
Promised Land. In fact, it had already been spied out by a
group led by Caleb, who had pronounced it a good land
ready to be taken with the Lord's help.

Wearily, Moses once again entreated God with long and
eloquent pleading. But this time, though God agreed to
pardon, a price had to be paid: a generation had lost the
Promised Land by making grumbling and rebellion their
way of life. In doing so, they had been steadily acting out a
spurning of God and of His promise for them. Therefore
they were told, "Tomorrow turn you, and get you into the
wilderness by the way of the Red Sea.... All... from twenty
years old and upward, which have murmured against
me... shall fall in this wilderness." [13]

Thus sadly, on the threshold of achieving their destination, the Israelites were turned back to wander in the desert for forty years. Their children would enter the Promised Land—but not those who had started out in such high hopes, those to whom God's glorious promises had first been made.

By this story, my eyes were opened to several truths. From the time the Chosen People first left Egypt, God had been trying to teach them some facts about Himself: first, He was (and is) a personal God. "I will walk in and with and among you, and will be your God, and you shall be My people." [14] Thus as a Father, no detail of His children's lives was beneath His notice—from the dimensions of the wilderness tabernacle or the tassels on the hem of the priests' robes, to the adjudication of the minutest quarrel between neighbors.

It follows that when the Israelites or any of us have really accepted God as our Father in the personal way He means it, then we are going to trust the circumstances He permits us to have. That is why our grumbling about God's provision is at the least attributing more power to circumstances and to evil than to God. And murmuring and rebellion can lose us our personal Promised Land. Our Promised Land means God's will perfectly done in our life and affairs. It means the supplying of every provision— spiritual and physical—for our every need. We can miss all of it through complaining.

On a larger scale the same principle applies to modern nations just as much as to the Israelites. Greed and lack of gratitude stemming from the grumbling spirit could eventually cost us or any nation the blessings of God.

What the Israelites needed—and what I believe we who build our lives around criticalness need today—is to see that the antidote to negativism is the power of God. It is a transforming power in and over the world He has made. On the reality of that power Scripture never backs down or gives ground. From the time God called Moses to lead His people, through the plagues visited on the Egyptians, through the parting of the Red Sea, through many miracles in the desert, God was saying, "I do have power. I am the God of the supernatural. You are to trust Me for more than you would expect through 'natural' law or 'natural' causation."

Power over what? Precisely those factors about which the Israelites were murmuring—the harsh desert, the difficulties of their trek, physical ailments and illnesses, and the hostility of their enemies. In other words, over the external conditions of life.

Rebellion of a far different sort—against dishonest United States government inspectors—turned into a surprisingly positive experience for two Florida businessmen several years ago. At that time the Meloon family boat business, Correct Craft, Inc., owed $500,000 to 228 creditors and faced financial disaster.[15] The trouble had begun when Walter Meloon and his brother Ralph were awarded a government contract to build 3,000 assault boats.

Shortly afterwards they were called upon by a member of the three-man team who would inspect the boats. "Did you know," the inspector asked Walter, "that you are one of only two companies in the Southeast that does not have someone on their payroll who takes care of their inspectors' expenses?"

Walter shook his head, knowing that the government paid all the inspectors' expenses.

The two brothers talked it over and decided to dismiss the overture as an ill-considered remark rather than as a request.

Soon, they learned differently.

Correct Craft, founded in 1925, had always been proud of producing quality boats. But now, as the sleek 18-foot fiberglass boats began coming down the assembly line, great numbers were being rejected by the government inspectors—many for tiny flaws allowable under the contract.

One day the brothers quietly took one of the rejects, cleaned off the inspector's chalk marks and sent it back through the line. It was passed.

It was now clear what they faced. In desperation they went to the inspector's superiors, but to no avail. As the silent war continued, they foresaw financial disaster for Correct Craft and for over a hundred employees and their families.

Temptation whispered to Walter, "Why not pay those men off? It really isn't much compared to what the company stands to lose."

No, it wasn't the money, Walter knew. Something far deeper. At night he would wrestle with the problem. Trying not to disturb his wife Anne, he would slip out of bed to think and pray.

"Lead me, Lord. Tell me what to do." By the little bedroom lamp, words glowed on the printed page open on the table. "Trust in the Lord with all thine heart; and lean not to thine own understanding. In all thy ways acknowledge Him, and He shall direct thy paths."

To pay off the men would not be trusting the Lord.

Walter crawled back into bed. "All right, Lord. We'll just try harder to build perfect boats."

Then one gray afternoon came the final blow. A flatcar had just been loaded with forty boats, each stamped "approved" by the inspectors. As Walter watched the switch engine back up to it, the inspector came out.

"I don't like their looks," he said flatly. "They've got to be unloaded and refinished." Walter waved the engine away and turned wearily to his car.

The brothers had reached the end of their rope. The contract had already cost them $1,000,000. They had delivered 2200 boats with 600 rejects stacked in their storage yard.

Walter found himself battling his bitter animosity against the surly inspector. He knew that Christ has told us to forgive our enemies. He tried his best to forgive the man, only to stay awake for hours with his mind seething with fury.

Then one night the Lord spoke. "I love that man too. I died for him as well as for you." The words were like a cooling hand on Walter's brow. After that, he was able truly to forgive the inspector.

Then what seemed like wild thoughts came to Walter. . . . *God has allowed the inspectors to reject all those boats. Then God has something that He wants us to learn out of this. We will learn it only when we stop rebelling against all this and begin to look to Him in thanksgiving.*

As the Meloon brothers accepted this concept and acted on it, God answered with an explosion of miracles. First, a loan came unexpectedly from business friends in Norway. The second miracle came from Pakistan. The minister of defense ordered six boats for $139,000. With the first shipment Correct Craft sent along one of their "rejected" assault boats, explaining they had more. Back came an order for 239.

The third miracle came in the form of an idea which God put into Walter's mind. The brothers were led to set up five factory warehouse distribution centers in different parts of the country. Each would operate as an autonomous company selling Correct Craft boats to dealers in their area. A boating industry innovation, those centers proved successful in tapping new markets. In effect, the five satellite companies acted as flotation barges around a sinking ship, lifting the company to the surface.

God was not only teaching the Meloon brothers how to handle temptation and adversity constructively, He was giving them a basic business lesson: no company can exist on a solid foundation with only one big customer. The government might have stopped buying their boats for a perfectly legitimate reason.... Indeed, His ways are wondrous.

Today the business is a healthy and growing Orlando concern. Walter can say, "As I look back, I praise the Lord for those dark days. They helped us become a much stronger company. More important, our faith has been greatly strengthened to the point where I will confidently walk with Him anywhere."

With an approach like Ralph's and Walter's, we are at the opposite of the critical spirit. Here we have trust and praise as the antithesis of complaint and rebellion.

We have seen this is in so many situations.... When Ellie Armstrong faced the crisis of the $300 mortgage payment due with only $50 in the bank and no motel guests for five consecutive nights, she might have felt justified in rebelling against such a predicament. Instead, she acted out her praise of God for His provision by giving away the $50 as He had told her to. That same night the motel filled up, stayed filled, and the payment was made on time.

In my battle of the sleeping pills, when I stopped rebelling and sought God even at the point of sleeplessness, then I was given the praise-filled message of the old hymn:

> Blessed assurance, Jesus is mine!...
> This is my story, this is my song,
> Praising my Saviour all the day long.

In retrospect I could see the steps—from rebellion, to acceptance, to praise, to God changing the situation. I began to see more clearly too why God sets Himself so seriously against a disobedient or rebellious or judgmental spirit: this is the precise frame of heart and mind which blocks His loving intervention on our behalf.

The wisdom of Solomon tells us, "Out of it [the heart] are the issues of life." [16] Jesus enlarged on this: the human heart and will are the main problem, He kept explaining. Every true reform in civilization involves a change of heart followed by a change of mind of human beings. So how can we get our hearts set right?

Traditionally men have tried to change the minds of other men in two ways—neither of them Jesus' way. The basest effort is the use of physical force to compel another person or an entire nation to do what the opponent wants. The trouble with this method is that the "victory" usually leaves untouched and unchanged the hearts and minds of the vanquished. No military victory could have been more complete than the Roman legions' over tiny defenseless Palestine in Jesus' day. Yet the Jewish fractiousness and insurgentism were worse than ever.

The second, more civilized technique is to use words and the power of personality to try to change the other person's mind and heart. Governments employ many tools to this end: controlled news media, education biased until it is a mere political tool; every imaginable form of pressure and propaganda, every skill of the advertising profession in what amounts to buying a change of mind.

In our times the art of persuasion has been developed to an all-time high, but there has been a curious result. Though a veritable frenzy of words is being spoken over millions of television sets as well as pouring from the presses, modern men seem less trustful of words than ever. It would also appear that both the spoken and the written word are less effective. "As a poet," W. H. Auden once wrote, "there is only one political duty, and that is to defend one's language from corruption. And that is particularly serious now. It's being so quickly corrupted. When it's corrupted, people lose faith in what they hear, and this leads to violence."

And to obscenity, Auden might have added. As the printed page, along with movie and stage scripts, is increasingly pepperd with four-letter words, we can't help wondering: isn't the obscenity really our frustration at the poverty of language that no longer really communicates or works any changes in people's minds and hearts? Perhaps then, the subconscious reaction goes, people can be *shocked* into paying attention—and so the foul words pour out.

There are other signs of the increasing ineffectiveness of

persuasion.... In the last decade "credibility gap" has become one of our favorite terms.

The lecture method of teaching is increasingly under suspicion.

The great issues before Congress are seldom debated any more on the floor of House or Senate.

Presidential speeches are similar casualties. For a quarter of a century television has provided the unprecedented advantage of intimate chats in every living room. Yet these speeches—almost always written by hired speech writers, tailored to computer-determined political requirements—make us wonder, where have great speeches and speakers gone? What has happened to the passion of a Patrick Henry, the sober sincere honesty of a George Washington, the homespun grandeur of an Abraham Lincoln, the flaming oratory of a William Jennings Bryan or a William Gladstone, the persuasive logic of a Woodrow Wilson, the person-to-person warmth of a Franklin D. Roosevelt, the rolling thunderous cadences of a Winston Churchill?

It would seem that the harder we have tried our "modern" techniques of persuasion, the more breakdowns in communication we have been experiencing on all fronts—between parents and children, between the races, between government and people, between nations. Our frustration then breeds more rebellion.

Psychologist Paul Tournier in his book *The Whole Person in a Broken World* diagnoses the prevalence of rebellion in our society not as a healthy sign of progress nor a means to needed reforms. Rather, Dr. Tournier sees rebellion as a neurosis of epidemic proportions startlingly comparable to adolescent neurosis. [17]

In normal adolescence, the storms and stresses—the negative self-assertion, the customary disparagement of established mores—are ultimately worked through to integration: adulthood. But in cases where this integration is unduly delayed, psychiatrists call the resulting illness the "neurosis of defiance." "Something like this," Dr. Tournier maintains, "has taken place in the development of human history since the Renaissance...."

He cites the classic signs of neurosis in the individual. First, anxiety. We do not have to look far to see much anxiety today. Restlessness and dissatisfaction with oneself and others are epidemic. In society the flood of criticism may be in part an effort to hide a deep anxiety. Jean-Paul Sartre went so far as to say "Man *is* anxiety." [18]

The second sign of neurosis, individual or societal, is sterility. "Big dreams do not produce the fruit.... True values do not play an effective role in the destiny of society...."

The final characteristic of the neurotic is inner conflict—ambivalence; the classic adolescent's awkwardness when everything he tries gets botched, and more often than not he gets the opposite result from the one he sought.

Certainly there are marked signs of ambivalence in our society. We undertake the war in Vietnam to keep peace in Asia and to ensure the good life for the South Vietnamese; we end up with the longest war in American history and the devastation of the Vietnamese homeland.

Protestors of that war march for an end to violence, and clash violently with the police.

The present administration sees protestors as traitors to law and order. But the Watergate investigation ends up showing that same administration in flagrant violation of the law.

The government seeks to avoid inflation by controlling the economy; the result is runaway prices and a devalued dollar.... The ambivalence and contradictions go on and on.

Since our ways are achieving the opposite of what we intend, perhaps we are ready to ask, what is Jesus' way? The first move, He told His disciples who asked Him the same question, has to be made on behalf of the inner man. You have problems in your lives, problems in society, But you must see that

> "...from within, out of men's hearts, come evil thoughts of lust, theft, murder, adultery, wanting what belongs to others, wickedness, deceit, lewdness, envy, slander, pride, and all other folly... they are what pollute you and make you unfit for God." [19]

Anger in the heart and the contempt of one human being for another precedes the act of murder. Lust in the heart precedes the act of adultery.[20]

The last thing God wants for us men is conflicts and neuroses that tear us apart. His primary concern is the healthy integration of man's heart and will. This health He measures by whether we are still running from Him in rebellion, or are reunited with Him, having found our way back to our heart's home.

The closer I looked into the dilemma of our rebellion, the more this central truth stood out for me: underlying all cleavage amongst us, behind our broken human relationships, lies a basic break—between God and us. We do not often recognize this, being inclined to blame any dislocation in our lives on other people, or on "circumstances," and to look for the remedy anywhere but in a reconciliation with God.

Since we human beings are rooted in God, rebellion against Him is like revolting against part of ourselves. Of course we are not able to "find ourselves" when we are such divided beings!

That is precisely what our adversary Satan wants for us. He was the original instigator of rebellion. Revolt was Satan's sin too. In the Garden of Eden he succeeded in luring Adam and Eve to join him in rebellion. And ever since Satan has whispered to us that the way to improve our lot is to rebel.

But if this is Satan's way, what is God's way? That was

essentially the question the thoughtful scholar Nicodemus came asking Jesus during their quiet midnight talk. The Master's answer was, "Those deep inner changes are never going to come about through men's efforts in trying to change the thinking or patch up the old person. There's only one way, Nicodemus: *'except a man be born again, he cannot see the Kindgom of God.'*"

And when Nicodemus probed and questioned, "How *can* these things be?" Jesus pointed him to a cross. How well He knew that soon He would hang there suspended between earth and heaven. And there, if we will recognize it and allow it to be so, our old selves can die too so that the new person can be born.

Can the way of the Cross do in men's hearts what force and persuasion and all man's artifice fail to do? A few years ago during a trip to Austria I heard a true story which suggests that it can and does. A Lutheran pastor, a former Nazi storm trooper, gave me this account of how he, trained in hatred and destruction, had been changed into a follower of Christ....

In December 1941 the trooper was with the German armies invading Russia. In the Crimea, in heavily wooded terrain, the battle began going against the Germans. As they had to fall back, the German found himself within the Russian lines, separated from his regiment. Alone he made his way through the forest, fearful at every minute of being captured. Suddenly, he saw a thin cloud of smoke coming from the chimney of a hut. Creeping up warily, gun in hand, he knocked on the door. It was answered by a tiny elderly Russian woman.

Shoving past her and searching the hut, he satisfied himself that the woman lived alone. Apparently, her menfolk were off fighting—perhaps had already been killed. To the German's surprise, the woman offered him food and drink. Neither spoke a word of the other's language, but in the end the Russian woman hid the soldier, feeding him and caring for him for three days and nights. The German grew increasingly baffled. Certainly, no worse enemy than he, a Nazi, could have come to the door here in Russia, where Germans murdered more civilians than the total number of Jews killed in all of Europe. The woods swarmed with Russian troops; surely she knew that if she were caught harboring a German she would be shot.

Out of his mounting desire to communicate, he managed through sign language and facial expressions to convey his question, "Why have you risked your life to hide and befriend me?"

The old woman looked at him for a long moment in silence, then turned and pointed to a crucifix on the wall above her bed.

Telling me the incident, the Lutheran pastor added, "After I escaped back to the German lines, try as I would I couldn't forget what had happened. I hadn't known love like that was possible. In the end, I was drawn irresistibly to the One who enabled the little Russian lady to prefer another to herself—even when that other was a cruel and deadly enemy. I wanted to know the power of the Cross in my life too. That's why I'm a Christian today."

The way of the Cross, Jesus' way. The way that puts others ahead of self. What would be the difference in our world today if we began to let the Cross work its change in our hearts?

Ezekiel's prophecy could come true for us individually and collectively as a society,

> A new heart also will I give you, and a new spirit will I put within you: and I will take away the stony heart out of your flesh, and I will give you an heart of flesh.
>
> And I will put my spirit within you...and ye shall be my people, and I will be your God.[21]

Rebellion and mutiny would be seen as a paltry playing at life as we enter into the glorious liberty of the children of God. What that liberty could mean for us was spelled out

long ago at the beginning of God's dealings with the
Israelites. It is a vision that has haunted us ever since....

The good earth, its seas, lakes, rivers, and streams, the
air, the trees, the animals, will no longer be ravaged by
man.

Crops would be blessed and be sufficient to end hunger
for all mankind. The nation that produces plenty would
rush its aid and know-how to those countries with less.

Happiness would reign in homes across the world. Marriage and family life would thrive and be blessed. Once
again babies would be wanted and cherished.

In the words of Isaiah, "Violence shall no more be heard
in thy land, wasting nor destruction within thy borders." [22]
Wars will end.

In real and practical ways, men will recognize that this
really is one world. With an effective world organization,
destructive and fear-motivated nationalism will disappear.
As the nations no longer need to spend most of their
substance on armaments, creative research will burgeon.
The cure will be discovered for cancer, for rheumatoid
arthritis, for multiple sclerosis, arteriosclerosis, heart disease, emphysema, and the myriad of other diseases that
have defeated research and plagued mankind.

In all branches of the arts, the new creativity will bring a
renaissance—music, art, writing, the theater, crafts.

Mourning shall be ended as men everywhere begin to
understand that because ours is a God of love, submission
and obedience to Him is not only our greatest good, but the
way "to enjoy Him forever."

13

Run for the Strong Tower

Recently I opened the newspaper to read headlines on a major article:

VIOLENCE

As Crime Soars, a Puzzled
Nation Asks, "Why, Why?"

The first paragraph read:

It is an age of fear—a stark, pervasive, gnawing, mind-numbing, gut-wrenching fear.[1]

Fear and anger are universally recognized as the two most destructive emotions in man. Yet it seems that year by year fears are growing and striking deeper as we—individually and collectively— are increasingly frustrated in our efforts to deal with our problems. In our newspapers we read almost daily of events like a grocer murdered for $20; rapes and killings of young girls in the Boston area;

stabbings and holdups in Washington and in London; a grandmother stomped to death by two youngsters; kidnapings and skyjackings.

Long articles are written suggesting ways the average citizen can protect himself: replace spring-type door locks with deadbolts; put chains and peepholes on doors; have keys made by licensed locksmiths recommended by a city Burglary Squad; install bars or ornamental metal grillwork on windows; buy one of the many burglar alarm systems now on the market; bring into the family unit a trained police dog; keep lights burning in stores, warehouses, and homes throughout the night.

Commonsense precautions are certainly necessary. But there come times when all the safeguards man has devised can't stand between us and the raw evil loose in this world. It is then that we discover a surer protection, the only final protection there is. This was dramatized for me by what happened not long ago to a neighbor in Delray Beach, Florida....[2]

It was a beautiful sunshiny June morning. Gene Klinger started out in her car for Delray Beach to take her final teacher's examination. As she turned from Military Trail down Fourth Street, she noted the time on her watch. It was 8:50. Good! She'd be at school by nine.

Fourth Street near Military Trail is a lonely stretch of road until it runs into the residential area. Just ahead of Gene was a light-colored pickup truck. It slowed down, then pulled over to the side of the road. An arm out the car window signaled to Mrs. Klinger to pull over too. She did so instinctively, wondering if the other driver had noticed a flat coming on in that left rear tire she'd been worried about.

A big burly man wearing a sports shirt open at the neck strode up to her window. "Lady, can you tell me how to get to Dixie Highway?"

Mrs. Klinger was unsuspecting. After all, it was broad

daylight. "I'm so sorry. I don't live in Delray. I'm just on my way to school here. Afraid I can't give you directions."

The man was looking at her intently. Suddenly the expression on his face changed. Jerking open the car door, he pressed a hard metal object into Gene's back. When she sat there paralyzed, he shoved her to the other side of the seat and climbed in beside her.

Instinctively, she screamed, then reached over and pressed hard on the horn. But there was not a car or pedestrian around.

He pressed the object harder into her back. "Don't try that again or I'll kill you," the man growled. Fear, panic, terror washed in waves over her.

Gene admits that she has always had many fears. Sensitive, intense, vivacious, she feels deeply. Long ago she determined to face up to her fears and to search for ways to eradicate them. Her search led her to seek God for His help in freeing her from these shackles. She had asked that in certain circumstances He help her do the things she feared or found difficult. This led her to apply for teacher training at the Montessori School.

During an early session there she confided to her instructor that she had not yet learned how to deal with her fears. The instructor gave her a copy of a printed prayer that has been widely circulated. The words soon became part of the fabric of Gene Klinger's life....

> The Light of God surrounds me.
> The Love of God enfolds me.
> The Power of God protects me.
> The Presence of God watches over me.
> Wherever I am, God is.

Upon arising that June morning, as every morning, she had prayed that prayer of affirmation. Thus at the crisis moment, sitting beside the threatening man in the car, when panic and terror almost overcame her, she discovered in herself this mighty prayer resource. Gene cannot remember the exact words she used, but she knows their essence.

"How can you force yourself on me this way?" she cried. "You are a child of God. God's love is in you. He cares about you. And I am His child too, and completely under His protection. His love and protection surround me...."

As she spoke the words, she felt warmed. "There was a kind of aura around me," she said later. "I could see it, feel it. It was like a soft light."

"Then a strange thing happened," she recalled. "Into my mind there came the clear picture of the face of the janitor at my school, one of the kindest, most gentle men I'd ever known, beloved by everyone. It was as if God was saying, 'You told the man sitting beside you that he is a child of Mine. To help you feel that as well as know it, superimpose the janitor's face and image on this other man.'"

"I followed directions and sure enough, after that, I could actually sense God's love flowing to my abductor."

The result was immediate. The man suddenly appeared confused. Lust seemed to leave him. He removed the metal object from Gene's back. Then she saw that it was a key case.

He started Gene's car and drove on in silence for a while, little trickles of perspiration running down his face as his confusion increased. Then he drew over to the side of the road and stopped. "Get out," he ordered. Quickly Gene opened the door and jumped out. The man turned the car around and drove off, careening down the road.

He was no sooner out of sight than the police car she had so desperately longed for pulled up. "Something the matter, lady?"

She and the officer found her car abandoned on down the road and the pickup truck gone. At the police station she was shown a group of photographs. With a start she recognized one of them as the very man who had halted her. As she opened her mouth to identify him, something on the inside of her would not let her say anything except, "I'm not sure." The man had no police record except a series of traffic violations. "I know it seemed weak, uncooperative with the police," she said later. "I only know something stopped me from identifying him."

Despite the ordeal, Gene Klinger continued on to the school, took her examination, passed it. She was glad to share her experience because she believes it may point to the most important protection for all of us.

"I am the light of the world," Jesus told us. In the past we have usually considered this symbolic, even exaggerated imagery. Now I wonder!

In this era of artificial light and of increasing energy shortage we are very aware of the merit of lighted areas for protection. Banks and business establishments are now commonly lighted throughout the night. A group of women in Indianapolis, crusading for years to make their streets safe again, have discovered that crime goes down as much as 85 percent when street lighting standards go up.

Was Jesus speaking figuratively only when He said:

> For everyone that doeth evil hateth the light, neither cometh to the light, lest his deeds should be reproved.[3]

I wonder if Christ means for us to take His "I am the light of the world" more literally than we do. Of course, the statement also points to a theological truth. But He who created the atom and the sun [4] remains the power center, the dynamo of the physical universe. And as Light, He is also Protection—largely unrealized, untapped, unresearched.

An increasing number of people are experiencing Jesus' contemporary Presence in this way. To me it is significant that Gene Klinger felt "a soft light" around her and that her attacker either could not or would not penetrate it.

> Let us therefore cast off the works of darkness and let us
> put on the armour of light.[5]

Could the apostle Paul, so often the target of hostile
crowds, have experienced the Light of Christ as actual
armor?

In promise after promise, the Bible seeks to teach us that
in God and in His resources there is physical protection
surer than any weapon or defense known to man. Other
descriptions of this protection are given in addition to light,
such as this one from the days of walled cities....

> The name of the Lord is a strong tower: the righteous
> runneth into it, and is safe.[6]

Short of magic or hocus-pocus, the question is, how
could there be enough power (as the world understands
power) in the invoking of a mere name to be a genuine
safety factor to anyone?

All through Scripture there is the insistence that a man's
name is never just a casual handle for identification pur-
poses. Rather, concentrated in a man's name is the essence
and character of the person. Thus when God was allowed
to enter a man's life and control it, more often than not the
man's name had to be changed because the character-
focus of the man was then different. So Abram became
Abraham; Jacob became Israel; Simon became Peter; Saul
became Paul. Frequently the Bible tells us the meaning of
names. Seth, for instance, means "granted"; Noah means
"relief"; Isaac denotes "laughter"; Moses means "to draw
out (of the water)."

There is great significance in the many names Scripture
gives to Jesus Christ, among them:

The Last Adam	Light of the World
Saviour	Bread of Life
The Good Shepherd	Cornerstone
The Door	Counsellor

King of Kings   The Prince of Peace
The Lamb of God   Great High Priest

When we think of Jesus' ringing statement after His
resurrection, "All power is given unto me in heaven and in
earth..." [7] we see why many descriptive words are needed
to cover "all power." But all of them are caught up and
comprehended in the name of Jesus. Again and again we
are assured that the power to save, to redeem, to heal, to
guide, to give wisdom, to protect, is wrapped up and
focused like a laser beam in this "Name."

> And whatever you ask in my name, I will do it, that the
> Father may be glorified in the Son. [8]

When we pray "in Jesus' Name," we are not simply
verbalizing a word or a phrase; rather, our petition is to the
complete character of the Lord and all of the power
implicit in His Name. The Scripture abounds in "holy
mysteries" and the full meaning of praying in the Name of
Jesus is one of those mysteries. In heaven, the mystery is
understood; on earth, we shall probably never know it fully.
Yet as we step out in faith using that Name, we do learn bit
by bit. Even some of Christ's first followers, the seventy
whom He sent out two-by-two during His earthly ministry,
discovered early that His Name had power indeed:

> And the seventy returned again with joy, saying, Lord,
> even the devils are subject unto us through thy name. [9]

Surely here is the real reason that men with evil in their
hearts back off so quickly when confronted by this Name:
evil has always recognized and reacted against the power of
this word, often more incisively than "religious people."

A short time after my friend Gene Klinger's experience, I
came upon a similar incident. [10] Roberta Lashley, a young
girl of Mount Savage, Maryland, was fortunate enough to
have learned about the power of Jesus' Name prior to a

desperate crisis-moment. One night she had stayed later than she realized at an interesting church meeting. When the bus let her out on a lonely country road, there was still a twenty-minute walk to the Lashley home.

She thought with distaste of the steep climb to her house on Bald Knob Road. It was not until a car drew up beside her on the dark road that she realized how tired she was. "How about a lift?" a man's voice asked from the car.

In the dim light Roberta assumed that this was a neighbor. She climbed into the car gratefully, then realized she had been mistaken: the driver was a stranger. Even so, in that rural community sharing rides was such an accepted practice that the seventeen-year-old girl felt no alarm. She thanked the driver but noticed that he made no reply.

They drove in silence until Roberta pointed out her house. Still the man said nothing and there was no decrease in speed.

"That's my house," the girl repeated, small prickles of alarm alerting her.

Was it her imagination or were they actually going faster? "There's a lane ahead where we can turn around," she told the driver, trying to keep panic from her voice.

The car was gaining speed, careening up the twisting mountain road. The last house was behind them now.

"Stop the car!" Roberta cried. "Let me out!"

Without slowing, the car swerved up a bumpy side road that led to an abandoned coal mine high on the mountain.

The girl looked wildly at the trees whizzing past them. A person could be killed and hidden forever in one of those deserted shafts. Her hand closed on the door handle.

But as her fingers gripped the handle, suddenly she remembered something she had heard at the church service several weeks before. A missionary to the Philippines had said that Jesus Christ has dominion over the evil in man, but that we have to call upon that dominion. *We must ask.*

Shutting her eyes, Roberta tried to remember the exact

words the missionary had used. Then very slowly and clearly, addressing the evil intent within the man, she said in a firm and clear voice, "I rebuke you in the Name of Jesus Christ."

For the first time the man looked at his passenger. "What do you mean?" he asked. "What's 'rebuke'?"

"I mean," she replied, "that Jesus Christ has absolute authority on this earth and that I am under His protection. He's protecting me this very minute."

They had reached the abandoned mine shaft. The car stopped. Time stopped too as Roberta felt her pulse pounding in her temples. The driver remained motionless, hands still on the wheel.

"I didn't know," he said at last. The force that had gripped him was gone. He started backing up, then turned down the steep mine road to the main highway. The crisis was past; waves of relief washed over Roberta.

"I'm not really so bad," the man went on as he headed the car down the mountain. His voice sounded almost pleading. "I've been to church some. It just never made any sense to me."

The girl beside him was never sure afterwards that all she said to the man in the next five minutes made sense either. But in the time it took to reach her house she poured out her heartfelt conviction of Christ's love for each of us, how much He loved the bewildered man beside her, and of the need for Him in every life.

The car stopped at the Lashleys' driveway. With relief Roberta got out, then ran trembling into the house to find her mother waiting up for her.

"God took care of me," was all she could say. "God took care of me," over and over again like a child waking up from a nightmare.

The words Roberta Lashley spoke to her mother stirred a slumbering childhood memory in me. As a little girl, I had suffered what seems now like a long period of fear of the dark. Night after anguished night I would lie rigidly in bed, eyelids screwed shut, afraid to breathe for fear of what lurked in the dark corners.

Looking back I am surprised that I didn't share it with my mother. Pride was fierce in me. And I was much too young to reason out that faith was the opposite of fear. As I tried to handle the fears myself, what helped me most was the chorus of a hymn I had learned in Sunday School:

> God will take care of you
> Thro' every day, in all the way:
> He will take care of you,
> God will take care of you.[11]

As I would lie there singing this softly over and over to myself, an ease would flow into me, assurance and confidence that nothing else supplied. For one little girl the childlike words of the hymn became at once both an affirmation of faith and also her response to Him—her prayer.

When I mentioned this childhood experience and the "God Will Take Care of You" hymn in a recent article, to my astonishment letters came flooding in from readers. Most wanted to share a similar experience. My words had apparently evoked half-forgotten scenes and impressions, childhood experiences still charged with so much emotion. Clear impressions rising again to the surface—the panic we felt as children followed by the relief of the particular word of consolation.

Sometimes we like to think of fear as an emotion that belongs to the childhood of the race, or perhaps to the child who still lives in every adult. Yet fear resides in the strongest, the most resourceful of men. They learn to handle fear not by hiding it, but through learning an important fact about evil: it has a cowardly side. I find a striking example of this in the life of David Livingstone, the

Scottish missionary-explorer who opened up and mapped so much of Africa.

In 1865 Livingstone was facing one of the gravest perils of his sixteen years in the Dark Continent. He had to pass through the wild country of the local chief Mburuma. The chief was not only hostile himself, but was seeking to rouse the whole countryside against the white man's expedition. Warning after warning had been given to Livingstone by runners going ahead of the expedition. There were reports that warriors were in the jungle creeping toward his camp.

Alone in his tent, Livingstone opened his Bible to the promise on which he had staked his life so often. Then he wrote with such stirring eloquence in his journal: [12]

> January 14, 1856. Evening. Felt much turmoil of spirit in view of having all my plans for the welfare of this great region and teeming population knocked on the head by savages tomorrow. But I read that Jesus came and said, "All Power is given unto Me in Heaven and in Earth. Go ye therefore, and teach all nations... and lo, I am with you always, even unto the end of the world.
>
> It's the word of a Gentleman of the most sacred and strictest honour, and there's an end on it! I will not cross furtively by night as intended ... Nay, verily. I shall take observations for latitude and longitude tonight, though they may be the last. I feel quite calm now, thank God!

During the hours of darkness nothing happened. The next morning Livingstone, still calm, directed the crossing of the river for his 114 men and their oxen while Mburuma and his tribesmen watched from the jungle's edge.

Deliberately, the missionary reserved for himself the last place in the last canoe. One of the party, fond of Livingstone and fearful of treachery, pleaded with him not to give the chief a chance to shoot him in the back.

"Tell him to observe that I am not afraid," Livingstone

replied. Then with dignity he thanked the astonished
tribesmen, wished them God's peace and walked very
slowly to the canoe, never looking back. No shot was fired,
no hand raised against him.

For me the incident has great personal significance.
About two years before Peter Marshall's death, one day I
noticed a strange inscription carefully written on the flyleaf
of his favorite Bible....

> It's the word of a Gentleman of the most sacred and
> strictest honour, and there's an end on it!
>   David Livingstone

Then underneath Livingstone's name, Peter had signed
his own.

When I asked Peter about the inscription, he told me of
the incident in Livingstone's life. It meant much to Peter
not only because this giant of the nineteenth century was
born in the village of Blantyre not far from Peter's home in
Scotland, but also because he too had often staked so much
on the trustworthiness of the promises in this Book.

Occasionally God can provide the necessary confident
poise to overcome evil with such an overflow of good that it
takes on a sort of gay exuberance. That's the way it was for
Brother Bryan of Birmingham, Alabama, a man whose
memory is almost legend to many Southerners. His real
name was James Alexander Bryan, and for more than forty
years he was the pastor of the Third Presbyterian Church
of Birmingham, located at 22nd Street and Avenue G in a
downtown section of the industrial city.

Citizens of all sorts—policemen, firemen, the ill in
hospitals, those in jail, the hungry and the poor, the black
people, businessmen—had long since stopped caring what
denomination the preacher was, what color, what social
class, just that he was "Brother Bryan," chaplain to the

entire city. Since 1934 there has been at the heart of Five Points in downtown Birmingham with traffic flowing on every side of it, a white marble larger-than-life statue of Brother Bryan. He is kneeling in prayer, wearing a baggy old overcoat with a scarf half sliding off his neck, just as the sculptor Georges Bridges had seen him so often.

For Brother Bryan had a way of praying in most unlikely places at most unlikely times. Many a Birmingham citizen had heard his "Brother, let us pray" and couldn't wait to relate the latest Brother Bryan story....[13]

One Thursday night he had been detained late after a prayer meeting at the church and had to walk home alone. As he was crossing a dark narrow alley between business buildings, a man slipped out, stuck a gun in Brother Bryan's face and ordered, "Hands up." Obediently, his hands went up.

The thief methodically went through the preacher's pockets, extracted all the money he found, and removed his watch. Then he almost dropped the watch when his victim said calmly, "Brother, you and I are going to pray about this right now...." Then the pastor lifted up his face and said, "Lord, here's a man who needs Your help in the worst way. I ask You to show him a better way to live, help him make a new start. Lord, You love this man, make him feel Your love right now."

Slowly the gun was lowered. The thief thrust the money and the watch back into Brother Bryan's hands. "Go on home," he said. "The likes of you is not for me."

We might wonder where Brother Bryan's kind of cool-headedness comes from. I know only one possible source—an utter trust in God that turns into a total form of protection.

"Fear not" is one of the most reiterated exhortations in Scripture. The Bible denounces fear over and over and describes this deadly brew as one of humanity's major ills....

> For God hath not given us the spirit of fear; but of power,
> and of love, and of a sound mind. [14]

> For ye have not received the spirit of bondage again to
> fear; but ye have received the Spirit of adoption, whereby
> we cry, Abba, Father. [15]

It is helpful to understand the basis on which the Bible
regards fear as a sin of disbelief in God. Most of us moderns
are resistant to the term "sin" since it implies condemnation. Yet Jesus stated categorically that He did not come
into the world ever to condemn men and women but to
save us. [16] Therefore, if we have God's view of sin, it is
"missing the mark," missing out on the good things He
wants us to have and experience.

Thus any emotion or attitude that disorients or dis-
integrates human personality so that we "miss the mark" is
certainly therefore a sin—a negative to be gotten rid of.
Whether at its simplest level when fear "roots us to the
spot" or causes our knees to buckle, or a more sophisticated
form of jealousy-fear, or the fear of hardship or disaster in
times of economic depression, it destroys coordination,
riddles personality, blocks logical thinking, and makes
creative solutions to problems impossible.

When we see fear through Jesus' eyes, it is the acting out
of our disbelief in the loving Fatherliness of God. By our
worrying and fretting, we are really saying, "I don't believe
in any God who can help me, and I do not trust Him."
Thereby we are sinning against God by impugning His
character and calling Him a liar.

At that point there is only one way to get rid of fear; like
any sin, we must recognize it, confess it in true repentance,
claim God's sure promise of forgiveness, cleansing, and
renewal, accept these gifts, rise and get on with life.

As Jesus walked the earth and so frequently felt fear in
men around Him, again and again we hear that cry of His,
"O men, how little you trust Him!" [17] In the cry there was

more than a little rebuke and sorrow along with a sort of marveling astonishment that men could be so blind: "Why are you afraid? How little you trust God!" [18]

Behind Jesus' sharp reaction to our faithless fears lay His consistent viewpoint that this is our Father's world still in His control. Nor did Jesus ever use the word "Father" lightly out of slick sentimentality. He taught that God deals with each of us personally in the way the best of fathers would. Therefore, the kind of love necessary to bring His kingdom on earth is not brotherly love, but fatherly love. When we take Jesus' teachings (for example, the last four Beatitudes) in the light of this fatherly love, what has before seemed hopelessly idealistic becomes practicable and possible.

Our Father never forgets the way we humans really are. He knows well that we, His children, are beset with fears. Therefore, in almost every example of God breaking into life on earth, the opening words are, "Fear not"... "Fear not, the Lord will go before thee"... "Have no fear, I am with thee"... "Fear not, nor be dismayed"... and a hundred variations. Our Father knows that, like small children, we need constant reassurance.

Whether small children or grown-up children, we need to develop a sense of dependence on the Fatherliness of God. It may seem to us at first thought that any dependence is the opposite of strength or a mature personality. But when we look closely at Jesus, we see that this is not so. Always the Master gave the impression of a moment-by-moment companionship and dialogue with the Father, yet here was a Man afraid of nothing. Not fearing men's opinions of Him, He spoke the truth bluntly. He was not afraid of unpopularity because He knew that when we are true to our real self, it is impossible to please everyone. He did not cringe when He walked through the mob at Nazareth. Here was a truly dangerous mob-lynching scene. Yet with Jesus' faith in the Father, He strode through the midst of them with such assurance that the crowd simply faded before Him.

When we look at His constant dependence on God alone, we begin to suspect that we may be teaching our sons a false basis for manliness. So long as we are in these bodies, we are going to be subject to the limitations of flesh and we shall always know a degree of loneliness. To ignore these facts of life is not to nurture independent manliness, but to suppress fears and cram them into the unconscious where they do further harm.

The Nazarene asks for strong men—the tensile strength of the inner spirit. He would seem to be telling us that much of our bravado is artificial. He is forever calling us to a simpler, sturdier faith.

Faithlessness makes us suffer multitudinous troubles that we never do, in fact, face. Not many of us are actually going to be called on to face the spears of African tribesmen or look down the barrel of a gun or confront a would-be rapist. But untold thousands suffer diminished lives through the fear of all the things that might happen.

"I...have known a great many troubles," the humorist Mark Twain wrote when he was an old man, "but most of them never happened." [17]

Peter Marshall was fond of telling a fairy tale to illustrate how fears have a way of growing smaller and then evaporating when we resolutely face up to what we fear most. It is the story of Miobi, the boy who lived far to the south beyond the Third Cataract, and how he went on his journeys to overcome his fears....[20]

> Miobi had come to a village where the people were doing nothing else but moan and wail. The fires were not lit, the goats were not milked, because all the villagers were expecting to be eaten shortly by the Monster on the Top of the Mountain.
>
> This monster had the head of a crocodile and the body of

a hippopotamus and a tail like a very fat snake, and smoke came from his fiery breath.

But Miobi said, "I will go up the mountain and challenge the monster."

There he was, sure enough.

But as the boy climbed and came nearer, the monster looked definitely smaller.

"This is very curious indeed," he said. "The further I run away from the monster, the larger it seems, and the nearer I am to it, the smaller it seems."

When the boy reached the cave, he found no monster— but a quiet little thing as small as a frog, which purred; and he brought it home as a pet.

When the villagers saw him return, they wanted to make a hero of him for killing the monster, but he explained just what had happened and how he had brought the monster home as a pet.

What was its name?

The monster answered, "I have many names. Some call me famine, and some pestilence; but the most pitiable of humans give me their own names."

It yawned and added, "But most people call me What-Might-Happen."

Is Jesus a tower-light of protection against this kind of fear? Yes, because Jesus is Light and that Light can melt and dispel these submerged incapacitating fantasies.

Sometimes it helps to write down one's fears, then hold them up one by one to the light of Christ's clear understanding. Never is Jesus as the Light of the World more clear than in these murky areas of our semiconscious fears, most of them unreal and psychotic. The trouble with the imaginary fears is that they can, if allowed to go on and on unchallenged, really destroy. As we talk over each fear on the list with Christ, He will illuminate for us some steps to expose them for what they really are....

For a woman with husband and children away from home who has always been afraid of spending even one night alone, God may simply tell her to try it for one night and trust Him.

He may provide a man who is terrified of public speaking with an opportunity, directing, "Don't duck it. Step out on faith and make that talk. Trust Me to help you with the flow of ideas and words."

A person who has some physical discomfort and is reluctant to go for a medical examination, fearful of fatal disease, may be told to pick up the phone immediately for an appointment with the doctor. This is the objective attitude, the opposite of that preoccupation with self that is one of the fear-dragon's breeding grounds.

He may simply direct the one who is frightened of flying to make reservations and board a plane.

Not only new confidence but real growth in character follows this facing up to what we fear. Provided we are acting under God's direction.

Scripture tells us that the real enemies we should fear are not what or whom they seem to be....

> For we are not fighting against people made of flesh and blood, but against... the evil rulers of the unseen world ... and against huge numbers of wicked spirits in the spirit world.[21]

The question here is, were Gene Klinger's and Roberta Lashley's real antagonists the men who wanted to harm them? Or were these men merely being used by "the evil rulers of the unseen world"? Were Livingstone's real enemies a group of African tribesmen, or were they spiritual forces using the ignorance of the natives as their tools for evil?

Our spiritual enemies take a variety of forms and use many devices. In our family we experienced a curious example of this in 1968 at Evergreen Farm in Virginia, my mother's and father's home for their retirement years.[22]

During the first years at the farm we had happy times with Bessie and Hank Reid who lived in the tenant house. In the years since they left, the little house on the hill seemed to fall on evil times. It was almost as if the house was drawing people of unhappy, violent temperament to it.... There was Mr. K., who turned out to have a vicious temper. It erupted with frightening intensity at anyone not white and Anglo-Saxon.

Then Mr. K. left and Mr. and Mrs. W. came. Soon there was trouble in their marriage. One day Mr. W. came home from his job as manager of a grocery store and found his wife and children gone with their clothes and most of the family furniture. Several months later a man entered the grocery store and shot Mr. W. dead. The police never discovered the murderer or the motive.

Three other couples followed, all of whom had financial and marital troubles. A stretch of ten years of acute unhappiness plagued the Little House.

In the living room at Evergreen the family prayed about it. Part of the prayer took the form of questions. "How can we break the chain of downbeat and tragic events? Is some sort of cleansing needed here?"

We had to wait several months for the answer. Eventually it came in two parts: first, we were sent an unusual couple, the Rodriguezes. They had emigrated from Spain several years before. People with a great spirit, they love family life and love the land. Of course, Isabel and Jacinto knew nothing of the history of the Little House.

Certain that God had sent them to us, we began cleaning the house, repainting and furbishing it for its new tenants. As we scrubbed and painted, our conviction grew that the house had suffered a kind of pollution that oceans of soap and gallons of paint couldn't remove. And we could not bear the thought of the delightful Spanish couple moving in to face any such threats.

"Are we imagining this or being superstitious?" we asked ourselves. How is it that buildings can take on the aura and character of the persons and events that their walls have held? Who can tell! But here is something that most of us have experienced: we step into certain church buildings and are immediately warmed and blessed; going into others we are chilled and no inspiration flows to us, only sterility.

We walk through the door of some homes even when the occupants are away, and know instantly that love is in this place. On the other hand, I've been in beautiful houses from which I wanted to turn and flee, later to find out that discord, strife, or tragedy of some sort had occurred there.

It must be then that the living patterns of those who dwell in these houses are being affected by those "evil rulers of the unseen world" Scripture warns us about.

We knew well that Jesus' authority is the only one which evil must finally obey. It happened that Edith and Peter John Marshall were at Evergreen at the time, so Peter led our assault on the Little House. Len and I, Peter and Edith, paused for our first prayer at the doorway of the house. There Peter, using the Apostle John's great words,[23] asked that every sin ever committed within the house to violate the peace and purity and sanctity of a real home, be cleansed "through the blood of Jesus who cleanses us from all sin."

Walking through and around the scrub buckets and paint pails, we went from room to room, in each one pausing for a prayer for cleansing, followed by thanksgiving that all darkness and evil would from henceforward pass over the house. Finally, we asked the Lord to bless the house and its occupants.

All of us felt a strange power in this procedure. We left that day knowing that something important had happened: all would be well. And events since then have borne this out. Light entered that home and abides there still. Jacinto and Isabel and their little daughter Maria Dolores love their home and have known a lot of happiness there. When Mary Elizabeth Marshall, age five, comes to Evergreen, she and Maria spend hours together happily playing "house" there with their tiny china dishes and their dolls.

Faith is the Strong Tower into which we can run for protection today. It isn't a physical place but the Light of a protecting Presence. It makes the unreal fears vanish and gives us literal protection against the real ones.

But something is required of *us*:

> Let us therefore cast off the works of darkness and let us put on the armor of light.[24]

In other places in the Bible the pieces of our armor are described. Integrity is our coat of mail, truth is our belt, salvation is our helmet. Our shoes are the stability of the gospel of peace. And above all, faith is our shield.[25] This kind of armor suggests that every hour of every day we are in the thick of battle. Not only must we put on that armor of light, but we must practice walking in it on ordinary days when we think we feel no danger. Gene Klinger was doing exactly that as she daily saturated her mind and heart with the words about the light of God. We are putting on the coat of mail when we resolutely expel dishonesty from our lives. We are sharpening our spiritual sword as we memorize some of the great passages of Scripture and seek out the life-giving promises.

But when evil pursues, challenges, persists—at those crisis-moments we need to seek out His light, and to speak out His Name in ringing tones.

There in the Strong Tower we shall be safe. "It's the word of a Gentleman of the most sacred and strictest honour."

14

The Helper

That night at the dinner table our son was almost too busy talking to eat. He had flown in from Taylor University that afternoon, having just finished his freshman year.

"Pops," Chester's voice was excited, "you wouldn't have believed the scene in the Notre Dame football stadium last weekend."

"Football in June?" his father asked quizzically.

"No—lots of singing and prayer and praising the Lord ...25,000 people. It was fantastic!"

"What was the occasion?"

"A big meeting of the Catholic Jesus People. A bunch of us students drove up from Taylor. Six hundred priests came pouring onto the field from where the players enter, singing, carrying banners. The whole place was clapping and singing. I've never seen people so excited."

Later that week we read *Time* magazine's coverage of the event.... First, men in business suits or sports coats carrying banners aloft: THE SPIRIT OF JESUS AMONG US, emerging from the football team's tunnel onto the Notre Dame field; then the double moving line of priests in white robes and clerical stoles singing, their arms raised heavenward, hands open, palms up. The excitement of the crowd built, erupting into applause. Then as eight Roman Catholic bishops, followed by Leo-Jozey, Cardinal Suenens of Belgium, resplendent in brilliant red chasubles came into view, the clapping exploded into a mighty roar. From 25,000 voices "Alleluia! Alleluia!" rocked the stadium.

Commented *Time*:

> The ceremonies at Notre Dame last week made it clear that the fastest-growing force within the church is that of the Pentecostals—or as many prefer to be called, Charismatics. Originating as an off-campus prayer group at Pittsburgh's Duquesne University in 1967, Catholic Charismatics form the third major group of Pentecostal believers.... There are probably more than 200,000 of them in the U.S. today, organized in more than 1,100 prayer groups. The movement has taken root in foreign countries more recently and is growing even faster....
>
> To the crowd of 25,000 in the stadium Cardinal Suenens said, "The Pentecostal renewal is not a movement. It is a current of grace... growing fast everywhere in the world. I feel it coming. I see it coming." [1]

One portion of a sentence in that report leapt out at me: "Originating as an off-campus prayer group at Pittsburgh's Duquesne University in 1967..." Yes, I remembered about that. I had heard the story from Kevin Ranaghan, at that time still a Catholic layman.

The seedbed of the Catholic Pentecostal movement was a group of four or five laymen (all members of Duquesne's faculty) who had begun meeting together in the fall of 1966. A book that fell into their hands led them to ask for the gift of the Holy Spirit for themselves: David Wilkerson's *The Cross and the Switchblade*, written by John and

Elizabeth Sherrill. The story concerned David Wilkerson and his street ministry to gangs and dope addicts in the New York Bedford-Stuyvesant area.

"By February of 1967," Kevin Ranaghan told me, "the four Catholics from Pittsburgh had received a release of the great gift of the Holy Spirit. They began to witness quietly but joyfully among close friends." Some of these friends were at Notre Dame University. Beginning there with small informal groups on whom the joy of the Holy Spirit has fallen, the movement has gathered momentum like a prairie fire.

The Catholic Holy Spirit movement has the official sanction and approval of the Pope and church fathers. Their attitude is that the baptism of the Holy Spirit is completely scriptural and nothing new; it simply "makes operative" the ancient sacraments of Baptism and Confirmation. This sanction has lent a freedom and an openness to Catholics in the Holy Spirit movement not always enjoyed by their fellow Christians in Protestant churches.

In reporting the June mass meeting *Time* went on:

> Catholic Charismatics form the third major group of Pentecostal believers.... The "classical" Pentecostal denominations...grew up around the turn of the century and are by far the largest group—some 2.4 million in the U.S. alone.

> A "Neo-Pentecostal" movement has developed over the past 20 years within mainstream Protestant churches—Episcopal, Presbyterian, Lutheran—and is still spreading.

"Spreading" is right!

It is difficult to estimate how far the Holy Spirit movement has spread. A conservative estimate would be that at least 300,000 members of mainline Protestant churches in the United States have found fresh springs of faith and vitality in the surge of the Spirit. By 1970 so many Presbyterian clergymen were caught up in the movement that the highest governing body of the church, the General Assembly of the United Presbyterian Church, appointed a Special Committee to investigate. The gist of that report, as adopted by the 1970 Assembly was:

> (1) We cannot follow the view... that the purely supernatural gifts (of the Holy Spirit) ceased with the death of the apostles....
>
> (2) ...know the misuse of mystical experience is an ever-present possibility, but... [see] no reason to preclude its appropriate use....
>
> (3) [believe that when such] experience clearly results in new dimensions of faith, joy, and blessings to others, we must conclude that this is "what the Lord hath done" and offer Him our praise.

The Protestant movement has been quieter than its Catholic counterpart because there has been more resistance—even persecution, with some pastors in various parts of the country asked to leave their churches. One of the earliest (now classic) cases was that of the Episcopal priest Father Dennis Bennett, asked to resign in 1960 from the 2,500 member St. Mark's Church of Van Nuys, California. He went on to a rundown mission church, St. Luke's in Seattle, now large and thriving.

Unprecedented growth has gone on anyway, in spite of such resistance. And perhaps it is time for the whole of this branch of Christendom to ask ourselves if this approach to the topic of the Holy Spirit is healthy and does honor to the Third Person of the Trinity.

Either the coming of the Holy Spirit into individual lives and upon the Church is Jesus' own teaching with His authority behind it, intended to result in sound and fruitful Christians—or else it is heresy that has no place in Christianity at all. I, for one, can see no middle ground.

What then did Jesus Himself tell us about the Holy Spirit?

Back in 1945 a personal health crisis led me to seek an answer to that question. Using a concordance and a notebook, I began methodically looking up all the references I could find on the Third Person of the Trinity. Gradually I worked the findings into a logical outline in the notebook. The part of it directly bearing on the question above could be summarized like this....

During the Last Supper conversation Jesus made it clear that the promises He was making that night were not meant just for the eleven men within the sound of His voice, but for "future believers" as well. [2] And what He promised for the future could scarcely be more exciting:

> It was "expedient" that He "go away." [3]
>
> When He went away, He would send the Holy Spirit to be "poured out on all flesh." (In contrast to the Old Testament way of a few chosen people—prophets, priests, kings.) [4]
>
> He Himself would be the Giver (or Baptizer) of the Spirit. [5]
>
> His plan was that this Spirit would dwell (with our permission) in our bodies. This would be God the Father coming closer to man than He had ever been before. [6]
>
> The apostles and all believers who would follow them down through the ages were, from the moment of Jesus' ascension, entering a new era—the era of the Holy Spirit. This would last until His second coming in physical Presence back to planet Earth. [7]
>
> The Spirit would make Jesus' continuing Presence and His teachings real to us. He would always turn the spotlight on Jesus and glorify Him. [8]
>
> The chief hallmark of the Holy Spirit would be *power* for service and ministry to others. [9]

The Spirit would be our Teacher; Guide; Comforter; Counsellor; Prayer-Intercessor; Giver of joy, of freedom, of many spiritual gifts, of eternal life.[10]

The Spirit would not ever be totally operative in an individual alone, but primarily in the fellowship of Christ's Body on earth—the Church.[11]

The apostles and those who would come after must expect a degree of resistance, cleavage, even persecution and expulsion from their synagogues (or churches) because "the world cannot receive Him—the Spirit of truth." [12]

After His resurrection and ascension the apostles were "to go into all the world and preach the Good News to everyone, everywhere...." [13]

They were not, however, to leave Jerusalem or start telling the Good News or attempt any ministry of any kind until *they had received the Holy Spirit.*[14]

Jesus promised that He *would* "manifest Himself to us." [15]
And that He *would* lead us into further truth—all truth.[16]

As I put all of this together back in 1945, it shed new light on the account of what happened next. That story is told in the Book of the Acts—really the Acts of the Holy Spirit. The Spirit's first great miracle was to transform the erstwhile timid, cowardly, and contentious disciples into bold men moving with power and authority. Thus the infant Church was born.

Jesus' explicit promises both to manifest Himself to us human beings and to lead us into further truth began to be fulfilled immediately. Old religious mores and set habit patterns had to be broken.

Virgin truth is always unexpected, often shocking. Though Jesus had spoken often of the Holy Spirit to the apostles, I could find no record that He had mentioned

details of the Pentacost to come such as the sound of a
roaring wind or flames of fire, or the sudden speaking of
languages they had never learned. Nor were these disciples
prepared for the "further truth" such as that Jewish food
taboos were no longer necessary,[17] or that the Gentiles
were also beloved by the Father and chosen by Him to
receive the Spirit.[18]

In fact, it seemed to me that Jesus' promise of "further
truth" gives us clear reason to believe that not all the truth
and instruction Christ has to give us is contained in the
canon of the Old and New Testaments. How could it be?
He who *is* Truth will never find the people of any given
century able to receive everything He wants to give.
Because the Holy Spirit is a living, always-contemporary
Personality, down all the centuries there must be an
ever-unfolding manifestation of Jesus, His personality, His
ways of dealing with us along with new, fresh disclosures of
the mind of the Father. I found this concept endlessly
provocative...and I still do.

At that point in my study some action on my part was
clearly indicated. I had already summarized how we receive the Spirit:

(1) By going directly to Christ for Him.

(2) By asking for the gift of the Spirit.

(3) By receiving the Spirit by faith (the only way to
receive any gift from God).

(4) By entering upon the discipline of hourly, daily
obedience to Christ and the Spirit.

So very simply, I asked for the gift of the Helper,
thanked Him for granting this, and entered upon that
fourth step—the daily living out of this new relationship. I
experienced no waves of emotion or ecstasy. Even when
eighteen years later, I was given the gift of a heavenly
language (glossolalia), it was with no particular fanfare;

rather as a divine quartermaster might casually hand out a tool for a job, "Here. You'll need this."

When I had asked myself, "Can we expect a manifestation of the Spirit?," I had little idea how to answer. Since the Helper is a Person, I reasoned, then of course He has personality traits, and presumably, these traits will show themselves. How or in what way, I could not guess.

Manifest Himself He did, though not in a way I could have guessed. As I stepped out in faith back in 1945, day by day listening to the inner Voice for instructions, the first discipline He gave me was a leash for my tongue. For others the Spirit may give torrents of ecstatic speech; I needed the discipline of not speaking the careless or negative or discouraging word. For weeks I was put through the sharp training of opening my mouth to speak and hearing from the Teacher "Stop! No, don't say it. Close the mouth."

Many other experiences followed which I have described elsewhere[19] such as the joy of discovering the Helper's concern with guiding us in the details of everyday life; the reality of His guidance; the way He brings us to life at the emotional level. None of this I could have predicted. My experience was rather a solitary one. In 1945 I knew no one who was experimenting along the same line.

I realized that my husband Peter had already been given the Helper along with the unmistakable gift of preaching. Unlike me, he had not been seeking the Spirit per se, rather what God's specific will for his life was. Probably the Helper had come to Peter at the same time he was "tapped on the shoulder by the Chief," as he liked to put it, and told to emigrate to America to enter the ministry. Having long known the Spirit's presence and help in so many ways, Peter did not feel the need for conscious search that I did.

Later, at the time of my husband's sudden death, I shall be forever grateful that I was able to know the Spirit as Comforter during those days. Without Him, I might have survived, but only as a truncated person and without ever knowing the grace and splendor of the Comforter's presence on this, one of life's starkest frontiers. Not only did He comfort me, but in one practical step after another, He showed me how to handle the devastation of widowhood.

By 1950 I was in need of another kind of help. I was under contract to deliver the manuscript of *A Man Called Peter* by May 1st, yet had never had a single course in the craft of writing and almost no practice except scribbling in personal diaries and journals. In that extremity, the Spirit became my Instructor in creative writing. For instance, He took me by the hand and showed me that the opening pages must present Peter Marshall in the framework in which the public knew him—through his Senate chaplaincy. Only then could I flash back (I did not even know the term "flashback") to Peter's early life in Scotland and come forward.

I tried to outline the book and knew that it was not right. When I asked my Teacher the right way of outlining the book, I was told that Peter's biography would have no lasting significance apart from what his life demonstrated about God—His goodness, His revelation of truth, His ways of dealing with men. "Outline the book *that* way," was the instruction. I did, and the material fell into place.

My Teacher showed me how to construct a book, what to include out of the totality of one man's life, what to omit. All the way through He kept insisting on the importance of the light touch and humor as the way to emphasize greatness.

Now I experienced all the emotion I had *not* felt when I'd first asked for His presence—plus much much more. "No creative work," He told me, "has final impact unless it touches the reader at the level of the emotions." As I worked on the manuscript, He poured through me a stream of strong emotion, yet permitted me none of the sentimentality into which I was tempted to slip.

So functional and effectual was the Teacher's guidance that I had fewer editorial suggestions, less outside help

with *A Man Called Peter* than with any book since, and I
wrote it more swiftly.

Little did I dream that some sixteen years later I would
see the rise of a major surge of the Spirit like a groundswell
across the world.

It came in 1966–1967 when a rising tide of evil had
plunged our world into a mess. The young, already disillusioned with war, were convinced that humanism had
failed. High school and college students were more clear-
eyed about man's failure than were most liberal theolo-
gians. Liberal churches and seminarians who mostly told
us what *not* to believe, were still teaching the sad doctrine
that any reform—humanitarian, sociological, political, ra-
cial, or religious—must be made by human effort alone. To
which the younger generation's consistent reply was, "No
way! Human effort alone hasn't worked, and never will."

So out of the vacuum of churches "holding the form of
religion but denying the power of it" [20] the young groped
their way—some of them through the jungle of drugs or the
occult or Eastern religions they didn't really understand, to
become "Jesus people." They not only carried Bibles, they
feverishly read them. They waded into the ocean or into
backyard swimming pools to be baptized. All over the world
they formed communes or "communities." And throughout the Jesus Revolution ran highly charged emotionalism—hand-clapping, hugging, singing, religious rock music, filled with words like "wow!" and "far-out!"

Of course some of these youthful experimenters were
not serious and soon drifted away. Yet many—like Carrie
and Jeff Buddington—were permanently healed of long-
standing hang-ups and had their lives turned right side up.

Like most adults I've had emotions ranging from delight—to wonder—to perplexity about all this. Yet surely
these young people have been saying something important
that the rest of us need to hear: we could use more joy and
more love in our spiritual lives; perhaps we have become so

occupied with worshiping God with our minds that we have forgotten that the rest of our beings, including the physical body, need to worship Him too.

Self-forgetfulness, a sort of joyous holy abandon, is indeed one of the Helper's trademarks. An experience Len had in 1962 is still vividly present with me....

During our Chappaqua, New York years we were part of a group of six or eight couples who met once a week in one another's homes for sharing, Bible study, and prayer. I remember that Len came to a particular meeting that spring discouraged and frustrated. An individual with whom he worked professionally was being difficult. In addition, he and I were having problems with our teen-agers.

That evening Len shared some of his problems and asked for prayer. Two members of the group especially seemed led to respond. With obvious concern, they stood by his chair, lightly rested their hands on his shoulders and head, and prayed. The particular request, as I recall, was that the power of the Holy Spirit would free Len of all resentments and antagonism. He told me later that he felt warmth coming from their hands. The prayer ended and he ex-pressed gratitude. The meeting broke up.

Hours later, after we were in bed, Len spoke softly, "Catherine, I hate to wake you up, but I have the strangest feeling."

A little alarmed, I asked, "How do you mean?"

"There's this rushing, headlong joy inside me! It started in the pit of my stomach after I got in bed, then has kept bubbling up right into my head. I've been lying here thinking how silly it is to be so joyous when I should be asleep, but I can't control it. Catherine, I'd like to pray about it."

"Well, fine," I responded sleepily. "Go ahead—pray."

"But it isn't enough just to lie here. I'd like to kneel."

So both of us knelt beside the bed.

Len's prayer began quietly enough. First, he expressed

gratitude for the friends who had cared enough to pray for him. Then he thanked God for our life together. After that he expressed love for each member of our family near and far. In between he kept telling the Lord how much he loved Him. Heartfelt love rose from the depths of his being for each person who had been a human thorn in Len's side. Afterwards he began God-blessing everyone he could think of, as if this love were so great it had to encompass the whole universe.

Always before Len's prayers had been short, even abrupt. Well thought out, words carefully chosen, but quite unemotional. In contrast, that night words poured from him lavishly, exuberantly repetitious, a geyser of deep emotion, unabashedly expressed. Like a bird uncaged, his emotions were darting, wheeling, soaring, wanting nothing so much as to keep on flying forever.

Minutes passed—half an hour, an hour, as the love and joy kept pouring from Len. Finally, becoming aware of me kneeling there too, Len interrupted himself long enough to say reluctantly, "This isn't fair to you, Catherine. I'd like to go on and on, but you need some sleep."

In the morning he reported, "It was the most cleansing experience I've ever had. I got to thinking it was almost like a car engine being overhauled. It's as though negative emotions—my frustrations and anger—had built up a residue in the body just like carbon deposits foul up spark plugs. That love and joy pouring through me was like fresh warm sudsy water washing away the bitterness. This morning I have—I don't know—a scrubbed feeling."

In the years since, on two other occasions Len has felt the same kind of rushing flowing love. In between time, he has tried seeking it on his own—to no avail. We know now—this kind of love is the Spirit's gracious gift, not something we humans can achieve on our own.

In 1970 I received as a gift a very old (1885) copy of *The*

Christian's Secret of a Happy Life by the Quaker Hannah Smith in whom I have been intensely interested for years. As I eagerly turned the yellowed old pages—but what was this? A chapter on the Holy Spirit. I had many editions of *The Christian's Secret* in my library, knew this book practically by heart, and there was no such chapter.

Why the deletion, I wondered?

I couldn't wait to read the chapter. As usual, Hannah Smith first turned to the Bible to summarize what it taught about the Spirit, then took a middle-of-the-road position liberally seasoned with common sense. The gist of her conclusion went something like this....

We make the mistake of looking upon the "baptism of the Spirit" as a single experience rather than a life, as an arbitrary bestowment rather than a necessary vitality.

It is plain from Scripture that we can't possibly enter into a new life in Christ or be a child of God at all without knowing the Spirit.[21] However, there is a big difference between being indwelt by the Spirit and being "filled" with His presence. For years (sometimes a lifetime) a Christian can keep the Spirit at a sub-basement level by the insistence on running one's own life. Then through teaching or need—or both—the person consciously recognizes his divine Guest's presence, opens the hitherto closed doors into certain rooms in his being so that the Spirit can enter there too. Thus the individual now deliberately abandons himself to the Helper's control.

"The result of this when done suddenly," Mrs. Smith explained, "is what many call 'the baptism of the Holy Spirit.' "[22] It can be but isn't always, a very emotional and overwhelming sense of His presence.

"In seeking for the baptism therefore, it is not God's attitude toward us that needs to be changed, but our attitude toward Him. He will not give us anything new; rather we are to receive in a new and far fuller sense that which He has already given at Pentecost. The Holy Spirit is the world's sunlight, its energy and power. Sunlight can be kept out only by erecting barriers against it. All we need do then, is to take down our shutters and barriers and walk out into the sunlight already given."

But then Hannah Smith issues a strong word of warning. "Baptism means," she says, "far more than emotion. It means to be immersed or dipped into the Spirit of God, into His character and nature. The real evidence of one's baptism is neither emotion nor any single gift such as tongues, rather that there *must* be Christ-likeness in life and character: by fruits in the life we shall know whether or not we have the Spirit."

Nor does this mean instantaneous holiness. The disciples had to learn that right after Pentecost, and so do we. Ananias and Sapphira [23] could still lie and cheat, and so can we. In practical fact, our life with the Spirit is a walk, a growth, an unfolding, as we learn to trust Him, and open more and more of our being to His presence and control.

To me this seemed such solid teaching that I wondered all the more why the chapter had been deleted from all more recent editions of the book. Intent upon unraveling the mystery, I sought the story behind this chapter. These are the facts as I dug them out of Hannah Smith's letters and writings and more recent books about the Smith family. [24]

Hannah was born in Philadelphia on February 7, 1832, into a Quaker family who were eminently successful glass manufacturers. Though Hannah grew up a lively girl in a happy home, by age sixteen she was writing of "the aching void in my heart." This was in part adolescent drama, but the spiritual hunger was real enough, so much so that for the rest of her long life she was an eager, open-minded spiritual researcher. Like John Wesley in the century before her, she would listen to anybody with a religious experience to relate; she read constantly, investigated tirelessly.

Such eagerness might have led this Quaker girl straying down dead-ends and into paths of heresy. Fortunately, she possessed qualities to balance her insatiable zeal—a thorough knowledge of Scripture and a high degree of common sense.

Hannah had long since arrived at the conclusion that the only solid ground of our faith is the character of God—who and what He is. The only sure route for us humans to know Him and experience His love and guidance resides "not in the region of the emotions, but in the region of the will—not 'How do I feel?' but always 'What does God say?'" Though initially she had set out on "a feverish search for emotional religion," she soon grew mistrustful of emotionalism in religion.

In 1865 Hannah and her husband, Robert Pearsall Smith, and their children moved to the village of Milltown, New Jersey, where Robert took charge of a branch of the family glass business. There Hannah met a group called "the Holiness Methodists."

Some of the most penetrating and valuable parts of *The Christian's Secret,* a book helpful to generations of Christians, was to come from what Hannah learned from this group. She was able to translate their teaching from its in-language to fresh everyday vernacular. No mean accomplishment!

Eventually Robert Smith was as caught up as his wife in all this. One summer the Smiths went to a ten-day Holiness Camp Meeting at a woodland campsite along the New Jersey coast. The purpose of these meetings, in Hannah's words, was "to open our hearts to the teachings of the Holy Spirit and His coming into seekers' hearts." But it was Robert rather than his wife who received an extraordinary emotional experience. As Hannah later reported it: [25]

After the meeting my husband had gone alone into a spot in the woods to continue to pray by himself. Suddenly, from head to foot he was shaken with what seemed like a magnetic thrill of heavenly delight, and floods of glory seemed to pour through him, soul and body, with the

inward assurance that this was the longed-for Baptism of
the Holy Spirit.

The whole world seemed transformed for him, every leaf
and blade of grass quivered with exquisite colour....
Everybody looked beautiful to him, for he seemed to see
the Divine Spirit within each one.... This ecstasy lasted
for several weeks, and was the beginning of a wonderful
career of spiritual power and blessing.

Naturally, this made Hannah renew her efforts to receive
similar joy. She described how she "went forward" to the
altar night after night in the meetings, then would go with a
smaller group to one of the tents, where they would spend
hours kneeling in the dark, pleading and wrestling in
prayer. For Mrs. Smith all this effort seemed of no avail.
Not then or ever did she have an emotional experience of
the type that had meant so much to her husband.

At first Hannah was disappointed. Then she realized that
what had been given her was a "real revelation of God that
made life to me a different thing ever since." She wanted
emotions and was given conviction. She "wanted a vision
and got a fact."

Later, Mrs. Smith came to feel that the difference
between what she and her husband experienced was largely
a reflection of the difference in their natures: Robert was
emotional, inclined to feel response in physical sensations;
Hannah was a more reserved and analytical person.

In 1873 the Smiths emigrated to England to become one
of America's most famous expatriate families with their
lives intertwined by marriage or friendship with Bertrand
Russell, Bernard Shaw, Beatrice and Sidney Webb, Bernard Berenson, the great art critic, and Henry James. For
some years the Smiths carried on a remarkable joint lay
ministry in England, especially in aristocratic circles.
These meetings became known as the Higher Life Movement, and much of their teaching was carried on at house
parties in some of England's great country places.

In the spring of 1875 Robert also traveled to Germany,
where he held highly successful evangelistic-teaching
meetings before large crowds, always in a highly charged
emotional atmosphere. "All Europe is at my feet," exulted
Robert in a letter to his wife. When engraved pictures of
him were offered for sale, eight thousand sold immediately.

Then the blow fell. Gossip began about Robert Pearsall
Smith's improper conduct with female admirers. No one
then or now knows the exact truth of the matter. The
emotionalism so appealing to Smith had apparently gotten
out of hand. It seemed that Paul's instruction to "Salute
one another with an holy kiss," had here spilled over to the
physical.

The rumors got into the press. Meetings scheduled in
England were canceled by their sponsors and for a time the
Smiths returned to New Jersey. Hannah quietly stood by
her husband. She wrote a friend of their "heart-scale" and
of the "crushing blow"[26] that had befallen Robert.

And crush him it did. He gave way to discouragement,
disillusionment, and to a degree of cynicism. Robert sank
into a joyless old age, while Hannah went on from strength
to strength, her quiet deep faith carrying her triumphantly
over all sorts of trials and difficulties.

With this story as background for the Smiths' experience
of the Helper, we begin to see the many forms and results
His coming into the life can have. Each opportunity for
Christian growth, each step forward, brings new temptations and dangers. In Robert Smith's case, tragedy resulted
when he succumbed to the temptation to idolize emotion
instead of worshiping Jesus. With Hannah Smith, no
ecstasy was apparent but a quieter joy from the fruitage of
her convictions about God.

As for the missing chapter, clearly editors had been
afraid of the subject. It was fire. Hadn't Robert Smith been
burned? Safer to omit it, they must have concluded.

As Len and I pondered Hannah's story, we agreed that

the modern surge of the Spirit in America may stand poised at the edge of this same problem—too great a love affair with emotion, too little grounding in Scripture, too wanting in garden-variety discipline, too small an emphasis on purity, strict honesty, morality—Christ's own life living in us.

What is needed, of course, is balance: plenty of solid teaching—but plenty of joy as well. Let's admit that over-emotionalism is the last problem most of us face in our mainline denominational churches. We shall achieve a proper balance between the emotions and the mind when we are truly led by the Helper—"always a Gentleman."

It may well be that the missing element in Robert Pearsall Smith's experience was a small corrective fellowship of other Christians like that of the infant Church in Acts 5. What was still missing in the late nineteenth century was a body of wisdom concerning the Holy Spirit movement and the Scriptural teaching of group submission. Recent experience is teaching us that as we go adventuring in the Spirit, we must deliberately make ourselves subject one to the other, be willing to be checked and corrected as well as encouraged and strengthened.

Thinking back to his own bubbling joy that memorable night in Chappaqua, Leonard commented, "It was heady stuff. No wonder people at Pentecost thought the disciples were full of new wine! No wonder Robert Pearsall Smith got himself in trouble! I have no intention of stopping at this point, just with waves of emotion, I mean. The emotion's great, but—well, a quiet day-by-day rooting and grounding in love and obedience is far more important."

The excising of Hannah Smith's chapter on the Holy Spirit points up the real question, why are we afraid of the Helper?

Something that happened to Elizabeth and John Sherrill illustrates just how fearful our society can be. In 1962 the Sherrills published *The Cross and the Switchblade*, the previously mentioned story of David Wilkerson's work with

New York drug addicts and warring gangs. For religious circles the book was clearly a departure necessarily depicting foul lives and some raw violence. The question in the Sherrill's minds was, would the public really be interested in reading about drug addiction in the big city? In those years it seemed like a remote sort of subject.

The publisher received a large order from one of the major denominational accounts. However, a condition was attached to the order: two chapters—21 and 22—which described the Baptism in the Holy Spirit, must be deleted "because such material would not be acceptable to our readers." The crime and violence the Sherrills had worried about was apparently perfectly permissible; it was the Spirit who was suspect!

The order was a temptation because the number of books in question was so large and the title was not expected to sell well. However, to Wilkerson and the Sherrills these chapters on the Baptism contained the point of the book, the secret of the amazing success of Wilkerson's work. To hold out a promise of help and then not tell how to obtain it would have been cheating. They declined to make the deletions. As it turned out, *The Cross and the Switchblade,* with the "unacceptable" chapters, became one of the best-selling religious books of the decade— including enormous sales to the denomination in question. To date *The Cross and the Switchblade* has sold a total of eleven million copies, domestic and foreign.

Some of us are afraid. Could we be terrified that if we invite the Holy Spirit into our hearts, we will lose control of our own emotions or the guidance of our individual life? Or are we afraid that the comfortable structures we have known may be altered or even blown to bits? Still others say they want to stay in safe areas that won't offend anybody, thus avoiding controversy and divisiveness.

There are dozens of theological dugouts in which people hide such as, "When I became a Christian I received everything there is to receive." Or "All those experiences in the Book of the Acts were just for the first century. Our time is different. We don't have the same needs today." Or again, one hears over and over, "I want my faith to remain middle-of-the-road *orthodox* Christianity. That's good enough for me."

The odd part of this latter statement is that I can think of nothing more central to Christianity or "orthodox" than the doctrine of the Trinity: God, our Father; Jesus, our Saviour and Friend; the Holy Spirit—Comforter, Counsellor, and Helper, who mediates the Father and our Lord to us. What Jesus Himself taught us must be central to "Christianity." Since He Himself bade us "Be filled with the Spirit" and told us that He personally would be the Baptizer, we can't very well extirpate the Third Person of the Trinity and still be "orthodox."

Part of our fear may also be that instinctively we know that the Spirit means power, and power makes all of us acutely uneasy. We're like people who have always lived with candles and campfires. We've heard rumors of electricity, but because we've never seen electric lights and are not certain we would know how to handle electric power, we'd rather make do with candles all our days.

As for churches, they must choose whether they wish to remain ecclesiastical monuments to Christ as just another historical figure—a great teacher whose brief life was cut short in 29 or 30 A.D. (Those churches would be limited to such things as liturgy, organizations, and a degree of social action.) Or the alternative is the church as the close fellowship of followers of the living Christ, the contemporary Lord, that fellowship made alive and operative by His Spirit, marching to His now-orders.

Until the surge of the Spirit began in the 1960s, far too many churches had chosen to be ecclesiastical monuments. A churchman like Dr. Carl Henry has warned about the danger of making the Holy Spirit "a displaced person": "Whenever the Church makes the Spirit of God a refugee," Dr. Henry wrote, "the Church—not the Spirit—becomes the vagabond."

Once we understand what Jesus told us would happen in the Era of the Spirit, we next ask, are these miracles of grace, restoration, guidance, new teaching, healing, rescuing, and all the rest actually happening today?

The account of what took place in the life of someone like Tay Thomas points up what a resounding "Yes" can be answered to this. Tay is Mrs. Lowell Thomas, Jr.; her husband is the son of the famed radio and television commentator and world traveler. The Thomases live in Alaska, where Lowell is one of Alaska's state senators.

Good Friday, 1964, began as such a happy day for the Thomas family. The snow which had been coming down steadily for two days finally let up. Lowell could fly from Spenard to a meeting in Fairbanks, and get back so that the family could spend Easter together. David Thomas was then six; Anne, eight. The story is best told in Tay's own words: [27]

"The children and I waved goodbye as Lowell drove off to the airport, then shut the door quickly because it was still below freezing outside. About five o'clock, feeling lonesome for him, Anne, David, and I went upstairs to watch TV. We took off our shoes so we could sit on the bed.

"It was half an hour later that I heard a rumbling sound. Although we frequently hear a similar roaring—the firing of guns at a nearby Army base—I knew instantly that these were no guns.

"I leapt off the bed, yelling 'Earthquake!' Grabbing Anne, I called to David. We had gotten as far as the front hall when the house began to shake. As we ran outside into the snow, David was crying, 'Mommy, I'm in bare feet!'

"We were about ten feet beyond the front door when we were flung violently to the ground, which was jolting back and forth with unbelievable force. The hallway we had just run through split in two. We heard the crashing of glass, the ear-rending sound of splintering wood. In front of us a great tree crashed full length. Our garage collapsed with a sharp report.

"Now the earth began breaking up and buckling all about us. Suddenly between Anne and me a great crack opened in the snow. I stared in disbelief as the trench widened, apparently bottomless, separating me from my child. I seized the hand she stretched out to me in time to pull her across the chasm.

"We were left on a wildly bucking slab. Suddenly it tilted sharply, and we had to hang on to keep from slipping into a yawning crevasse. Now the earth seemed to be rising just ahead of us. I had the weird feeling that we were riding backward on a monstrous Ferris wheel, going down, down toward the water (our house had stood on a high bluff overlooking Cook Inlet). The entire face of the bluff had fallen to sea level. A few feet away, at the water's edge, lay the roof of our house.

"All I could think of was that the water would rise as earth tumbled into it and we would be trapped. The cliffs above us were sheer, with great sections of sand and clay still falling.

"The children both were hysterical, crying over and over, 'We'll die! We'll die!' I realized we'd have to find a way up that cliff, but the children were too frightened to walk.

"I looked up at the leaden gray sky, the bleak clouds, and silently cried out, 'Jesus, where are You—I thought You'd be with us at the end.' *Suddenly, I felt a sense of peace so intense that I knew beyond all doubt He was with me—not way up in the air, but right there inside me.* It was a revelation that gave me a tremendous courage.

"We clambered up and down the great slabs of earth and snow, our bare feet aching and raw in the cold. I found a large tree leaning against the cliff and thought for a few moments that we might be able to shinny up it, but we gained only a few feet.

"Suddenly a man appeared above us. 'Help!' we called to him. He shouted down that he would hunt for a rope, then disappeared. As we waited we were aware for the first time that we were soaked to the skin, the children shaking and their lips blue.

"At least six or eight men appeared at the top of the cliff. One of them, a stranger to us, started down, finding one less steep spot. The children threw their arms around him as he reached us. He took off his black wool jacket, put it around Anne, then boosted David into his arms and led us all back up along the rope. At the top, when I turned to thank our rescuer, he had gone."

Tay Thomas went on to describe the mounting suspense during the hours when Lowell and his family could not communicate; then the drama of their reunion. For so many hours Lowell had not known whether his family was dead or alive.

The earthquake experience bound families and neighbors together as never before. For Tay it was another in a series of spiritual adventures that have been part of her life's search.

In 1954 she and her husband had flown around the world together in a single-engine Cessna plane named "Charlie." They spent long days with bearded Afghan nomads and Pygmies of the Congo; they sailed in a primitive dhow on the Persian Gulf; they put in an appearance at the birthday ball of the Emperor of Ethiopia.

On the dashboard of the plane Tay had pasted this poem:

> Peace be in thy home
> And in thy heart.
> Or if thou roam
> Earth's highways wide,
> The Lord is at thy side,
> To bless and guide.

In 1958 the Thomases had put three-year-old Anne in "Charlie's" back seat and taken off on three months' work on a television film documentary on Alaska, the new forty-ninth state. It was an area pulsing with vitality, full of the promise of the frontier and of undeveloped resources. Tay's book *Follow the North Star* is a vivid account of traveling in a small plane through wilderness areas with a small child.

Out of this trip had come the Thomases' decision in 1960 to make Alaska their home. Soon Lowell was elected a state senator, Tay to the Anchorage School Board, and to the important Land Use Planning Commission.

Tay's spiritual search had begun two years after the move to Alaska. Her family, the Sam Pryors, had been lifelong Episcopalians in the traditional manner. But intermittent years of roaming the world had deprived Lowell and her of a church home. Suddenly Tay realized that the children were old enough for Sunday School and that the time had come to find a church. Within a few weeks she found Saint Mary's Episcopal Church, a small wooden structure sitting on a hilltop, with windows looking out over Alaska's magnificent mountains. But it wasn't the building that won over the Thomases—it was a warm, loving, informal congregation and pastor. To Tay, Saint Mary's meant the finding of what she calls her "faith ladder."

In 1963 she climbed up the first of two most important rungs. It happened the night she heard the visiting pastor, Dennis Bennett, talk in a crowded school auditorium. Tay's whole life was changed that night. In her own words...

While driving home I realized that Christianity wasn't just going to church on Sunday and trying to follow the Ten Commandments—that I actually had to commit my life to Jesus, to give up all of my own personal ambitions and desires and let Him take over, using me in whatever way He saw fit. At first I was frightened, scared to death of letting go the "command" of my own life. But I did, talking to Him while driving, "I am Yours, Lord, do with me what You wish." My fear was suddenly replaced by such a joyful, peaceful feeling that I sang praises all the way home.

Once I had climbed onto that first rung of my faith ladder, life changed in many ways. I was happier, I prayed informally often, all during the day whenever I felt the need for support or guidance, and with missionary zeal I plunged headlong into a massive load of community social work.

I'm so grateful that I had achieved that first rung of the ladder before the trauma of the earthquake. But it was traumatic, and while it taught me that God is a present power, I knew that I needed something more. That was when I embarked on my search for what step would take me up the second rung of my ladder. The second part of the search took almost five years.

One day, after many hours of reading and searching through the Bible, the answer came to me. The original apostles had Jesus as their constant companion and guide, but when He was about to leave them, He promised to send the Comforter, one who would continue to be with them in everything they did—the Holy Spirit. I had always considered the Biblical story of the day of Pentecost as an historical happening, but now, as I read through the letters of Saint Paul, I knew I was wrong—the Holy Spirit had been promised to all people for all time, bringing to all believers the same gifts and fruits of the Spirit as in those earliest Christian days.

I longed to be filled with the Holy Spirit because I could see what His presence was doing for friends and for the many Spirit-filled people I was reading about. But who isn't afraid of the supernatural!

As I prayed more and more about my dilemma, one Sunday our minister announced that there would be a Wednesday evening prayer meeting at the home of a parishioner and his wife who I knew were having real experiences of the Spirit. I had the immediate realization that here was my chance to step up onto that next rung of the faith ladder. I was so excited by Wednesday I was ready for anything—all reticence gone. An uncanny coincidence of timing, perhaps, but I still think that Jesus has His eye on our movements up that ladder.

That night I received the laying on of hands, felt the joyful inpouring of the Holy Spirit. Needless to say, my elation increased until I thought I'd burst with joy, a state of euphoria which lasted for several weeks. Once I had returned to a more normal emotional level, I realized that many startling changes in my life were coming one after another.

I was fascinated to hear from Tay what those changes were. For the first time, she knew Jesus as a close personal Friend, that same closeness which she had experienced briefly during the Earthquake. There was a great strengthening of her private prayer life—she could talk to and praise God in a way and a language she had never known before. Gradually she was learning to listen to that "still small voice." Then there was the new dimension of answered prayer, though not always in the way Tay wanted or expected. She also saw some miraculous healing through prayer and experienced it herself. There was a new relationship to other people, a deeper love and understanding which helped immeasurably in Tay's community work— old habit-patterns of anger, frustration, and irritation were gone, leaving her more energy and enthusiasm.

One of the changes that startled Tay Thomas most had to do with her old reticent Episcopal solemnness toward worship in church. In the beginning she resisted the folk

mass, the new liturgy, the general informality of worship.
Her inclination had been to go to the altar for Communion
in reverent silence, to pray quietly by isolating herself in
the pew. In her new life she was startled to find herself in
the midst of the loudest singing during services, the words
of the prayers, old and new, took on a deeper meaning, and
she almost danced on her way to the altar. She has laughed
and cried during folk masses and at retreats, and along with
this great release of emotions, has no hestiation about
sharing the new growth of her faith with others.

Tay Thomas has been amazed at what has been happening recently in her state. "In just the last five years," she
wrote us recently, "the Holy Spirit has roared through
Alaska from the Panhandle to the tiny Arctic villages.
Many churches are open about the wonderful experiences
felt by so many people of all denominations.

"I don't see how this tremendous and exciting Power can
be stopped" she told me, "when it is so clearly supported by
the Bible and so firmly supported by so many 'conservative' people of traditional background. Anyway, as for me
I feel strongly that it's time for me to speak up and be
counted.

"We're told there was an earthquake on the First Good
Friday too. But then dawned the calm and the victory of
Resurrection morning. What happened on the first Easter
morning made possible all the good that has come out of
our Good Friday earthquake, for me perfectly captured in
the lines from an old hym:

> Speak through the earthquake, wind and fire,
> O still, small voice of calm.[28]

There is a sense in which every page of this book is about
the Helper. Jesus told us He would send Him to us—and
He has. As Comforter and Teacher He was with Edith and
Peter John and me in that little Cessna 205, tenderly
brooding over Peter Christopher's tiny white casket, saying

to us, "I have many things to teach you. Walk softly, with heads up. This too will teach you."...

Nancy De Moss's friend Ginny learned what Jesus meant when He promised, "He—the Spirit—will tell you about the future." The Helper knew about that fire. The baby Brandon must be saved. "Go and get Brandon," He directed Ginny.

"It's the risk in *not* obeying the Helper that gives me the shivers now," Nancy De Moss reflects.

That day in the little church, the Spirit came to Pat Baker in His role as Counsellor. He spoke through the young preacher's lips, "He's ready to deal with your problem of nicotine."

How does he know that?

"It started when you were a teen-ager. The problem grew out of the soil of rebellion."

So He does know! Wise Counsellor....

That bitterly cold winter in Oregon it was the Helper who rescued Carrie and Jeff Buddington and their friends by alerting the men up the road in the Christian community, "Go—and saw wood."

"Saw wood, Lord?"

"Yes, saw wood. I was a carpenter, I know all about wood. Remember? But the woodpile will be only the beginning."

Or I think of Gene Klinger and Roberta Lashley who got an intimate look at how swiftly and ingeniously the Helper comes to protect from immediate danger those who ask Him, even as David Livingstone experienced the same protection a century ago in Africa.

And Maude Blanford, so grievously ill of cancer, knows now how surely Jesus fulfills His promises about the Helper. "He, the Spirit of truth, is come, He will guide you into all truth."

"The truth is," the Helper told Maude, "your life is in danger. See, your body-house has no roof. Without Jesus as your covering, you have no protection."

"But how do I get the roof back on my body-house?"

"Here I am—I, the Lord thy God, to loose the bonds, to let the oppressed go free. I will lead you out step by step."

Yes, a healthy Maude Blanford knows that the Spirit is also this, the Great Physician, Lord of the body.

You and I are living in rough times. We must make our way through minefields of evil, booby traps of deception, brush fires of sickness and disease, wastelands of economic disaster, burning deserts of disappointment. "I won't take you out of this world," Jesus told us. "But don't be afraid, because I've overcome that world of dangers. All power is Mine. I promise to be with you always."

"How, Lord? How are you with us?"

"Through the Helper."

It is true. He is here. We who in moments of desperation have asked, "What can I do? What is there left?" have felt His answering presence and experienced His help...We know now...always He holds out to us the exciting promise of something more.

Notes

Chapter 1 Yes, God Is in Everything

1. Acts 4:20
2. Job 1:21
3. Hannah W. Smith, *The Christian's Secret of a Happy Life* (Westwood, N.J.: Fleming H. Revell Company, 1962), pp. 148, 149
4. I Thessalonians 5:18
5. Hannah W. Smith, *The Christian's Secret of a Happy Life,* pp. 144, 146, 147, 149
6. Romans 8:28
7. Shakespeare, *Hamlet* IV. v. 78
8. This story and other examples of relinquishment are included in Catherine Marshall's *Beyond Our Selves* (New York: McGraw-Hill Book Company, 1961), chapter 6, "The Prayer of Relinquishment".
9. Luke 18:10–14
10. Matthew 10:29–31
11. Matthew 25:37–46
12. Acts 9:4, 5
13. Matthew 18:5
14. Frank C. Laubach, *You Are My Friends* (New York: Harper and Row, 1942), p. 22
15. Mark 1:40. James Moffatt, *The Bible: A New Translation* (New York: Harper & Row, 1935)
16. Matthew 18:12–14

Chapter 2 The Golden Bridge of Praise

1. Merlin R. Carothers, *Prison to Praise* (Plainfield, N.J.: Logos International, 1970)

2. Psalm 22:3

3. I Thessalonians 5:16–18

4. Colossians 4:2

5. See also I Peter 2:9; Philippians 4:4–6; Romans 1:21

6. Hebrews 13:15

7. *The Random House Dictionary of the English Language* (New York: Random House, 1966, 1967)

8. Habakkuk 3:17, 18

9. II Chronicles 20:21, 22

10. The Acts 16:19–40

11. Luke 10:20

12. Isaiah 12:2, 3

13. Philippians 4:11 *(Revised Standard Version)*

14. Philippians 4:4–6

15. II Corinthians 11:23–30

16. Ephesians 5:20

17. This incident has also been told in Corrie ten Boom's *The Hiding Place* (Washington Depot, Conn.: Chosen Books, 1971), pp. 180–181.

18. Though the material here (and at several other places) is set in much the same style as Peter Marshall's sermons, I have borrowed the style but not the material.

19. Both in Greek or Hebrew the most common word for "thank" or "praise" is also often translated "bless": Ps. 63:3,4; Ps. 69:30; Luke 1:64. Note also the clear thrust of Luke 15:11–32 that man's actions can make God happy.

20. Hebrew for "hand" is *yad*; for "thanks" *yadah*. *Yadah* is used for "thanksgiving" 40 times in the Old Testament; for "praise" 53 times; for "confess" 19 times. (King James Version)

21. Scripture's use of the same Hebrew root for "praise" and "confession" makes sense. Confession is the recognition that we have sinned—an offense against God. Thus both praise and confession are an acknowledgment that God is God.

Chapter 3 Forgiveness: The Aughts and the Anys

1. Mark 11:25

2. John 16:8

3. Catherine Marshall, *Beyond Our Selves*, pp. 47–48

4. Matthew 18:18

5. Matthew 22 : 37,38 *The Living Bible* (Wheaton, Illinois: Tyndale House Publishers, 1971)

6. Luke 15 : 25–32

7. Matthew 17 : 20

Chapter 4 The Law of Generations

1. Deuteronomy 28 : 41

2. Biblical scholars generally agree that Moses' towering spirit, along with his remembered and recorded words, was the inspiration for Deuteronomy. As usual, there is disagreement about the actual date of the book. Some would place it as late as Josiah's reign, about 638 B.C. Others offer evidence that the book discovered in the Temple and read to the people as told in II Kings 22,23 was the book of Deuteronomy.

3. Deuteronomy 30 : 15,19 *The Amplified Bible* (Grand Rapids: Zondervan Publishing House, 1965)

4. Romans 12 : 5

5. Exodus 20 : 5

6. Malachi 4 : 6

7. Ephesians 6 : 17,18

8. Hebrews 4 : 12

9. Luke 4 : 18

10. II Corinthians 3 : 17

11. Romans 8 : 21

12. Starr Daily, *God's Answer to Juvenile Delinquency* (St. Paul, Minnesota: Macalester Park Publishing Company, 1953), pp. 43–51; 132–142

13. Matthew 18 : 19

14. Matthew 6 : 4

15. Starr Daily, *Love Can Open Prison Doors;* (Worster, England: Arthur James, 1943); *Release;* (New York: Harper & Row, 1942); *Faith, Hope, and Love* (St. Paul, Minnesota: Macalester Park)

16. Matthew 6 : 33

17. Acts 10 : 28

18. This and the material that follows is taken from Elisabeth D. Dodds' *Marriage to a Difficult Man* (Philadelphia: The Westminster Press, 1971).

19. Exodus 20 : 6

20. Acts 2 : 39

Chapter 5 The Joy of Obedience

1. Art De Moss is founder of National Liberty Corporation, a life insurance company.
2. Matthew 7:24,25
3. John 14:21–23
4. Hebrews 5:9
5. John 7:17
6. Matthew 12:50
7. John 14:23
8. John 14:21
9. Acts 5:32
10. James 1:25; I John 3:22
11. John 14:21
12. Titus 3:1; I Peter 2:13–17; Romans 13:1,2; John 19:11
13. I Peter 5:5
14. Hebrews 13:17; I Peter 5:1–5
15. I Corinthians 11:3
16. Ephesians 5:21–24; I Peter 3:7; I Samuel 3:13
17. Ephesians 5:25–33; I Peter 3:1–7
18. Colossians 3:20
19. C. S. Lewis, *The Screwtape Letters* (New York: The Macmillan Company, 1943), p. 21
20. The existence of both a sleep system and a wakefulness (activating) system in the brain is now generally acknowledged. The sleep-inducing mechanisms have been experimentally demonstrated in the lower brain stem, the descending limbic hypnogenic circuit, and the neocortex; the reticular arousal system is thought to be in the brain stem. For more on this, see J. Edward Murray, *Sleep, Dreams and Arousal* (New York: Appleton-Century-Crofts, 1965)
21. Such as the sleep experiments of the Sleep Research and Treatment Facility of the Milton S. Hershey Medical Center, Hershey, Pennsylvania
22. Hymn *Blessed Assurance* by Fanny J. Crosby
23. Hannah W. Smith, *The Christian's Secret of a Happy Life*, p. 208
24. Genesis 12:1,2

Chapter 6 "To Sleep! Perchance to Dream…"

1. Numbers 12:6,8 *(Revised Standard Version)*
2. Matthew 27:19
3. Research typical of sleep laboratories is the research of Dr. Charles Fisher as summarized in "Psychoanalytic Implications of Recent Research on Sleep", *Journal of the American Psychoanalytic Association,* Vol. 13, p. 20 (April 1965).
4. Morton Kelsey, *God, Dreams and Revelation, A Christian Interpretation of Dreams* (Minneapolis: Augsburg Publishing House, 1968, 1974)
5. John A. Sanford, *Dreams: God's Forgotten Language* (Philadelphia: J. B. Lippincott Company, 1968)
6. John 2:25
7. See pages 90–94
8. Glenn Clark, *How to Find Health through Prayer* (New York: Harper and Row, 1940), pp. 105–108
9. Lewis's fiction works (New York: Macmillan) include *Out of the Silent Planet; Perelandra; That Hideous Strength; Till We Have Faces.*
10. See page 87
11. See page 87
12. Joel 2:28; Acts 2:17

Chapter 7 The Fallen Angel

1. C. S. Lewis, *Mere Christianity* (New York: The Macmillan Company, 1943), p. 40
2. Isaiah 14:12–14
3. Revelation 12:4
4. For a summary of current research in an effort to solve the mysteries of memory, learning, and consciousness, see "Exploring the Frontiers of the Mind," *Time* (January 14, 1974).
5. Genesis 3:5
6. Genesis 1:28
7. Hebrews 2:7,8 is quoted from Psalm 8:5,6
8. Matthew 4:4
9. Edna St. Vincent Millay, *Collected Poems* (New York: Harper and Row, 1934), p. 91
10. C. S. Lewis, *The Screwtape Letters*, pp. 68, 96, 97

11. John 12:19

12. Derek Prince, "Spiritual Conflict" (from the Cassette Teaching Series, Derek Prince Publications, Fort Lauderdale, Florida)

13. John 18:37

14. C. S. Lewis, *Mere Christianity*, pp. 55, 56

15. Ephesians 6:12,13, *(The Living Bible)*

Chapter 8 The Unholy Spirit

1. Out of this interview also came Catherine Marshall's "An Answer to Drugs," *Guideposts* (May 1970)

2. Lysergic acid diethylamide (LSD)

3. The amphetamine drugs

4. *Life* (July 18, 1969)

5. *Time* (February 11, 1974) and *Newsweek* (February 11, 1974)

6. Zechariah 12–14

7. This and the quotations below from the graduate student and from Professor Eliade are from Andrew M. Greeley, "There's A New-Time Religion on Campus," *The New York Times* (June 1, 1969)

8. I Peter 5:8 *(Revised Standard Version)*

9. John 8:44

10. Luke 13:16; Mark 9:25,26

11. Job 1:2,5,18,19

12. Job 1:9–11

13. Derek Prince, "Deliverance and Demonology," from the Cassette Teaching Series, Derek Prince Publications, Fort Lauderdale, Florida

14. James 4:7

15. I Corinthians 10:13

16. Matthew 28:18

17. John 8:34

18. John 14:30

19. Romans 13:12

20. Isaiah 9:2

21. Ephesians 5:8

22. Joshua 7:11–13

23. John 3:20,21

24. Luke 8 : 28

25. II Peter 2 : 9 (*The Living Bible*)

26. Luke 10 : 19

27. Revelation 3 : 10

28. I John 1 : 7–9

29. Colossians 2 : 14, 15 (*The Bible: A New Translation*)

30. Catherine Marshall, *A Man Called Peter* (New York: McGraw-Hill Book Company, 1951) pp. 120, 121

Chapter 9 The Enigma of Healing

1. As this book goes to press Kent Ghost is still an outpatient at NIH in Bethesda, Maryland. The happy ending of the crisis was but one of the many episodes in an eight-year battle with leukemia. The end of the story is not yet. C.M.

2. John 6 : 38; 14 : 9

3. Acts 10 : 38

4. Luke 4 : 18; Matthew 4 : 23; Matthew 12 : 15

5. John 5 : 1–14

6. Luke 5 : 12,13; Mark 9 : 22–24

7. Matthew 5 : 3–11

8. III John 2

9. John 14 : 12. See also Mark 16 : 15–18; Hebrews 13 : 8

10. Matthew 8 : 16–17; Mark 3 : 7–11; 6 : 53–56; Luke 6 : 17–19

11. Mark 3 : 1–5

12. John 5 : 1–14

13. Romans 3 : 23

14. Deuteronomy 9 : 5

15. Titus 3 : 5

16. John 5 : 14 (*The Living Bible*)

17. Ruth Cranston, *The Miracle of Lourdes* (New York: McGraw-Hill Book Company, 1955)

18. One compilation of these case histories: (*The Miracle of Lourdes*)

19. Dr. Carrel's own account of this is: Alexis Carrel, *The Voyage to Lourdes* (New York: Harper and Row, 1950)

20. Catherine Marshall, *A Man Called Peter*, pp. 175–177

Chapter 10   The Roof on the House

1. John 16:13
2. Isaiah 64:6
3. Romans 3:20; Philippians 3:8,9
4. John 5:19
5. John 8:29; 5:30
6. John 6:38 *(The Bible: A New Translation)*
7. John 4:34
8. For other instances of relinquishment, see Catherine Marshall, *Beyond Our Selves,* chapter 6
9. Fritz Kunkel and Roye E. Dickerson, *How Character Develops* (New York: Charles Scribner's Sons, 1944), pp. 116, 120
10. Luke 8:43–48
11. Mark 2:1–12
12. Luke 18:1–8
13. Matthew 4:4,6,7
14. John 5:19 (*The Living Bible*)
15. Luke 10:9

Chapter 11   The King's Treasury

1. Edith Schaeffer, *L'Abri* (Wheaton, Illinois: Tyndale House, 1969), p. 126. Other books by Mrs. Schaeffer describing the L'Abri community are *Hidden Art* and *Everybody Can Know.*
2. Francis Schaeffer, *The God Who Is There* (Downers Grove, Illinois: Inter-Varsity Press, 1968). Dr. Schaeffer is also the author of thirteen other books including *Escape from Reason, Death in the City, True Spirituality, The Church at the End of the 20th Century, He Is There and He Is Not Silent, Pollution and the Death of Man.*
3. Philippians 2:5
4. In late 1973 after nineteen years of living with almost no privacy in the Chalet les Mélèzes, the Schaeffers now have a private home. Yet typically they wrote me, "At last we have the space to share in a new way with endless teas, meals, conversations, meetings, Bible studies, discussions."
5. Matthew 6:33
6. Psalm 24:1

7. I John 3:1

8. Philippians 4:19

9. *The National Geographic* (May, 1974)

10. Matthew 20:32 *(The Living Bible)*

11. Luke 6:38

12. Malachi 3:10

13. Peter Marshall, *Mr. Jones, Meet the Master* (Westwood: Fleming H. Revell Company, 1949), pp. 63–74

14. Billie Davis first told this incident in "I Was a Hobo Kid," *The Saturday Evening Post* (December 13, 1952)

Chapter 12 The Dilemma of Our Rebellion

1. I Corinthians 4:5 *(The Bible: A New Translation)*

2. Joyce Maynard, "My Parents Are My Friends," *McCall's* (October 1972)

3. This and the quotation that follows are from Agnes Sanford, *Sealed Orders* (Plainfield, New Jersey: Logos International, 1972), pp. 51, 52

4. Matthew 5:21

5. Matthew 26:52

6. Matthew 5:22

7. Matthew 5:25

8. Matthew 6:15

9. Luke 6:36 *(The Living Bible)*

10. Hebrews 1:9

11. Luke 6:27 *(The Living Bible)*

12. I Corinthians 10:10,11 *(The Living Bible)*

13. Numbers 14:23,25,29,32

14. Leviticus 26:12 *(The Amplified Bible)*

15. *Guideposts* (November 1973)

16. Proverbs 4:23

17. Paul Tournier, *The Whole Person in a Broken World* (New York: Harper and Row, 1947), pp. 2–12

18. Walter Kaufmann, *Existentialism from Dostoevsky to Sartre* (New York: The World Publishing Company, 1956)

19. Mark 7:14–23 *(The Living Bible)*

20. Matthew 5 : 22

21. Ezekiel 36 : 26–28

22. Isaiah 60 : 18

Chapter 13 Run for the Strong Tower

1. David Shaw and Bill Hazlett, *The Miami Herald* (January 7, 1973)

2. *Guideposts* (November, 1966)

3. John 3 : 20

4. Colossians 1 : 16; John 1 : 3

5. Romans 13 : 12

6. Proverbs 18 : 10

7. Matthew 28 : 18

8. John 14 : 13

9. Luke 10 : 17

10. *Guideposts* (December, 1965)

11. Hymn *God Will Take Care of You.* Lyric by C. D. Martin

12. Schapera, ed., *Livingstone's African Journal 1853–1856*, 2 vols., (London: Chatto and Windus, 1963), vol. II, p. 374

13. Hunter B. Blakely, *Religion in Shoes* (Richmond, Virginia: John Knox Press, 1953), pp. 89, 90.

14. II Timothy 1 : 7

15. Romans 8 : 15

16. John 3 : 17

17. Matthew 6 : 30 (*A New Translation of the Bible*)

18. Matthew 8 : 26 (*A New Translation of the Bible*)

19. Ralph L. Woods, *The Modern Handbook of Humor* (New York: McGraw-Hill, 1967), p. 471

20. (Author unknown) *The Scarlet Fish and Other Stories*

21. Ephesians 6 : 12 (*The Living Bible*)

22. Catherine Marshall, *To Live Again* (New York: McGraw-Hill Book Company, 1957) pp. 299–325, and *Beyond Our Selves*, pp. 247–256.

23. I John 1 : 7–9 (*The Living Bible*)

24. Romans 13 : 12

25. Ephesians 6 : 16

Chapter 14 The Helper

1. *Time* (June 18, 1973), p. 91.
2. John 17:20 *(The Living Bible)*
3. John 16:7
4. Acts 1:4,5; 2:17
5. John 1:33b; Mark 1:8; Matthew 3:11
6. John 14:17; Galatians 2:20; I Corinthians 6:19; John 15:18–26
7. John 7:39; 16:7; Matthew 24:14,30,31
8. John 15:26; 16:13,14
9. Mark 16:15–18,20 *(The Living Bible)*; John 14:12
10. *Teacher:* John 14:26; Luke 12:12; I Cor 2:13
    Guide: Romans 8:14
    Comforter: John 14:16,26
    Counsellor: Matthew 10:19,20
    Prayer-Intercessor: Romans 8:26,27
    Giver of Joy: Romans 14:17; I Thessalonians 1:6
    Giver of Freedom: Romans 8:2
    Giver of Spiritual Gifts: I Corinthians 12:4–11; 27,28; Hebrews 2:4
    Giver of Eternal Life: Galatians 6:8; Ephesians 1:13,14
11. Ephesians 1:22,23; Romans 12:4,5
12. John 14:17; 15:20
13. Mark 16:15 *(The Living Bible)*
14. Acts 1:4
15. John 14:21
16. John 16:13
17. Acts 11:1–10
18. Acts 11:11–18
19. Catherine Marshall, *Beyond Our Selves*, chapter 14, "Journey into Joy," pp. 227–246
20. II Timothy 3:5
21. John 3:5,6; Romans 8:9; Galatians 4:6
22. Hannah W. Smith, *The Christian's Secret of a Happy Life* (Boston: Willard Tract Repository, 1885), p. 249
23. Acts 5:1–11
24. *Philadelphia Quaker, The Letters of Hannah Whitall Smith* (New York: Harcourt, Brace and Company, 1950); Logan Pearsall Smith, *Unforgotten Years* (Boston: Little, Brown and Company, 1939), pp. 30, 29; Ray Strachey, *Group Movements of*

the Past and Experiments in Guidance (London: Faber and Faber, Limited, 1928); Robert Allerton Parkes, *The Transatlantic Smiths* (New York: Random House, 1959)

25. This summary of the Smiths' experiences together with the exact quotations is taken from Hannah W. Smith, *My Spiritual Autobiography or How I Discovered the Unselfishness of God* (New York: Fleming H. Revell Company, 1903), pp. 288–296

26. Letter to Mrs. Henry Ford Barclay, June 3, 1876, Hannah W Smith, *Letters*, pp. 29,30

27. This portion of Tay Thomas's story was written originally for *Guideposts* (April 1965)

28. *Dear Lord and Father of Mankind.* Lyric by John Greenleaf Whittier

Index

Abraham, 94–95
Adam and Eve, 124, 126–127, 185, 239
Adler, Alfred, 98
Adolescent neurosis, 237–238
Adversity, handling, 234
Advertising profession, 236
Alaskan earthquake, 284–286
Alcoholics Anonymous, 37
Alcoholism, 3
Alienation, 60
Ambivalence in society, 238
American Revolution and seeds of violence, 225–226
Anger and hatred, 35, 239, 275, 289
   destructive emotions, 243
Antagonisms, 274
Anxiety, 238
Aquinas, Thomas, 186, 200
Armor of light, 248, 263
   defense against Satan, 152–155
Armstrong, Ellie, 212–213, 217–218, 235

Arts and creativity, 242
Astrologers, 143
Attitudes, effect of changes in, 68
Auden, W. H., 236

Baker, Pat, 90–93, 291
   dream interpretation, 101–103
Baptism in the Holy Spirit, 266, 276–277
   "believer's baptism," 49–50
   resistance to, 281–282
Beard, Rebecca, 3
Bennett, Father Dennis, 267, 287
Berenson, Bernard, 279
Bernadette of Lourdes, 167–168
Beyond Our Selves (Marshall), 187
Biblical references: conflict between good and evil, 130–131
   Deuteronomy, 59–60
   dreams, 97–98, 115–116
   law of the generations, 66–67
   obedience, 81–82
   praise to God, 20–22, 32

Biblical references:
  Scripture as truth, 155
  (*See also under* specific subject)
"Binding" and "loosing," 38
Bitterness, 35
Black magic, 144
Black Panthers, 27–28
Blanford, Maude, 177–184, 291–292
  drug crutch, 178, 183
Blatty, William, 144
Blessings or curse of the generations,
  58–77
Book of the Acts, 269, 283
Book of Malachi, 66
Boston Children's Hospital, 9
Botts, Mr., 161–164, 166
Bouhohartz, Louis-Justin, 168
Bridges, Georges, 255
Brown, Roland, 3
Bryan, Brother (James Alexander),
  254–255
Bryan, William Jennings, 237
Buddington, Carrie and Jeff, 137–143,
  273, 291
  commitment to God, 137–138
  on drugs, 137–140
  in hippie commune, 138–141
  unholy spirits and, 141–143

Calvin, John, 186
Campus revolution, 145
Cancer, 3, 242
Cape Cod congregation, 9, 137
Caring and compassion, 16–17, 251–
  252
Carothers, Merlin, 19–20
Carrel, Dr. Alexis, 168–170
  witnessed cure at Lourdes, 171–172
Case for Christianity, The (Lewis),
  121–122, 129
Catholic Church, 145
  Holy Spirit movement, 266–267
  Jesus People, 264–265
  Pentecostal movement, 264–266
  verification of cures at Lourdes,
  170
Change, effecting, 68, 225–226
  of heart and mind, 235–236

Chappaqua, New York, 274
  Fellowship-Prayer Group, 115
Charismatics, 265–266
Cheating, 3, 263
Child-rearing, 44–45
Christian commitment, 137–138, 203
Christian communes, 141–143
Christianity, 110, 273
  not inherited, 37
  orthodox, 283
*Christian's Secret of a Happy Life,
  The* (Smith), 3, 275–281
  missing chapter, 276–281
Christy (mother of Catherine Mar-
  shall), 31
Christy (Marshall), 44
  purchased for films, 10
Church of the Saviour, 43–44
Churches, 273, 283
  ecclesiastical monuments or close
    fellowship, 283
  liberal, 273
  membership, 43
  presence of the Holy Spirit, 269
Churchill, Winston, 237
Cigarette smoking, breaking habit,
  90–93, 291
Citizenship, concept of good, 222
Clairvoyance, 143
Clark, Dr. Glenn, 3, 103–105
Cleansing and healing experience,
  274–275
Communal living, 26, 43–44, 273
  Christian communes, 26, 141–142
  hippies, 26, 138–143
Complaints and complaining, 231
  trust and praise instead of, 235
Concentration camps, 36
  Ravensbruck, 28–30
Confession, 39, 171
Confirmation, sacrament of, 266
Conflicts and neuroses, 238–239
Congressional debates, 237
Contentment, 5
Controversies, 282
Conversions, religious, 65–66, 68–72
Cornerstone (fellowship group),
  Washington, D.C., 51

Cornwall, Judson, 20
Correct Craft, Inc., 232–235
Cosby, Gordon, 43
Counseling, 47
  nondirective, 37
Creativity, 212, 242
  making the most of one's talents,
    217
"Credibility gap," 237
Crime and violence, 243–244, 282
  (*See also* Violence and crime)
Crisis-moments in life, 245–246, 250
  protection of God, 263
Criticism, adverse effects of, 219–223
  cause of negativism, 220
  concentration on things that are
    wrong, 220
  dissatisfaction with life and, 220–
    222
  home training and, 219–220
  protest and dissent, 223–224, 226
Cross and the Switchblade, The
  (Sherill and Sherill), 265–266,
    281–282

Dachau extermination camp, 36
Daily, Starr, 3, 68–72
Darkness and light, 152–155
Davidson, Dr. Philip, 225–226
Davis, Billie and George, 210–211,
  217
Death and grief, 2–3
  acceptance of death, 10
  death of Peter Marshall, 6–7
  participating Presence of God, 15
De Moss, Nancy, 78–80, 291
Depression, 131, 220–221
Deuteronomy, 59–60
Devil worship, 145–146
Disappointments, 22, 292
Discontent expelled by appreciation
  and gratitude, 226
Discouragement, Satan's tactics, 131
Disease and sickness, 12, 292
  (*See also* Healing)
Dishonesty, 263
  in government, 223, 232–235, 238
Disillusionment, 273

Dissatisfaction, 238
Divisiveness, 282
Divorce rate, 58
Dodds, Elisabeth D., 73
Dowling, Tom, 111–114
  dream therapy experienced by,
    112–114
Dreams and dream interpretation,
    86–88, 96–116
  Biblical emphasis on, 97–98, 115–
    116
  characters in dreams, 101–103
  "the collective unconscious," 100–
    101
  effect of barbiturates on, 86–87
  Freud on, 97–98
  head-on-pedestal-stand dream, 96, 109
  importance of, 115–116
  interpretations by Morton Kelsey,
    105–111
  nightmare problem, 112–114
  of physical danger, 103–105, 108–
    109
  prayer-meditation and, 101–103,
    110–111, 115–116
  principles of interpretation, 106–107
    of promise, 89–90, 109
  psychiatry and, 96–97
  of rejection and danger, 87–88,
    103–105, 108–109
  symbolism, analogies, and images,
    99–101, 107
  therapeutical values, 111–114
  warnings of coming events, 103–105
  writing-down, 106–107
Drug abuse, 3, 52, 59, 137–143, 273
  bad acid trips, 139–140
  experimentation in 1967, 145
  hippie commune, 138–143
  ministering to addicts, 265–266, 282
  possession by unholy spirits, 140
Dryburgh Abbey ruins, 39–40
du Plessis, David, 37–39, 42
Duquesne University (Pittsburgh),
  pentecostal movement, 265

Earthquake experience of Tay
  Thomas, 284–286

Eastern religions, 273
Economic disaster, 292
 (*See also* Financial problems)
Education, 236
Edwards, Jonathan and Sarah, 73–76
 descendants, 75–76
Eliade, Mircea, 146
Elijah, 66
Emotional experiences, 273–278, 281
 negative, 275
 Robert Pearsall Smith, 278–280
 Tay Thomas, 288–290
Emotional involvements, fear of,
 64–66
Enemies, command to love, 228,
 233–235
Establishment, opposition to, 138–
 139, 273
Euland, Rebecca, 210–211
Evergreen Farm, Virginia, 51, 53,
 261–262
Evils and disasters, 3, 137–158, 292
 confident poise to overcome, 254–
 255
 effect of God's Presence, 32–33
 increase in, 145
 power of praise and, 17–18
 protection against, 149–157, 244–
 263
 resist not evil, 32–33
 Satan as personification of evil,
 117–136
Existentialism, 146
Exorcist, The (film), 144
Expectations, low threshold of, 207
Experiential literature, 3
Exploitation and exploiters, 36
Ezekiel's prophecy, 241

Faith, 12, 177, 258
 asking for gift of, 38, 171
 presumption differs from, 196
 protection from fears, 263
 relinquishment and, 194
 yielding of self, 186
Family relationships, 44–57, 133, 242
 Jonathan and Sarah Edwards,
 73–76

Family relationships,
 role of father, 70–72
Fatherliness of God, 17, 256–257
Fathers, role of, 70–72
Fears and phobias, 61–63
 of the dark, 251–252
 depending on the Fatherliness of
 God, 256–257
 destructive emotions, 243
 as disbelief in God, 256
 of emotional involvements, 64–66
 exhortations to "fear not," 255–256
 facing up to, 260
 inherited fears, 61–63
 invoking the name of the Lord,
 248–249
 lack of trust in God, 63, 256
 listing of fears, 259–260
 overcoming, 258–260
 prayers for dealing with, 67–68, 245
 semiconscious and imaginary,
 259–260
Fellowship-Prayer Group (Chappaqua, New York), 115, 274
Ferrand, Marie, 168–169, 188
Financial problems, 197–218
 experience of Schaeffer family,
 198–207
 and God's supply, 197–218
Fire and destruction, 3
 obeying God's will, 78–80, 291
Fisher, Bishop John, 39
Flying, fear of, 260
Folk mass, 290
Forgiveness, 35–57
 all-inclusive nature, 36
 Aughts against the Anys principle,
 35–57
 inability to forgive, 35–38
 means withholding judgment, 38,
 41–42, 55–56
 prayer of release, 43, 48, 50
 precondition of love, 42
 release from judgment, 55–56
 releasing of "aughts against all the
 anys," 36, 39, 48–50
 teachings of Jesus, 35–36
 unforgiveness and, 37–38

Fortune-tellers, 147, 157
Fosdick, Dr. Harry Emerson, 221
Foxe, John, 3
Free will, 7
protection against evil, 149–157
Freedom of choice, 149
repetition of downbeat choices, 151
Freedom of the press, 223
Freud, Sigmund, 98
The Interpretation of Dreams, 97
Friends and friendship, 212
Frustrations, 22, 275, 289
violence due to, 243–244

Gallo, Dr. Robert, 159–163
Gang warfare, 282
Generations, law of the, 58–59
Gentiles, 270
Ghost, Kent, 159–164, 166
Ghost, Sandra, 159–164
Giving and receiving, 208–212
"give, and it shall be given unto
you," 212–214
giving out of one's shortage, 212–
213
tithing, 214–217
Gladstone, William, 237
Glossolalia, gift of heavenly language,
270
God, 3–17
acceptance and relinquishment of
God's will, 11–12
Divine Alchemist, 7–8
Fatherhood of God, 17, 256–257
is in everything, 3–17
love for each man, 16–17, 72, 85–
86, 256–257
obedience and submission to, 78–
95, 242
power of, 16, 249, 292
praising God, 19–34, 235
Presence of, 3–17, 30–31
God Is Dead movement, 145–146
God Who Is There, The (Schaeffer),
198–199
Good and evil, 130–131, 145–146
reality of evil, 146
warfare period between, 145

Gospels, 7, 12
healing and prayer, 13
Government corruption, 232–235
Watergate offenses, 223, 238
Grace of God, 72, 85–86
Grandmother Sarah, 61–63
Gratitude and greed, 231
Greeley, Andrew, 145
Grey, Kenneth, 175
Growth and development, 20, 63
Guidance counseling, 37, 47
Guideposts magazine, 152
Writers Workshop, 111–114
Guilt feelings, 157
release of, 50
Guiness, Os, 144–145

Habakkuk, 21
Habit patterns, breaking, 151, 156
Happiness and victory, 7, 139, 242
Hatred, 35
Hayes, Dr. Oscar J., 177–178, 183–
184
Healing and prayer, 3, 9–10, 88, 110,
159–173
asking Christ for, 171–173
attitude of sick person, 167
Biblical references to, 165–166,
187–188
difference between faith and presumption, 196
experiences of Virginia Lively,
188–194
giving up self-will, 185
at Lourdes, 167–171
man at the Pool of Bethesda, 166–
167
of mind and body, 194
miracles, 167–171, 177, 289
need for relinquishment, 12–13,
173–177, 185
obedience to God in the totality of
life, 185
recovery of Maude Blanford, 177–184
recovery of Kent Ghost, 159–164,
166
search for spiritual laws governing,
165–171

Healing and prayer,
 through God's intervention, 159–
  164, 166–173
Health and disease, 12, 292
 effect of negativism, 220–221
Heart and mind, 194
 avoiding conflicts and neuroses,
  239
 effecting change, 235–236
Heartache or loss, 2
 acceptance of death, 10, 15
Helping other people, 93
Helplessness, 17
Henry, Dr. Carl, 283–284
Henry, Patrick, 237
Henry VIII, King of England, 39–40
Heredity, 58–79
 fears and phobias, 61–63
 law of the generations, 58–79
 sins or blessings of the fathers on
  the children, 66–77
 spiritual inheritance, 63
Heroes, 222
Higher Life movement, 279–280
Hippies, 26, 138–143
 in Christian community, 143
Holbrook, Stella, 103–105
"Holiness Methodists," 278
 camp meeting, 278–279
Holy Spirit, 37–38, 110, 264–292
 baptism of, 266, 276, 278–279
 as Comforter, 271–272
 counterattack by unholy spirit, 145
 emotional experiences, 273, 276–
  277, 281
  of Len LeSourd, 274–275
  of Robert Pearsall Smith, 278–
  280
  of Tay Thomas, 284–290
 gift of, 265–266
 gift of tongues, 270
 how to receive, 270–271
 manifestation of, 37–38, 271–272
 Pentecost and, 269–270
 power of, 142
 promises made by Jesus at the Last
  Supper, 268–269
 resistance to, 281–282

Holy Spirit movement, 266–267, 273
 danger of overemotionalism, 281
 growth of, 267, 283–284
 resistance to, 267
Hope, 77
Hopkins, Samuel, 74
Horoscopes, 143
Hostility and guilt, 157
 release of, 50
House blessings, 261–263
Household possessions, 212
Human relationships, 43–57
 (*See also* Family relationships)
Humanism, 186, 273
Hunger in the world, 242
Hunter, Frances Gardner, 20
Hussein, King of Jordan, 223

Ideas, 212
Indians, treatment of, 226
Infants, reaction to tensions and
 fears, 62
Iniquity, hatred of, 228
Insights, 94
Insomnia, 83
 and obedience to God, 83–90
Integrity, 263
Intellect and reason, 199–200
Irritations, 289
Isaiah, 242
Israelites, 229–232
 murmurings and grumblings
  against leaders, 230–232
Israel's six-day war, 145

James, Henry, 279
Jehoshaphat, King of Judah, 21–22
Jesus, 66–67
 Aught-Anys command on forgiveness, 35–36, 56–57
 caring and compassion, 16–17,
  251–252
 concern for everyday problems, 83
 death and resurrection, 127
 dependence on the Father, 176
 on evil and injustice, 227–228
 experience of the Risen Christ, 172
 face of, 190–192

Jesus,
  First Rebel, 229
  on forgiveness, 35–36, 56–57
  God-Man, 120, 126–127
  at Last Supper, 151, 268–269
  miracles, 3–4, 16
  names given to, 248–249
  observation of His personality, 172
  parable-stories, 99
  personification of Man, 120, 126–127
  role as Saviour, 14–16
  Way of Jesus, 238–239
Jesus People, meeting at Notre Dame, 264–265
Jesus Revolution, 273
Jewish people, 241, 273
  food taboos, 72, 98, 270
Job, 4
John the Baptist, 3
Jones, Sybil, 51–56
Joy, 143
  of Lord alive in one's life, 172, 174
  sources of, 22–23
  spiritual, 273–274
Judas Iscariot, 228
Judd, Dr., 104–105
Judgment and forgiveness, 38, 42–43
Jung, Carl, 98, 100–101

Kelsey, Morton T., 99, 105–111
Kerin, Dorothy, 3
Kingdom of God on earth, 217
  righteousness and, 204–205, 217
Klinger, Gene, 244–246, 260, 291
Kunkel, Fritz, 186–187

L'Abri (Christian evangelical community) in Switzerland, 198–207, 217
  prayer principles, 204
  total dependence on God, 206–207
L'Abri (Schaeffer), 198
Languages, gift of tongues, 270
Lashley, Roberta, 249–251, 260, 291
Last Supper, 151, 268–269
Laubach, Frank, 3, 14
Lawrence, Brother, 3

Laying on of hands, 289
League of Nations, 40
Lepers, 16, 182
LeSourd, Chester, 8, 44–45, 64, 264
LeSourd, Jeffrey, 8, 44–45, 64
LeSourd, Leonard, 31, 38–39, 41, 64, 206, 262
  gift of the Holy Spirit, 274–275
  marriage, 8, 44–45
  trip to L'Abri, 200–203, 206
LeSourd, Linda, 8–9, 45–50
  life changed by prayer, 48–51
Let Us Praise (Cornwall), 20
Lewis, C. S., 3, 83, 107
  The Case for Christianity, 121–122, 129
  That Hideous Strength, 109
  The Screwtape Letters, 126
Liberal churches and seminarians, 273
Life style, 43, 185
Light of Christ, 152–155
  armor of light, 152–155, 248, 263
  defense against Satan, 152–155
  protection against fear, 246–248
Lincoln, Abraham, 237
Literature, Christian, 3, 97–98
  dream interpretation in, 97–98
Lively, Virginia, 9, 188–194
Livingston, David, 252–254, 260, 291
Loneliness, 17, 258
Lourdes, healings at, 167–171
  miracles, 168–170
  scientific study of cures, 170
Love, 212, 240–241
  command to love one another, 72
  forgiveness precondition of, 42
  gift of the Holy Spirit, 274–275
  of God for man, 16–17, 72, 85–86, 256–257
Lucifer, Archangel, 122–124
Luther, Martin, 186
Lutheran pastor (former Nazi storm trooper), 240–241

Main, Dot, 113
Man, creation of, 123–125
  disobeyed God, 125

Man Called Peter, A (Marshall), 272–273

Manliness, 258

Marriage, 3, 58, 242
divorce rate, 58
of Fay Randle to Bart, 54–55
Puritan view of, 73
rejection of premarital chastity, 58

Marshall, Amy Catherine, 9–10
accepting death of, 17–20, 33, 48–49

Marshall, Catherine, 8, 44–45
asking Christ for healing, 171–173
Beyond Our Selves, 187
editing and writing, 8, 44–45, 215, 217, 272
financial problems, 215, 217
lung condition, 164, 171–173
A Man Called Peter, 272–273
marriage to Leonard LeSourd, 8, 44–45
Mr . Jones, Meet the Master, 8

Marshall, Edith, 1, 9–10, 50, 138, 262, 290

Marshall, Mary Elizabeth, 8–10, 263

Marshall, Peter, 37, 131
death of, 2, 6–7, 214–215, 272–273
editing sermons of, 8, 41, 272–273
on fears, 258–259
gift of the Holy Spirit, 271
on God's judgment, 157–158
heart attack, 41
on tithing, 216

Marshall, Peter Christopher, 1–2, 8, 290

Marshall, Peter John, 1–2, 9–10, 43, 51, 137–138, 215, 262, 290
house blessing, 262–263
prayer for release from fear, 67–68

Material needs provided by God, 207–210
exactness and timing of, 205–206
Schaeffer's experiences, 198–199, 203–207

Maturity, development of, 63

Mayo, Dr Will, 104–105

Mayo Clinic, 104–105

Mechanistic universe, concept of, 17

Melancholy, 220

Meloon, Walter and Ralph, 232–235

Melrose Abbey, destruction of, 39–40

"Methodists, Holiness," 278–279

Middle East politics, 222–223

Migrant workers, 224

Millay, Edna St. Vincent, 125

Missionaries, 221–223

Mr. Jones, Meet the Master (Marshall), 8

Money, 212
provided by the Lord, 197–218

Montecalvo, Pastor Lou, 27–28

More, Sir Thomas, 39

Moses, 59–60
lead Israelites to Promised Land, 229–232

Mosley, Rufus, 3

Movies, obscenity in, 236–237

Müller, George, 3

Name of the Lord, 248–251
power to overcome evil, 248–249

Nardozzi, Jean, 115–116

National Commission on the Causes and Prevention of Violence, 226

National Institutes of Health, 160, 163

Nationalism, 242

Nazi concentrations camps, 28–30, 36

Negative situations, reaction to, 207–208

Negativism, 220–221
antidotes to, 231–232

Neurosis, adolescent, 237–238

News media, 223, 236
constant criticism by, 223
government controlled, 236

Nicodemus, 240

Nobel Prize, 170

Notre Dame University, meeting of Catholic Jesus People, 264–265

Obedience, 78–95
based on love and trust, 81–95
Biblical references, 81–82
breaking smoking habit and, 90–93
healing and praise, 89

Obedience,
to law and governmental authority,
82
obeying hunches, 78–80
rejection and, 87–89
submission to God's will, 18, 242
understanding follows, 95, 110
Obscenity, spread of, 236–237
Occult, interest in, 59, 121, 143–144,
273
Exorcist fever, 144
Ouija boards, 147, 157

Parent-child relationships, 44–50
Biblical references, 59
Edwards family, 73–76
effect of changes in attitutde, 68–72
law of the generations, 58–79
miracles of restored relationships,
44–57
Randle's experience, 51–56
spiritual rehabilitation, 70–72
Paul the Apostle, 17, 33, 229, 288
conversion of, 57
imprisoned at Philippi, 22–23
on Light of Christ, 248
on prayer and praise, 22–23
Pendle Hill, Quaker study center, 216
Pentecost, 270, 277, 281, 288
Pentacostal movement, 265–266
Permissiveness, 55, 69
Persuasion, art of, 236
modern techniques of, 237
Peter the Apostle, 71–72
dreams of, 98
Philippi, Paul and Silas imprisoned
in, 22–23
Physical needs, 35
provided by God, 207–210
Pole, Margaret, 39
Port Allegheny Motel, 213–214
Positive thinking, 171
Positivism, revolt against, 145
"Poverty complex," 208–209
Power of God, 16, 249, 292
invoking name of Jesus, 248–251
Praise and praising God, 19–34, 235
Biblical references to, 20–22

Praise and praising God,
faith in action, 30
God's participating Presence, 30–33
for good and evil, 18
healing and, 80
illustrations of power of:
after death of Amy Catherine
Marshall, 18–20, 33
flea story in Nazi concentration
camp, 28–30
Gladys and Clem's story, 24–26
Redeemer Temple in Denver,
26–28
key to answered prayer, 19, 68
miracles wrought by, 22–23, 30
most powerful prayer of all, 17–18,
24
rejoicing in the Lord, 23–24
resist not evil, 32–33
as sacrifice, 20–21
for unhappy situations, 18–20
writings on, 19–20
Praise the Lord Anyway (Hunter), 20
Prayers and praying, 212
asking Christ for healing, 171–173
blocked by self-will, 175
extraordinary answers to, 9–10, 20
group prayer, 47–49
healing through, 9–10, 12, 171–175
for material needs, 197–207, 218
in the Name of Jesus, 249–251
power of praise, 20, 24, 68
principles used at L'Abri, 204
for release from fear, 67–68, 245
relinquishment of self, 11–12, 173–
174, 180
for those who are ill, 174–175
unanswered, 38–39
Precognition, 143
Presence of God, 4–5
Presumption, difference between
faith and, 196
Prince, Derek, 127, 147–148
Prison reform, 68
Prison to Praise (Carothers), 19–20
Propaganda, 236
Protest and dissent, 223–224, 229, 238
Protestant churches, 145

Protestant churches,
    critical judgments, 222–223
    Holy Spirit movement, 266–267
Protestant Reformation, 186
Psychoanalysis and dream interpretation, 96–97
Public speaking, fear of, 260
Puritans, 73

Ranaghan, Kevin, 265–266
Randle, Fay, 51–56
Randle, Loretta and Tim, 51–57
Rationalism, 222
Ravensbruck concentration camp,
    28–30
    flea story, 28–30
Rebellion, 12–13, 219–242
    built-in dangers, 227
    dilemma of, 219–242
    frustration and, 237
    instigated by Satan, 239
    mutiny and, 241–242
    neurosis of epidemic proportions,
        237–238
    reconciliation with God, 239–240
    trust and praise instead of, 235
Receiving and giving, 208–212
Reconciliation with God, 239–240
Redeemer Temple, Denver, Colorado, 26–28
Reform, effecting, 273
    techniques of, 223–224
Rehabilitation, spiritual program,
    69–70
Reid, Hank, 224–225, 261
Rejoicing in the Lord, 23–24
Relativism, doctrine of, 146
Religious conversions, 65–66
Relinquishment of self, 17, 173–177
    faith and, 194
    prayer of, 180
Research needs, 242
Resentments, 35, 50, 88, 274
    "Aughts against the Anys" principle, 54–55
Rest and refreshment, need for, 90
Restlessness, 238
Retreats, 9–10, 44

Reynolds, Barbara, 216, 218
Risen Christ, experience of, 172
Rockefeller Institute for Medical Research, 170
Roosevelt, Franklin D., 237
Russell, Bertrand, 279

Sacred, definition of, 146
Sacrifice, 90–92
    concept of prayer as, 20–21
St. Mark's Church, Van Nuys, California, 267
Sanford, Agnes, 3, 221–223
Sanford, John A., 99
Sartre, Jean-Paul, 238
Satan, 12, 15, 117–136
    archangel Lucifer, 122–124
    "the beachhead strategies," 149–151
    characteristics, 123
    danger from, 147–157
    defense against, 148, 152–158
    disbelief in existence of, 117–120,
        147
    exorcism and, 118
    external manifestations, 122
    harassment techniques, 131–136
    instigator of rebellion, 239
    lists of God's wants and Satan's
        aims, 133–136
    personification of evil, 120
    power of, 128–129, 141, 147–157
    publications on, 144–145
    renouncing, 157
    rise of Satan cults, 121, 143–144
    routed through praise, 28
    strategies of, 131–136
    truth as a defense against, 152–158
    unholy spirits, 137–158
    war against evil and, 133
Saturday Evening Post, 217
Saul of Tarsus, 56–57
Schaeffer, Edith and Francis, 60,
    198–207, 217
    material needs supplied by God,
        198–207, 217
Schmitt, Dr. Francis Otto, 123
Science, imperialism of, 17, 138,
    144–145, 164

Scientology, 143
Screwtape Letters, The (Lewis), 126
Scripture, authority of, 155–156
Secularism, 146
Self-gratification, 55
Self-pity, 131, 156
  evils of, 226–227
Self-righteousness, 13
Self-will, 185
  answers to prayers blocked by, 175
Sermon on the Mount, 14–15
Sexual attraction, 152–155
Sexual promiscuity, 58–59, 132
Sexuality, Freud's doctrine of, 98
Shakespeare, William, 11
Shaw, Bernard, 279
Sherill, John and Elizabeth, 115,
  265–266, 281–282
Sickness and disease, 12, 292
Silas and the Apostle Paul, 22–23
Simpson, A. E., 3
Sin, 7, 37, 256
  getting rid of sin, 256–257
  guilt feelings, 66, 157
  hidden sin, 154
  lack of trust in God, 63
  passed down from generation to
    generation, 63
  strained relationships and estrange-
    ments due to, 66
Sit-ins and protest rallies, 224
Sleep and sleeping, 83–87
  effect of calcium deficiency, 115–116
  periods of wakefulness, 86–87
  sleep mechanism, 86
  sleeping-pill battle, 83–85, 108–109,
    235
Sleep laboratories, 98
Slum conditions, 224
Smith, Hannah Whitehall, 3–6, 9,
  11–12, 14–15, 17, 94, 131, 154
  *The Christian's Secret of a Happy
    Life,* 4, 275–281
  early life, 277
  marriage, 278–280
  spiritual researcher, 277–278
Smith, Robert Pearsall, 278–281
Smoking habit, breaking, 90–93, 291

Social injustice, 223–224
Sorcerers and sorcery, 143
Spiritism, 143
Spiritual rehabilitation, 69–70
Spiritualism and mediums, 143, 147,
  157
Stephen, first Christian martyr, 56–57
Submission and obedience to God,
  242
Suenens, Cardinal Leo Jozey, 265
Suicide, 140, 221
Superstitious practices, 59, 121, 143–
  145, 157, 273

Talents, making the most of, 217
Tarot cards, 143, 147
Teen-agers, rebellious, 44–57
  runaways, 58
Telepathy, 143
Television, words becoming less ef-
  fective, 236–237
Temptations, 154, 280
  how to handle, 234
ten Boom, Corrie and Betsie, 28–30
That Hideous Strength (Lewis), 109
Thomas, Lowell, Jr., 284, 286–287
Thomas, Tay, 284–290
  Alaskan earthquake experience,
    284–286
  Follow the North Star, 287
  spiritual search, 287–290
Time magazine, 263–266
Tithing, 214–218
Tournier, Paul, 237–238
Trinity, doctrine of, 283
Trust in god, form of protection,
  252–255
Truth: defense against Satan, 155–158
  Jesus' promise of "further truth,"
    269–270
Twentieth-century civilization, 111

Unclean spirits (demons), 156
Unconscious, 87, 93–94, 258
  dream interpretations and, 97, 99
Underhill, Evelyn, 3
Understanding: follows obedience to
  God, 95, 110

Understanding:
self-will and, 185–186
Unholy spirits, 137–158
(*See also* Satan)
University of Chicago, 145, 170

Value-judgments, 36, 219
Vietnam-war opposition, 238
Violence and crime, 236, 242–243,
282
due to frustrations, 243–244
National Commission on Causes
and Prevention of Violence,
226
seeds of, 226

War, opposition to, 40, 238, 273
Washington, George, 237
Washington Post, 223
Watergate offenses, 223, 238
Webb, Beatrice and Sidney, 279
Wesley, John, 3, 277

Whole Person in a Broken World, The
(Tournier), 237–238
Wilkerson, David, 213, 265–266, 281–
282
Will, 124
free will, 7, 149–157
giving up self-will, 175, 185
total dependence on God's will, 7,
85–86, 175–176
Wilson, Woodrow, 40, 237
Winship, A. E., 75–76
Wisdom and understanding, 185–186
Witchcraft, 143–144, 145, 157
Wolff, Roy, healing of, 188–194
Working mothers, 58
World Friendship Center, Hiroshima,
Japan, 216
World organizations, 242

Youth Revolution, 48

Zwingli, Ulrich, 186

About the Author

Catherine Marshall is the author of four great best-sellers, *A Man Called Peter, To Live Again, Beyond Our Selves,* and *Christy.* Her books have sold two and one-half million copies in hard-cover editions alone; they include several collections of sermons and prayers by her late husband, Peter Marshall. She is now married to Leonard LeSourd, for twenty-eight years the Editor of *Guideposts* magazine. Her son, Peter John Marshall, is a minister, serving a church in New England. Catherine's life is centered on writing and family activities. (The LeSourds have three children: Linda, Chester, and Jeffrey.) She also finds time to serve as a roving editor for *Guideposts,* to handle a voluminous correspondence, to paint tropical scenes, and to make a few speaking appearances. She is widely known over the country as an attractive, provocative, and inspiring personality.